# Value Sensitive Design

# Value Sensitive Design

Shaping Technology with Moral Imagination

Batya Friedman and David G. Hendry

The MIT Press
Cambridge, Massachusetts
London, England

This book was set in ITC Stone Sans Std and ITC Stone Serif Std by Toppan Best-set Premedia Limited. Printed and bound in the United States of America.

Library of Congress Cataloging-in-Publication Data

Names: Friedman, Batya, 1957- author. | Hendry, David, 1962- author.
Title: Value sensitive design : shaping technology with moral imagination / Batya Friedman and David G. Hendry.
Description: Cambridge, MA : MIT Press, [2019] | Includes bibliographical references and index.
Identifiers: LCCN 2018028524 | ISBN 9780262039536 (hardcover : alk. paper)
Subjects: LCSH: System design--Methodology. | Human-computer interaction. | Computer programming--Moral and ethical aspects. | Computer programmers--Professional ethics.
Classification: LCC QA76.9.S88 F75 2019 | DDC 004.01/9--dc23 LC record available at https://lccn.loc.gov/2018028524

10  9  8  7  6  5  4

To Zoe, and Joe (in spirit)

To Eric and Karen

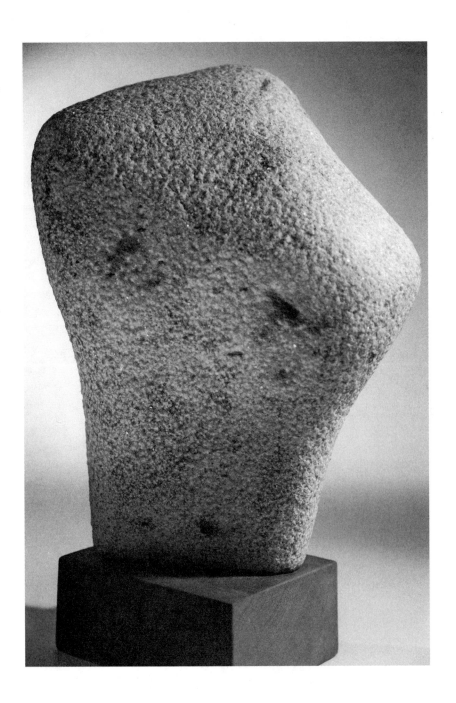

[We have to reject the] worshiping [of] the new gadgets which are our own creation as if they were our masters.

—Norbert Wiener (1954/1985, p. 678)

The human artifice of the world separates human existence from all mere animal environments, but life itself is outside this artificial world, and through life man remains related to all other living organisms.

—Hannah Arendt (1958/1998, p. 2)

Mankind is unique among animals in its relationship to the environment. ... Only mankind transforms earth itself to suit its needs and wants ... This job of form-giving and reshaping has become the designer's responsibility.

—Victor Papanek (1971, pp. 157–158)

What is wrong, I think, is that we have permitted technological metaphors ... and technique itself to so thoroughly pervade our thought processes that we have finally abdicated to technology the very duty to formulate questions. ... Where a simple man might ask: "Do we need these things?," technology asks "what electronic wizardry will make them safe?" Where a simple man will ask "is it good?," technology asks "will it work?"

—Joseph Weizenbaum (1972, pp. 611–612)

We encounter the deep questions of design when we recognize that in designing tools we are designing ways of being.

—Terry Winograd and Fernando Flores (1986, p. xi)

In contrast to analysts or critics, designers put things together and bring new things into being. ... Almost always, designers' moves have consequences other than those intended for them. Designers juggle variables, reconcile conflicting values, and maneuver.

—Donald A. Schön (1987, p. 42)

# Contents

# Preface and Acknowledgments

Value sensitive design emerged in the 1990s. The roots of the value sensitive design tripartite methodology can be found as early as 1992 in a paper by Friedman and Kahn (1992) in which they engaged in a conceptual analysis of human agency and responsible computer system design. That paper provided careful analyses of agency, human and machine; implications of that agency for moral action; and considerations for technical features in computer system design. The paper concluded with a call to bring an empirical understanding of people's moral psychology into the mix. The term "value sensitive design" first appeared in the mid-1990s with a perspective in the ACM *Interactions* entitled "Value-Sensitive Design" (Friedman, 1996), followed shortly thereafter by an edited volume published by Cambridge University Press and the Center for the Study of Language and Information, *Human Values and the Design of Computer Technology* (Friedman, 1997).

Two workshops funded by the US National Science Foundation helped to cultivate a research and design community in value sensitive design. The first workshop, held in Washington, DC, in May 1999 and attended by Edward Felten, Batya Friedman (organizer), Jonathan Grudin, Helen Nissenbaum, and Terry Winograd, sought to set a research agenda for value sensitive design (Friedman, Felten, Grudin, Nissenbaum, & Winograd, 1999). The second workshop sought to further develop and refine that research agenda and to stimulate research in this approach by cultivating a broad community of value sensitive design researchers. Held at the University of Washington in Seattle, Washington, in September 2000, the second workshop was organized by Alan Borning and Batya Friedman and attended by nearly 30 participants,[1] who, as a group, represented perspectives from cognitive science, computer ethics, computer security, computer-supported cooperative work, design, human-computer interaction, interaction design, participatory design, philosophy, social-psychological aspects of information systems, software development, technology, and ubiquitous computing. Many of the individuals who attended the 1999 and 2000 workshops have either contributed directly to the literature on value sensitive design or in other ways engaged explicitly with human values in their technical research and design work.

Also in 1999, Batya Friedman and Peter Kahn joined Alan Borning at the University of Washington, where they established the interdisciplinary Value Sensitive Design Lab. Their co-location and support from their respective units—the Information School, Department of Psychology, and Department of Computer Science and Engineering—provided a fruitful environment for developing value sensitive design.

Four prior synthetic accounts of value sensitive design provide a window onto its development. The first was a handbook chapter on human values, ethics, and design (Friedman & Kahn, 2003; rev. ed., 2008), which placed an early description of value sensitive design in a broader discussion of how values become implicated in technological design; other approaches to human values, ethics, and design; human values of ethical import; and professional ethics. The second was an entry on value sensitive design in an encyclopedia of human-computer interaction (Friedman, 2004). The third, a chapter devoted to value sensitive design that explicated some theory, three case studies, and heuristics on method (Friedman, Kahn, & Borning, 2006a; reprinted in Himma & Tavani, 2008 and in Doorn, Schuurbiers, van de Poel, & Gorman, 2013). The fourth, a survey article on value sensitive design methods that summarized core theoretical commitments, reported on 14 methods and provided heuristics for skillful value sensitive design practice (Friedman, Hendry, & Borning,

1. The following individuals participated in the 2000 workshop: Gregory Abowd, Alan Borning (organizer), Tone Bratteteig, Philip Brey, Gary Chapman, Edward Felten, Raya Fidel, Batya Friedman (organizer), Jonathan Grudin, Jim Gray, Chris Hoadley, Peter Kahn, Wendy Kellogg, Jennifer Mankoff, Elizabeth Mynatt, Clifford Nass, Helen Nissenbaum, Andreas Paepcke, Kurt Partridge, Karen Pettigrew, Steven Poltrock, Lodis Rhodes, Ole Smørdal, Deborah Tatar, John Thomas, Peter Paul Verbeek, Paul Waddell, and Terry Winograd.

2017). That survey article has been expanded and is now chapter 3 in this book.

Moreover, during the seven-year period of writing this book, review articles have also appeared in the literature, including one by Davis and Nathan (2014), who discuss applications, adaptations, and critiques of value sensitive design, and one by Huldtgren (2015), who reviews some of the methods and theoretical aspects of value sensitive design. Having received doctoral or internship training at the Value Sensitive Design Lab at the University of Washington, Davis, Nathan, and Huldtgren offer distinctive and insightful points of view in their review articles.

Most recently, two new workshops (Friedman et al., 2015; Friedman, Harbers, Hendry, van den Hoven, & Jonker, 2016) have taken up the charge of framing grand challenges for value sensitive design going forward. The first, titled "Charting the Next Decade for Value Sensitive Design," was a one-day workshop held in August 2015 at the Fifth Decennial Conference on Critical Alternatives in Aarhus, Denmark. Organized by Batya Friedman, David Hendry, Jeroen van den Hoven, Alina Huldtgren, Catholijn Jonker, and Aimee van Wynsberghe, the workshop brought together 19 researchers and designers from such fields as computer science, engineering, human-computer interaction, law, library and information science, and philosophy.[2] Focusing on human values and technology, workshop participants began a conversation on grand challenges for value sensitive design. A year later, in November 2016, the Aarhus conversation continued at a five-day workshop at the Lorentz Center in Leiden, The Netherlands. Similarly titled "Value Sensitive Design: Charting the Next Decade," the Leiden workshop was organized by Batya Friedman, Maaike Harbers, David Hendry, Jeroen van den Hoven, and Catholijn Jonker.[3] There were 41 participants in

2. The following individuals participated in the 2015 Aarhus workshop: Anette Andersson, Batya Friedman (organizer), Maaike Harbers, David Hendry (organizer), Jeroen van den Hoven (organizer), Alina Huldtgren (organizer), Sampsa Hyysalo, Catholijn Jonker (organizer), Michael Katell, Alex Kayal, Ian King, Lisa Nathan, Bryce Newell, Rose Paquet Kinsley, Jeremy Pitt, Luke Stark, Åke Walldius, Daisy Yoo, and Bieke Zaman.

3. The official website for the Lorentz Workshop, "Value Sensitive Design: Charting the Next Decade," can be found here: https://www.lorentzcenter.nl/lc/web/2016/852/info.php3?wsid=852&venue=Oort.

Leiden,[4] many of whom had also attended the Aarhus workshop. Along with paper presentations and numerous hands-on activities, distinguished conversations were held with Lisa Nathan, Sarah Spiekermann, Alan Borning, and Volker Wulf. The 2017 Lorentz workshop resulted in new research nuggets on recent work in value sensitive design and a set of grand challenges for moving the field forward over the next decade. These workshop outcomes will be published in a special issue of the *Journal of Ethics and Information Technology* (forthcoming).

Turning now to specific acknowledgments: many, many people have contributed to bringing value sensitive design to its current form. To all those, we are enormously grateful.

Early supporters who challenged, critiqued, and enabled the work include Ron Baecker, Suzanne Iacono, Sara Kiesler, Rob Kling, Ben Shneiderman, and Terry Winograd. Early collaborators include Sunny Consolvo, Edward Felten, Ken Goldberg, Peter Kahn, Clifford Nass, Helen Nissenbaum, Ian Smith, and John Thomas.

Alan Borning: no other person has contributed so much to value sensitive design over the years—intellectually, practically, and always with integrity. To Alan, first and foremost dear friend: deep respect and appreciation.

Our former students, now friends and colleagues—Norah Abokhodair, Janet Davis, Tamara Denning, Katie Derthick, Abigail Evans, Nathan Freier, Daniel Howe, Shaun Kane, Travis Kirplean, Predrag Klasnja, Milli Lake, Peyina Lin, Jessica Miller, Lynette Millett, Lisa Nathan, Bryce Newell, Trond Nilsen, Kari Watkins, Jill Woelfer, and Daisy Yoo—have contributed substantially to the development of value sensitive design while pursuing their own research interests and successful careers. Some of their work appears

---

4. The following individuals participated in the 2016 Lorentz Center Workshop: Tag Alshehri, Christian Bonnici, Alan Borning, Oliver Burmeister, Christian Detweiler, Batya Friedman (organizer), Christiane Grünloh, Maaike Harbers (organizer), Oliver Heger, Donal Heidenblad, David Hendry (organizer), Alina Huldtgren, Naomi Jacobs, Nassim Jafarinaimi, Catholijn Jonker (organizer), Ian King, Marjolein Lanzing, Qinyu Li, Nick Logler, René Mahieu, Noëmi Manders-Huits, Jason Millar, David Miller, Lisa Nathan, Bryce Newell, Bjoern Niehaves, Anne Nigten, Sarah Spiekermann, Luke Stark, Tjerk Timan, Ibo Van de Poel, Jeroen Van de Hoven (organizer), Peter Van Waart, Aimee Van Wynsberghe, Pieter Vermaas, Åke Walldius, Kari Watkins, Till Winkler, Volker Wulf, Daisy Yoo, and Annuska Zolyomi.

in chapter 4 of this book. Our current students—Stephanie Ballard, Michael Katell, Ian King, Rose Paquet Kinsley, Nicholas Logler, Lassana Magassa, and Meg Young—are opening new frontiers for value sensitive design and contribute every day to a stimulating intellectual atmosphere in the Value Sensitive Design Lab at the University of Washington.

Tadayoshi Kohno has been an innovative collaborator for nearly a decade, spearheading research and toolkit development around privacy and security. Emily Bender, a recent collaborator in computational linguistics, has raised deep questions about mitigating bias in natural language processing systems. Brian Gill on the faculty of Seattle Pacific University has been the long-standing and much admired statistician for projects in the Value Sensitive Design Lab.

The newer work on multi-lifespan design is a joint enterprise, begun with Lisa Nathan in 2007 and carried forward with Daisy Yoo in collaboration with a large and talented team.

Other new work bringing value sensitive design to tech policy is emerging through the University of Washington Tech Policy Lab, with marvelous colleagues Ryan Calo and Tadayoshi Kohno.

Over the years, we have had the privilege of engaging with many undergraduate and graduate students in value sensitive design. They have asked the hard questions, explored and improved method, and pursued projects with a passion that has inspired us. We thank them.

The Value Sensitive Design Reading Seminar comprised of Norah Abokhodair, Alan Borning, Katie Derthick, Shaghayegh Ghassemian, Tad Hirsch, Michael Katell, Ian King, Lassana Magassa, Trond Nilsen, Kyle Rector, and Daisy Yoo provided detailed feedback on an earlier version of this book.

From The Netherlands, Jeroen van den Hoven has led the integration of value sensitive design into the European context and the development of responsible innovation. Alina Hultdgren, Aimee van Wynsberghe, and Maaike Harbers were visiting scholars at the University of Washington Value Sensitive Design Lab and helped to foster an exchange of ideas with Delft University of Technology and other universities across the globe.

A broader national and international community of researchers and scholars has shaped the intellectual discourse and practice of value sensitive design, and is carrying value sensitive design forward in exciting and innovative ways. We would like specifically to acknowledge Oliver Burmeister,

Christian Detweiler, Ken Fleischmann, Catholijn Jonker, Michael Muller, Ibo van de Poel, Katie Shilton, Sarah Spiekermann, Åke Walldius, and Volker Wulf.

The Information School at the University of Washington has provided a superb home for the Value Sensitive Design Lab since 1999, welcoming colleagues and students from across the university and beyond. The US National Science Foundation has funded the development of value sensitive design from 1998 to the present through the following awards: IIS-0000567, IIS-9911185, SES-0096131, IIS-0102558, EIA-0121326, IIS-0325035, IIS-0849270, CNS-0905384, IIS-1143966, IIS-1302709, and IIS-1018008. Two gifts from Intel and an award from the University of Washington Center for Mind, Brain and Learning (now the Institute for Learning and Brain Sciences) funded additional projects. The Washington Research Foundation funded commercialization of the Envisioning Cards. Batya Friedman also thanks the University of Washington for a generous sabbatical that provided important time for reflection and writing of this book.

Value sensitive design theory drawings courtesy of the University of Washington Value Sensitive Design Lab. Photo credit for photos on pages vi, vii, viii, xxii, 18, 58, 104, and 166: Nell Carden Grey. Photo credit for photos on pages ix, 186, and 187: Batya Friedman. All photographs courtesy of Batya Friedman.

The aesthetic talents of Nell Carden Grey and Daisy Yoo have enriched this volume. Nell took exquisite photographs of Batya's stone carvings and imagined them in conversation, creating the elements of the photo poem that we assembled for the volume (see Envoi II). Daisy listened receptively to our visual intuitions for the theoretical constructs and transformed them into the visual language found in chapter 2 (and see Envoi I).

Finally, we acknowledge our primary intellectual advisors. Batya apprenticed with Elliot Turiel and John Ogbu at the University of California, Berkeley. David apprenticed with Tom Carey, The University of Guelph; Thomas Green, MRC Applied Psychology Unit, University of Cambridge; and David Harper, Robert Gordon University, Aberdeen. They taught us to think hard, appreciate theory, observe with care, and design with respect.

To our many intellectual partners, friends, collaborators, teachers, students, critics, and fellow travelers in the human-technology relationship and value sensitive design—sincere thanks for the conversations and work, past and future, which in time we hope will contribute to our common humanity.

Batya Friedman and David Hendry
September 2018
The Plank Table
Zoka Coffee, University Village
Seattle, Washington
United States

# 1  Introduction

The water vessel, taken as a vessel only, raises the question, 'Why does it exist at all?' Through its fitness of construction, it offers the apology for its existence. But where it is a work of beauty it has no question to answer; it has nothing to do, but to be.
—Rabindranath Tagore (1922, p. 5)

In these few words, Rabindranath Tagore gently points us to the human condition. We learn from Tagore that being with our tools gives consideration not only to functionality but also to human flourishing. Thus, retelling Tagore's story of the water vessel, we might say: Every human being is entitled to clean water to drink and a vessel from which to drink that water. And that vessel should be beautiful.

Technology is the result of human imagination—of human beings envisioning alternatives to the status quo and acting upon the environment with the materials at hand to change the conditions of human and non-human life. As a result of this human activity, all technologies to some degree reflect, and reciprocally affect, human values. It is because of this deep-seated relationship that ignoring values in the design process is not a responsible option. At the same time, actively engaging with values in the design process offers creative opportunities for technical innovation as well as for improving the human condition.

Our human imaginations have the potential to be moral—to imagine what constitutes lives of quality and societies of quality, human beings living well and other living creatures living well. Technology shapes our human experience and impacts all of nature. Thus, in Terry Winograd and Fernando Flores's (1986, p. xi) words, "in designing tools we are designing ways of being"—ways of being with moral and ethical import.

This book is about bringing our moral and technical imaginations into the designing and making of technology writ large. It is about expanding our imaginations and opportunities, our toolsets and methods, and our criteria for judging the quality of systems we build. While empirical study and critique of existing systems is essential, this book is distinctive for its design stance—envisioning, designing, and implementing technology in moral and ethical ways that enhance our futures.

All human beings have enduring desires—to survive, to explore the natural world, to be in community, to create and experience beauty through music and art, to dream, to live in health, to prepare for death. We look inward and we look outward, sometimes narrowly and sometimes expansively. These and other desires have led to a myriad of inventions, and those inventions then shape our lives going forward. This is familiar news.

Consider these technologies. The Internet has enabled new and particular forms of remote communication and, in so doing, transformed our ideas about and how we experience friendship, parenting, caring for our elderly, community, and social networks. Sophisticated search algorithms can also bring us closer to people who appear to be and think like ourselves, wherever they are physically located. On the one hand, such connection can foster community in the face of isolation; on the other hand, it can lead to social and information "bubbles," risking isolation from people with ideas, belief systems, and ways of being that differ from our own. The Internet of Things and related technologies enable smart cities that manage electricity consumption in more energy-efficient ways, but also further dependence of cities and societies on a 24/7 power grid that, in turn, requires an energy infrastructure. Algorithmic decision-making systems press on education, work, and law as they increasingly make college entrance, hiring, firing, and criminal sentencing, parole, and other institutional decisions. Over time, biases that become embedded in such systematic decision making have the potential to magnify existing structural inequalities. Computing and information technologies wrapped in the ephemeral language of "the cloud" and "Ethernet," working at the speed of nanoseconds, give the illusion of minimal physical, material, and energy impact. Yet, in reality, these technologies possess a large footprint in the form of server farms, e-waste, and vast amounts of energy consumption to produce hardware and run complex algorithms. Indeed, the impact of human activity amplified by our technology use on atmospheric, geologic, hydrologic, biospheric, and other earth systems has been so transformative as to lead some scientists to propose a new geologic epoch, that of the Anthropocene.

Similar observations extend to simpler and nondigital technologies used in urban or rural settings. Consider food: powdered energy drinks and other packaged foods now populate our markets, are regular parts of human diets, and have changed ideas about what it means to eat and drink healthy food. Or consider the water mill and its continued use by farmers in developing countries. Or consider durable goods and infrastructures in energy, transportation, warfare, health care, food systems, housing, water, and sanitation—such as wind turbines, bicycles, bombs, pill bottles, organic foods, energy-efficient dwellings, faucets, and plumbing. It is noteworthy that these tools and technologies may or may not be tied to information systems, as well, for example via embedded digital technology or by being part of global information-intensive supply chains. This, however, is not the main point. What matters is that a tool or technology is in an *interactive* relation to human beings. As Winston Churchill said in 1943, "we shape our buildings and afterwards our buildings shape us." We think the same is true, not just for buildings, but for any tool or technology.

There is a tightly coupled interaction between our experience of ourselves as human beings and our tools and technologies—so much so, that it makes little sense to speak of one without the other. Given this coupling, how then can researchers, designers, engineers, and policy makers engage in the design and development of tools and technology to support human flourishing in all its richness—to enable human beings to grow and develop, to make manifest what they value, and to act meaningfully and ethically in the world?

While there are surely many ways to approach a design and engineering process addressing this question and these aims, in this book we take up one approach, that of value sensitive design.

## Value Sensitive Design in Essence

Value sensitive design seeks to guide the shape of being with technology. It positions researchers, designers, engineers, policy makers, and anyone working at the intersection of technology and society to make insightful investigations into technological innovation in ways that foreground the well-being of human beings and the natural world. Specifically, it provides theory, method, and practice to account for human values in a principled and systematic manner throughout the technical design process.

Value sensitive design offers an organic and interactional way forward. Its processes are fluid and situationally responsive. Value sensitive design has come to rest on the following definition of human values: *what is important to people in their lives, with a focus on ethics and morality.* Work to date has emphasized human well-being, dignity, and justice.

Value sensitive design holds to a number of commitments, which come from the theory of value sensitive design and are used to shape design situations and processes. These commitments include the key proposition that the relationship between technology and human values is fundamentally interactional; analyses of both direct and indirect stakeholders; distinctions among designer values, values explicitly supported by the project, and stakeholder values; individual, group, and societal levels of analysis; integrative and iterative conceptual, technical, and empirical investigations; co-evolution of technology and social structure; and a commitment to progress (not perfection). We discuss these theoretical commitments in chapter 2.

The theory and methods of value sensitive design are to be used in concert with other existing technical methods. To do so requires skillful practice. Ultimately, value sensitive design asks that the technical, civil, and other communities broaden the goals and criteria for judging the quality of technological systems to include those that advance human flourishing. In this vein, value sensitive design emphasizes the following:

(1) *Proactive orientation toward influencing design.* Value sensitive design is oriented toward influencing the design of technology early in and throughout the design process.

(2) *Carrying critical analyses of human values into the design and engineering process.* Value sensitive design is committed to design and engineering methodologies that bring critical analyses of human values into the design process.

(3) *Enlarging the scope of human values.* Value sensitive design embraces a broad spectrum of human values that arise in the human context.

(4) *Broadening and deepening methodological approaches.* Value sensitive design's emergent methods draw on anthropology, design, human-computer interaction, organizational studies, psychology, philosophy, sociology, software engineering, and others.

As perhaps with any design process, the actual work of doing value sensitive design, while intricate, is practical, based on skills and experience. One key to value sensitive design is to meaningfully shape the design process by engaging the above theoretical commitments with sensitivity to the design situation. While the commitments are fairly abstract, their implications are entirely practical. To illustrate, we briefly explore two quite different projects, informed consent online and sustainable energy transition.

In the late 1990s, the US public was generally concerned with how the use of web browsers impacted individuals' privacy. Cookies, in particular, were a technical mechanism that, while crucial for creating personalized web experiences, could also be used to invasively track users and collect sensitive data related to identity, interests, and behaviors. Concern over the disposition and use of such data has yet to abate. One strategy for addressing the public's concern over data collection and use is to insert mechanisms of "informed consent" into browsers and web applications. Friedman, Felten, and colleagues investigated this possibility in a three-year project, begun in 1999. Concretely, to address the sociotechnical complexity of "privacy" and web browsers, the project pursued conceptual, technical, and empirical investigations. Seeking an enduring and value sensitive framing, the value of "informed consent" was carefully defined based on prior philosophical analysis, with "informed" being explicated in terms of "disclosure" and "comprehension," and "consent" being explicated in terms of "voluntariness," "competence," and "agreement" (Friedman, Felten, & Millett, 2000a). Two technical investigations were conducted: one retrospective, analyzing existing browser technology (Millett, Friedman, & Felten, 2001) and one proactive, developing novel mechanisms for realizing informed consent (Friedman, Howe, & Felten, 2002). This project showed how the tripartite methodology of conceptual, technical, and empirical investigations, along with some of the other commitments, could be brought together to shape a computing technology project.

Value sensitive design is intended to be useful no matter the particular sociotechnical context of stakeholders, values, and tools and technologies, from informed consent and web browsers to aesthetics and solar energy installations. In the second project, Mok and Hyysalo (2018) used value sensitive design to develop a strategic approach for transitioning to sustainable energy. Their aim was to examine how, if at all, solar arrays might be installed on the roof of a heritage building, the Dipoli, designed by the acclaimed architects Reima and Raili Pietilä and located at Aalto University's Otaniemi campus in Espoo, Finland. This was no straightforward matter, in part because the roof's silhouette, a key element of the building, might be disturbed with the installation of the solar arrays. Beginning with a conceptual investigation, the authors identified a web of values that were used to shape several empirical and technical investigations. These values included cultural heritage preservation, campus prestige and image, and ecological modernization, along with economic costs. Building on this conceptual investigation, architectural reviews and expert interviews with architects (empirical investigations) led to criteria for guiding a technical investigation. These criteria included "preservation yet modernization," "the identity of Aalto University as eco-conscious," and "producing renewable energy without greenwashing." Next, a technical investigation was conducted, where prototypes of solar arrays were placed on the roof of the Dipoli. These prototypes were studied in terms of their aesthetics and their expected energy production—values that are entwined, since the orientation of the solar arrays to the sun determines expected energy production but also impacts the aesthetics of the roof's silhouette. In summary, the integrative and iterative use of conceptual, empirical, and technical investigations led to the key concept of "subtle visibility," which refers to striking a balance between preserving the "roofscape" of the Dipoli while also allowing for substantial energy production.

These two examples are illustrative. Chapter 4 includes 10 in-depth reports of application domains, further showing how the theoretical commitments of value sensitive design can be put to practical use to meaningfully shape design processes. They show value sensitive design to be robust and actionable in its current form, while also being open to further discovery, enhancement, and improvement. The applications, as a whole, demonstrate a commitment to "progress, not perfection."

## Two Hard Problems and a Way Forward for Value Sensitive Design

Value sensitive design is concerned with what people consider important in their lives, with a focus on ethics and morality. Hence, moral and ethical theory matters. Yet moral discourse is rife with disagreement. Longstanding debates about human values and ethics permeate moral philosophy and the social sciences. In his book *Justice: What's the Right Thing to Do?*, the leading political and ethical philosopher Michael Sandel (2009) talks about the state of these debates in morality and law as revolving "around three ideas: maximizing welfare, respecting freedom, and promoting virtue. Each of these ideas points to a different way of thinking about justice" (p. 6). In the language of moral philosophy, these concerns reflect consequentialist, deontic, and virtue ethics perspectives, respectively. Adding to these Western-centric perspectives on justice, we can point to other non-Western worldviews that foreground, for example, harmony or community, as ways to organize and sanction societies. Depending on which perspective is taken, different implications for law and policy (and technology use) follow.

The complexity goes beyond abstract moral theory, connecting to the particulars of societies and technologies. To see this interconnection, think for a moment about practical systems of government and consider democracy as a specific example: the shape of communication technology that supports one form of democracy (e.g., direct democracy in a small town or city) may be quite different from that which supports another form of democracy at another scale (e.g., representative democracy spanning a continent). Moreover, even while democracies are developing, along with corresponding understandings of justice, technology is evolving, offering new ways of acting in the world.

Thus, the first hard problem: these complexities tied to moral and ethical theory are unlikely to be resolved any time soon. Technology and society will not stand still. Value sensitive design needs to chart a path forward, even while moral philosophers, legal scholars, social scientists, and others are still at work.

How then, will value sensitive design account for moral and ethical theory? It is not the intent for value sensitive design to solve these disagreements. Rather, the aim for value sensitive design is to position researchers, designers, engineers, and others to make progress in the design of technology through the foregrounding of human values even as these debates unfold and disagreements go unresolved. To do so, value sensitive design resists overarching normative directives, for example, about which ethical theory to adhere to or what particular design sequence to prescribe. That said, mechanisms exist through which normative elements can be embedded in value sensitive design. For example, a particular ethical theory could be employed in a given project, as van Wynsberghe (2013) did in her application of care ethics to robotic assistants for health care. Or, prescriptions for carrying out specific methods could be inserted into standard engineering processes, as Spiekermann (2015) did when integrating elements of value sensitive design into a waterfall model for software engineering. Interestingly, some moral philosophers, such as van den Hoven, Lokhorst, and van de Poel (2012), suggest that design approaches like value sensitive design, which cultivate both moral and technical imagination in the context of practical activity, could contribute to the moral discourse, perhaps paving the way for new insights in these long-standing debates.

The second hard problem concerns "robustness" in terms of the scope and transferability of value sensitive design. Two questions have motivated key strategies for developing value sensitive design: "How to design an approach that can account for a wide range of values, stakeholders, technologies, populations, contexts, and circumstances, and at different scales of human experience?" and "How to develop theory and methods that can be broadly applicable, readily transferring from one situation to another?"

These considerations of "robustness" pointed us toward a pragmatic way forward, one structuring the choice and framing of value sensitive design projects as a whole. Specifically, and counter to common practice, around the year 2000 we made the strategic decision *not* to specialize in a particular value, technology, population, or context. Thus, for example, we explicitly decided not to become specialists in privacy and security, or to specialize in human-robot interaction, or to work with young children or with the elderly, or in hospital settings. Rather, our intuition was that by working across a diversity of values, technologies, populations, contexts, and levels of human experience, we would both surface blind spots in the approach (and be positioned to mitigate them) and more readily characterize theoretical commitments and methods at a level of abstraction that would be widely useful (see figure 1.1).

Following this strategy led us to explore a broad set of values and to appreciate the interconnectedness of values in human experience. It led us to adapt and invent methods that work well not only in the hands of designers but also with clients and other direct and indirect stakeholders. It led us to explore those same methods successfully with personal technologies like implantable medical devices (Denning et al., 2010) and mobile

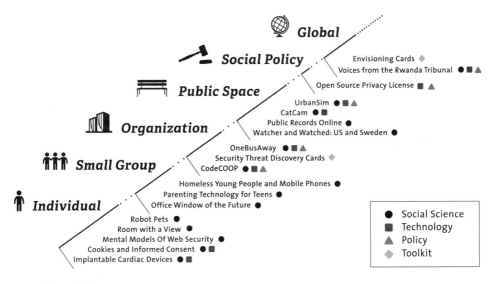

**Figure 1.1**
Projects that engage different levels of human experience. Slide reproduced from University Faculty Lecture, University of Washington (Friedman, 2013).

phone parenting technologies (Czeskis et al., 2010), as well as with new tools for data scientists working with machine-learning algorithms (Bender & Friedman, 2018) and information systems to support international justice (Yoo et al., 2016). Of course, the use of theory and method needs to unfold in a sensitive and responsive manner—each design situation is unique.

Value sensitive design, itself, was designed intentionally with this scope and transferability in mind: an approach that wouldn't break when presented with a new set of values, a new technology, a new population, or a new context or circumstance of use.

Related to robustness, in putting forth a new design approach with new processes, methods, and theoretical commitments, we considered carefully how best to "test" the approach and make the case for its effectiveness. Reflecting both on supporters and skeptics, we settled on the strategy of "proof-of-concept" projects that would first show, then tell, about the approach. That is, we argued for the viability of a value sensitive design approach through the making of artifacts that employed the approach to realized desired aims. Thus, those who would challenge the approach would need to argue not only with representations on paper but also with the existence of the built artifacts themselves. This strategy proved especially effective with those who initially thought such value sensitive design couldn't be done, as the artifacts clearly demonstrated otherwise. Moreover, because we often found ourselves treading new ground—the possibility for informed consent with web browsers in early 2000 (Friedman et al., 2000a; Millett et al., 2001; Friedman et al., 2002a; Friedman, Hurley, Howe, Felton, & Nissenbaum, 2002b); the possibility for social and moral engagement with robots in the mid-2000s (Friedman, Kahn, & Hagman, 2003; Kahn, Freier, Friedman, Severson, & Feldman, 2004; Kahn, Friedman, Alexander, Freier, & Collett, 2005); the possibility for gender differences in the experience of privacy in public (Friedman et al., 2006a; Friedman et al., 2008a); and so forth—we often found ourselves at the forefront of key issues concerning the moral and ethical impact of emerging information and computing technologies.

Stepping back, scholars engaged over several decades in developing any robust body of work will likely make adjustments along the way. How could that not be the case? If it were otherwise, no new knowledge, experiences, or approaches would have been discovered, invented, or expanded. Value sensitive design is no exception. From early on, we have been alert in framing value sensitive design to articulating the approach so that, as appropriate, it could accommodate elaboration, growth, development, expansion, and discovery. Our primary strategy is to be precise about our intellectual commitments without being overly prescriptive or constraining. While much of the initial framing of value sensitive design remains intact and methods developed early on are still useful, other changes have occurred as follows: theoretical constructs have been elaborated or expanded to address gaps; some theoretical constructs have been clarified or reframed in response to new knowledge or critique; many new methods have been developed or adapted; new ways of employing earlier methods have been explored; and open questions have been articulated. As appropriate in this book, we call attention to instances for which later articulation of value sensitive design theory, method, and practice diverge from earlier accounts.

## Situating Value Sensitive Design Historically

New ideas and ways of doing come about in response to what has been done before—in part building upon, in part reacting against. People bring to each new situation what they have experienced, perceived, and understood from their positions in culture, history, and time. So, too, the story of value sensitive design begins in a particular place and moment in time.

Sociotechnical change was afoot. Circa the early 1990s, particularly in the United States where value sensitive design has its roots, computing technology had moved out of elite universities and a handful of large companies into mainstream society. The convergence of at least three sociotechnical developments were in play. The first was the development and commercialization of the personal computer in the mid- to late 1970s. Personal computers put computing into the hands of "just plain folks." Next on the scene was the Internet, a national backbone enabling communication among computer systems. Commercial Internet services began to emerge in the United States in the late 1980s. Then, in 1989–1990, Tim Berners-Lee released a protocol that would underlie the World Wide Web, enabling information services that could run over the Internet and provide more intuitive ways to access, receive, and share information. With these three innovations—the personal computer, the Internet, and the World Wide Web—just plain folks (albeit those who could afford a personal computer and the cost of Internet service), from the comfort of their homes, schools, communities, organizations, etc., could access and share information as well as build online communities at will.

These decades were bursting with visions of "high tech, high touch," machines pervading everyday life, and the talk of such machines. Bill Gates called for a "computer in every home and on every desk." Intelligent tutoring systems, programming languages for young children (Logo), video games running on PCs, word processing in offices, and automation filled newspaper headlines, reflecting the public's fascinations and fears. Scholars were scurrying to study these sociotechnical phenomena as rapidly as they enfolded—in workplaces, in hospitals, in schools.[1] Sociologists

1. Batya Friedman was in conversation with many of these individuals in various ways. In her early twenties, she worked in computing education at the Lawrence Hall of Science, Berkeley, California, and participated in the first National Science

such as Rob Kling (1996) and Shoshana Zuboff (1988) were on the forefront, examining impacts on work, power, and social choice. Psychologists such as Sherry Turkle (1984) were asking questions about identity and the human spirit, and educators such as Seymour Papert and Cynthia Solomon (1971) were empowering kids with technology and laying the foundation for the maker movement. Philosophers such as Hubert Dreyfus (1972) were thinking about the fundamental limitations of artificial intelligence. Moral philosophers such as James Moor (1979) were asking, "are there decisions that computers should never make?" Ordinary life was becoming the purview of this extraordinary machine.

Continuing with our story, by the mid-to-late 80s, four research communities were engaging directly with one or more aspects of human values and computing and information technology, and doing important work: computer ethics, social informatics, computer-supported cooperative work, and participatory design (Friedman & Kahn, 2003). Yet none of these communities were directly taking up design and engineering questions of how to design responsibly and sensitively to human values in the context of widespread, diverse computing development and adoption. To understand the circumstances that motivated the development of value sensitive design, we consider the actors, focus, and contributions of each community below in turn, circa the 1990s.

Critical to any discussion of human values in relation to technology is the applied moral philosophical community, particularly those concerned with technology, and specifically computing technology. The computer ethics community (Bynum, 1985; Johnson, 1985; Moor, 1985), comprised primarily of applied moral philosophers, had begun to utilize existing moral theory to bring clarity to the issues at hand and—at appropriate times—to

---

Foundation-funded teacher-training workshops for Logo, bringing her into conversation with Seymour Papert and Cynthia Solomon. Shortly thereafter, as a graduate student at UC Berkeley, Friedman attended philosophy courses offered by John Searle and talks by Hubert Dreyfus. In the years that followed, she presented talks at the MIT Media Lab and developed a professional friendship with Sherry Turkle. Rob Kling was the acting editor at *ACM Transactions on Information Systems* who handled publication of Friedman and Nissenbaum's 1996 paper on bias in computer systems. Friedman and Kling also met at meetings around sociotechnical systems, debating possibilities for a more humanistic approach to computer science education.

prescribe norms of behavior, as well as to explore how such innovations might extend the boundaries of traditional ethical concepts, such as privacy and agency.

Complementing this more philosophical discourse, the social informatics community (Attewell, 1987; Iacono & Kling, 1987; King, 1983; Kling, 1980), at the time not yet coalesced under this label and comprised primarily of social scientists, emphasized the sociotechnical analyses of deployed technologies. As a community, they engaged in an interdisciplinary study of the design, uses, and consequences of information technologies that took into account interaction with institutional and cultural contexts. As a group, this body of work demonstrated how the introduction of computing technology into organizations changed the nature of work, communication, commerce, education, and so forth—and, reciprocally, how individuals and organizations worked around computing/technical features to (re)assert their values. Taken together, these studies laid important groundwork for an interactional understanding of technology and human values.

However, neither the philosophical work nor the social informatics work provided much guidance for designers and engineers engaged in addressing human values in their technical work. Indeed, at this time, only two communities were doing so, and both were working in well-defined contexts tied to the workplace.

The computer-supported cooperative work community (Galegher, Kraut, & Egido, 1990; Greif, 1988; Grudin, 1988) focused initially on the design and development of new technologies to help people collaborate effectively in the workplace—typically computer professionals working in relatively small groups and sometimes remotely. At the time, the values considered in computer-supported cooperative work systems were closely tied to group activities and workplace issues: cooperation, of course, but also such values as privacy, autonomy, ownership, security, and trust.

Finally, the participatory design community (Bjerknes & Bratteteig, 1995; Bødker, 1990; Ehn, 1988; Greenbaum & Kyng, 1991; Kyng & Mathiassen, 1997), comprised primarily of Scandinavian technologists and designers working (again, at the time) in an environment with strong labor unions and co-determination laws, developed a new approach to system design and development that fundamentally sought to empower workers' knowledge and a sense of work practice into the system design and development process. In terms of value considerations, participatory design historically had deeply embedded within it a commitment to democratization of the workplace and human welfare as well as techniques to address unequal power relations within workplace settings.

Value sensitive design emerged out of this intellectual landscape in the early to mid-1990s in response to the perceived need for a broad-based design approach to account for human values and social context. In contrast to the research communities above, value sensitive design specifically targeted the design and development process to enable technologists and others to be proactive about engaging human values in the design process, and it took a broad perspective on human values, type of technology, and context of use.

Why the name "value sensitive design?" Labels matter. During this period, a wide range of variations on the label were considered. Following labels popular at the time (e.g., user-centered design, usable design, human-centered design), some options included value-centered design and value-based design. However, these were set aside as they seemed to imply that values would dominate other considerations in the technical design process. From the beginning, value sensitive design was conceptualized as an approach that would be engaged alongside of and intermingle with existing, well-functioning technical approaches. A label was sought to convey that relationship—to bring forward (be sensitive to) human values, but at the same time not to supplant the important technical efforts in their own right. Hence, the name: value sensitive design.

In its earliest published form, value sensitive design appeared hyphenated with the first letter of each word capitalized—"Value-Sensitive Design." As the term gained some purchase in the literature, the hyphen seemed unnecessary and awkward, and was dropped; hence, "Value Sensitive Design." Then, as the approach moved beyond a small group of initial researchers to be appropriated more broadly, any earlier sense of the term as a brand for a particular set of people's work was supplanted to reflect wider use, and the initial capital letters dropped except for titles or to introduce the approach; thus, "value sensitive design." Notably, similar changes in capitalization and use can be seen for the terms "participatory design" and "computer-supported cooperative work."

## Bounding the Book

The value sensitive design literature is large and experiencing rapid growth. A Google Scholar search in January 2018 on the phrase "value sensitive design" returned over 3,500 works. A Google Scholar search on "value sensitive design" by year, from 2010 to 2016, returned 460 new works in 2010 and 935 new works in 2016, suggesting a growth trajectory. This is one reasonable, if imperfect, indicator of impact. In addition, the diffusion across fields appears to be significant, with publications ranging for example from workload management (Harbers & Neerincx, 2017) and digital journalism (Dörr & Hollnbuchner, 2017) to sustainable energy (Mok & Hyysalo, 2018).

Methodological development and innovation is rich within this body of work. Methods and theory engage, for example, transcultural and cross-cultural design (Alsheikh, Rode, & Lindley, 2011; Burmeister, 2013; Pereira & Baranauskas, 2015; Abokhodair & Vieweg, 2016); health informatics (Schikhof, Mulder, & Choenni, 2010; Huldtgren, Wiggers, & Jonker, 2014; Burmeister, 2016; Fitzpatrick, Huldtgren, Malmborg, Harley, & Ijsselsteijn, 2015; Novitzky et al., 2015; Pakrasi, Burmeister, Coppola, McCallum, & Loeb, 2015; Teipel et al., 2016; Grünloh, 2018); care robots in health settings (van Wynsberghe, 2013, 2015; Felzmann, Beyan, Ryan, & Beyan, 2016); empowerment and marginalization in crowd-work (Deng, Joshi, & Galliers, 2016); appropriation within action research (Weibert, Randall, & Wulf, 2017); embedding ethical and moral considerations throughout the software development lifecycle (Harbers, Detweiler, & Neerincx, 2015; Spiekermann, 2015; Ferrario et al., 2016); responsible innovation and value sensitive design (van den Hoven, 2013); and still other developments in varied application domains (e.g., Walldius, Sundblad, & Borning, 2005; Pommeranz, Detweiler, Wiggers, & Jonker, 2012; Shilton, 2012; van de Poel, 2013; Walldius & Lantz, 2013; Solomon, 2014; Stark & Tierney, 2014; JafariNaimi, Nathan, & Hargraves, 2015; Millar, 2016).

Furthermore, over the past 20 or more years, a large amount of work has been inspired by or developed in relation to value sensitive design. As a case in point, many different terms have been introduced to frame and describe work related to technology, values, and design, including: reflective design (Sengers, Boehner, David, & Kaye, 2005); value-centered human-computer interaction (Cockton, 2004); value-centered design (Cockton,

2005; Knight, 2008), later renamed worth-centered design (Cockton, 2006; Camara & Calvary, 2015); value-conscious design (Belman, Nissenbaum, Flanagan, & Diamond, 2011; Manders-Huits & Zimmer, 2009); values at play (Flanagan, Howe, & Nissenbaum, 2005); values for design (van den Hoven, 2005); values in design (Flanagan, Howe, & Nissenbaum, 2008; Knobel & Bowker, 2011); and, most recently, value-inspired design (Purao & Wu, 2013), ethical, value-based IT system design (Spiekermann, 2015), and values in computing (www.valuesincomputing.org). Simply put, this work largely seeks to move user-centered design, and more generally human-computer interaction, toward an even greater focus on human values—that is, what people believe to be important (Bannon, 2011; Harper, Rodden, Rogers, & Sellen, 2008).

Much additional literature is relevant to value sensitive design. Early interest in technology, values, and design can be found, for example, in the work of Mumford (1934), Wiener (1954/1985, 1985), Papanek (1971), and Kling (1980). Fields such as computer ethics, information systems, media studies, and science and technology studies are also relevant (for a review, see Snyder, Shilton, & Anderson, 2016). Numerous perspectives on design, moreover, are highly relevant to the theory, method, and practice of value sensitive design, including ability-based design (Wobbrock, Gajos, Kane, & Vanderheiden, 2018); adversarial design (DiSalvo, 2012); collapse informatics (Tomlinson et al., 2013); contestational design and surreptitious communication design (Hirsch, 2008; Hirsch, 2016); critical design (Malpass, 2013; Bardzell, Bardzell, & Stolterman, 2014); feminist design (Bardzell, 2010; Rode, 2011); empowered design (Marsden, 2008); ludic design (Blythe et al., 2010); positive computing (Calvo & Peters, 2014); postcolonial computing (Irani, Vertesi, Dourish, Philip, & Grinter, 2010; Philip, Irani, & Dourish, 2012); privacy by design (Koops & Leenes, 2014); sustainable interaction design (Blevis, 2007; Nathan, 2012); and systems for human benefit (Venable, Pries-Heje, Bunker, & Russo, 2011), among many others. In addition, participatory design has continued to evolve vigorously (Ehn, 2008; Binder et al., 2011; Vines, Clarke, Wright, McCarthy, & Olivier, 2013), and its older and more recent contributions to the literature are highly relevant to value sensitive design.

It is beyond the scope of this book to pursue a thorough analysis of this large literature (for a review, see Shilton, 2018). Instead, our goal is to bring together in one place a current articulation of value sensitive design.

Beginning with theory, we discuss the underpinnings of value sensitive design. Then, we bring together 17 value sensitive design methods, showing how theory and method go hand in hand. We discuss each method and explore how it can be used to address values in the research and design processes. The book also includes reports on applications from 10 technical domains, each authored by leading researchers in that domain. We conclude with a discussion of several published critiques, with an assessment of the robustness of the current state of value sensitive design, and lastly with some reflections for furthering and deepening value sensitive design. We end with a commitment to progress, not perfection.

## 2   Theory

Value sensitive design rests on a core set of theoretical commitments. Some speak to technology (*tools and technology*), some to human beings and societies, human and nonhuman (*stakeholders*), some to values (*human values; value tensions*), and some to their interrelation (*interactional stance*). Finally, others speak to design practice (*tripartite methodology; co-evolving technology and social structure; multi-lifespan design; progress, not perfection*). These commitments should be understood to be mutually constitutive. Together, the commitments clarify the human relationship with technology and set the stage for design.

### Tools and Technology

Tools and technologies are fundamental to the human condition.[1] They do no less than create and structure the conditions in which we live, express ourselves, enact society, and experience what it means to be human.

The boundary between tools and technology is not a sharp one. As a heuristic, one might think of *tools* in their simpler sense as human-scale physical artifacts that augment human activity. The stone axe head, the wooden plough, and the paring knife are a few. *Technology* extends our ideas about tools to include the application of scientific knowledge to solve practical problems, including the specific methods, materials, and devices employed. Factory robots and tractors fit this characterization, as

1. Other intelligent, nonhuman species may also be toolmakers and users (Savage-Rumbaugh, Williams, Furuichi, & Kano, 1996; van de Waal, 2006; Hart, Hart, McCoy, & Sarath, 2001). Perhaps as our understandings of these species develop in the future, including their technology, culture, and society, value sensitive design may be meaningfully extended.

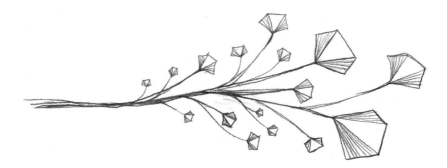

do computers, spaceships, and nuclear power plants. Some might wish to argue that even stone axe heads, wooden ploughs, and paring knives belong here as well, since they, too, involve the application of at least some sort of rudimentary scientific knowledge. In any case, there is clearly a continuum. A sharp stone used for shaping wood is a tool, as is, presumably, a mechanical hand drill. What about an electric drill? A computer-controlled milling machine? We would prefer not to belabor this point; the difference is at most one of degree. To tools and technology, we then add *infrastructure*— the basic physical and organizational structures and facilities needed for the operation of a society or enterprise. This includes the buildings, roads, energy sources, and other structures that enable complex societal activities such as communication, transportation, and information flow. Taken together, tools, technology, and infrastructure comprise what some might term a technological system. When speaking of one—tool, technology, or infrastructure—it is nearly impossible not to speak of the others. For purposes of this book, we will use the term technology as a shorthand to refer to all three and their interdependencies.

We tend to view technology in terms of artifacts. But it is also possible to view policy in this light—particularly as some combination of tool and infrastructure. After all, policy also shapes, albeit through law and regulation, human activity. For purposes of value sensitive design, we currently consider policy to be a form of technology.

The design and diffusion of technologies typically involve diverse actors and relationships. One kind of relationship exists between the actors in the design and use contexts (Albrechtslund, 2007). Here, clients, co-designers, designers, field-testers, inventors, and so forth imagine and develop technology that, later, is appropriated and integrated into society by other kinds of actors. Limited in part by the human ability to foresee, designers simply cannot anticipate the many ways a technology will be adopted, appropriated, or, in the extreme, used subversively; nor can designers fully anticipate the consequences of a technology on social life. That said, we shall see that value sensitive design offers methods (e.g., direct and indirect stakeholder analysis, value scenarios, Envisioning Cards) that position designers to envision the many actors and relationships that emerge through the technology design process.

At its core, value sensitive design is technology agnostic. That is, in principle the theory, method, and practice of value sensitive design are not tied to any specific technology. They could just as well be applied to the development of brain-machine interfaces as to technologies for agriculture, energy, or water treatment. That said, the vast majority of early work in value sensitive design concerned information technology. For example, projects engaged with artificial intelligence and autonomous agents (Friedman & Kahn, 1992; Friedman & Nissenbaum, 1997); computer algorithms (Friedman & Nissenbaum, 1996); web browser security (Friedman, Howe, & Felten, 2002); human-robot interaction (Kahn et al., 2007; Kahn, Friedman, Perez-Granados, & Freier, 2006); location-aware mobile devices (Czeskis et al., 2010; Friedman, Smith, Kahn, Consolvo, & Selawski, 2006c); large-scale urban simulation (Borning, Friedman, Davis, & Lin, 2005; Davis et al., 2006); and groupware knowledge systems (Miller, Friedman, Jancke, & Gill, 2007). With the emergence of the Internet of Things, we see an increased blurring between information systems, on the one hand, and physical systems on the other. Here value sensitive design has been applied to "things" such as wireless implantable cardiac devices (Denning et al., 2010) and public transportation information systems (Watkins, Ferris, Malinovskiy, & Borning, 2013b). More recently, value sensitive design has been applied to non-information technologies and processes such as wastewater treatment (de Kreuk, van de Poel, Zwart, & van Loosdrecht, 2010; van de Poel, Zwart, Brumsen, & van Mil, 2005) and wind turbine parks (Oosterlaken, 2015). It remains an open practical question how (if at all) the theory and method of value sensitive design developed primarily with information technologies will need to be adapted or extended to account for human values in the design process of other non-information technology.

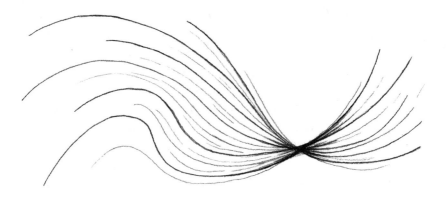

## Human Values

We turn now to explicate how the term "human values" has been understood within value sensitive design.

In 1997, in the introduction to her edited book on *Human Values and the Design of Computer Technology*, Friedman provided a working definition of human values as follows:

In some sense, we can say that any human activity reflects human values. I drink tea instead of soda. I recently attended a Cezanne exhibit instead of a ball game. I have personal values. We all do. But these are not the type of human values which this volume takes up. Rather, this volume is principally concerned with values that deal with human welfare and justice. (p. 3)

This framing placed an emphasis on human welfare and justice—what some might call moral values. Moreover, Friedman pointed to ways in which culture and context inform people's understandings and experiences of both welfare and justice (e.g., in Western societies, most people believe that if a person chooses to wear a bathrobe that is a personal choice; but if a person wears a bathrobe to a dignitary's funeral, many people would judge that event not only as a conventional violation, but a moral violation as well—a sign of disrespect). Following Turiel (1983), Friedman further drew on the psychological literature to distinguish among three broad domains of social knowledge: moral, conventional, and personal. Here, the moral domain refers to prescriptive judgments that people justify on the basis of considerations of justice, fairness, rights, or human welfare. The conventional domain, in contrast, refers to judgments concerning behavioral uniformities that help to promote the smooth functioning of social interactions, and the personal domain to judgments seen as under the jurisdiction of the self. Friedman concluded her discussion with the rationale for focusing on human values rather than more narrowly on only moral ones.

The human values addressed in this volume principally refer to moral values. But I prefer to use the broader term "human values" instead of simply moral values to highlight the complexity of social life, and to provide a basis for analyses wherein personal and conventional values can become morally implicated. (p. 5)

Thus, from its earliest conceptions, value sensitive design sought to emphasize moral and ethical values, but to do so within the complexity of social life and with recognition for how culture and context implicate people's understanding and experience of harms and injustice.

A decade later, Friedman et al. (2006a) expanded the discussion of values within value sensitive design to emphasize *what is important to people in their lives*. Within this broad and gentle conceptualization of "value," they also reaffirmed a focus on ethical and moral values, while at the same time calling attention to the long and ongoing contentious history of framing human values. They wrote:

In a narrow sense, the word "value" refers simply to the economic worth of an object. For example, the value of a computer could be said to be two thousand dollars. However, in the work described here [value sensitive design], we use a broader meaning of the term wherein a value refers to what a person or group of people consider important in life.[1] In this sense, people find many things of value, both lofty and mundane: their children, friendship, morning tea, education, art, a walk in the woods, nice manners, good science, a wise leader, clean air.

This broader framing of values has a long history. Since the time of Plato, for example, the content of value-oriented discourse has ranged widely, emphasizing "the good, the end, the right, obligation, virtue, moral judgment, aesthetic judgment, the beautiful, truth, and validity" [Frankena, 1972, p. 229]. Sometimes ethics has been subsumed within a theory of values, and other times conversely, with ethical values viewed as just one component of ethics more generally. Either way, it is usually agreed [Moore, 1903/1978] that values should not be conflated with facts (the "fact/value distinction") especially insofar as facts do not logically entail value. In other words, "is" does not imply "ought" (the naturalistic fallacy). In this way, values cannot be motivated only by an empirical account of the external world, but depend substantively on the interests and desires of human beings within a cultural milieu.

[1] The Oxford English Dictionary definition of this sense of value is: "the principles or standards of a person or society, the personal or societal judgment of what is valuable and important in life." (Friedman et al., 2006a, p. 349)

Since 2006, reflection on completed and ongoing work has led to this current working definition of "value" within value sensitive design: *what is important to people in their lives, with a focus on ethics and morality.*

Over the years, critiques have surfaced about how value sensitive design has conceptualized "human value." They take primarily two forms, largely reflecting debates in moral philosophy and the social sciences. For those who seek normative positions (these tend to be moral philosophers), the current formulation of human values within value sensitive design is underspecified (see, for example, Albrechtslund, 2007; Manders-Huits, 2011; van de Poel, 2009). Conversely, for those with leanings toward culture-, community-, or individual-specific positions—or who believe that value sensitive design should accommodate researchers with these views— the current formulation of human values within value sensitive design may imply too great an underlying universality (Borning & Muller, 2012; Le Dantec, Poole, & Wyche, 2009). Granted, both types of dissatisfactions are understandable. After all, the working definition of "human values," while retaining moral and ethical sensibilities, does not spell out *what* is important to people in their lives. That work is left to individual researchers and designers as they move forward on specific projects. For example, some might wish to draw on ethical principles from Buddhism, others from a care ethics, still others from a consequentialist or deontic position. At the same time, the working definition is intended to hold a commitment to moral and ethical sensibilities. Thus, it is incumbent on those working from a culture-, community-, or individual-specific perspective to establish the basis for and bring forward the ethical and moral dimensions within that perspective.

Given the complexity of social life, the technological development process, the commitments of designers, and the unresolved nature of debates on morality, this working definition provides an appropriate balance. That is, it positions value sensitive design to engage with important moral and ethical considerations in light of technology design and legitimates other considerations that are important to people in their lives; it leaves the explication of both to the details of any particular design project. For example, van Wynsberghe (2013) engages value sensitive design from a perspective of care ethics, Cummings (2006) from that of a just war. In these respective perspectives, both authors pay careful attention to the moral and ethical aspects of the technology under study, employing the working definition for human values put forth here. Moreover, in the sections below, we shall see that through certain theoretical constructs, as well as through certain methods, value sensitive design provides some explicit checks and balances on the design process. For example, the commitment to explicitly surface and engage direct and indirect stakeholders extends human dignity and moral standing to those affected by a technology.

Perhaps these debates will never be resolved. However, if, over time, aspects of these debates on morality are resolved, then refinements that reflect those new understandings could be incorporated into a future working definition of human values for value sensitive design.

*On the interconnection among human values.* We also make the observation that within lived life, human values do not exist in isolation—with, for example, privacy over here and security or community over there. Rather, in the complexity of human relations and society, values sit in a delicate balance with each other. One useful metaphor might be that of centrifugal force, where the tensions among values, reasonably balanced, work together to hold each respective value in place. For example, consider the case of public records in the United States, such as campaign finance contributions (Munson et al., 2012). Historically, these records were made public to help provide transparency and support the democratic process; however, access was constrained by the resources and effort needed to travel to the civic buildings where the records were stored. Thus, a balance between transparency on the one hand and privacy on the other hand was maintained through ease (or lack thereof) of access. As current civic offices are putting their public records online and ease of access is increasing, the earlier balance between transparency and privacy is being disturbed. Whether or not the new balance is a positive change remains to be seen. Our point here is that in addressing one value, likely others will be implicated. One methodological implication of this observation is that not only do individual values need to be understood and studied vis-à-vis any given technology, but the balance among relevant values must be engaged as well.

*On heuristic lists of human values.* The question arises whether it would be helpful to provide initial heuristic lists of human values with corresponding working definitions from which others could build (see also Borning & Muller [2012] for a discussion of pros and cons, including engagement with

Le Dantec et al., 2009).[2] Providing any specific heuristic list of human values runs the risk of privileging or reifying those values over others and, correspondingly, those stakeholder groups who feel themselves well reflected in that particular list of values, either by the inclusion or exclusion of certain values. Moreover, any list of human values would likely be incomplete. In response to this concern, an alternative process might allow for stakeholder groups to identify their own list of values. That said, naming no human values and providing no working definitions misses an opportunity to legitimate at least some human values in the design of technology and to help bring those human values into the conversation. It also misses an opportunity to build on previous work, otherwise requiring each new effort to engage the time-consuming process of identifying and developing working definitions of values from scratch.

Acknowledging the former and mindful of the latter, in 2003, Friedman and Kahn discussed a set of 12 specific values with ethical import. They were careful to call out limitations of this approach, including the incompleteness of the list as well as this particular list's roots in deontological and consequentialist moral orientations. Moreover, writing at a point in time where human values received very little attention and resources in the design process, they had hoped by providing such a set they would help to legitimate substantive engagement with human values in the design process. Toward that end, they wrote as follows:

We review and discuss 12 specific values with ethical import. ... [B]y including these values here, we highlight their ethical status, and thereby suggest they have a distinct claim on resources in the design process. (p. 1187)

Notably, here, in the phrase "and thereby suggest *they* have a distinct claim on resources in the design process" (italics added) the word "they"

---

2. Of note, within the capabilities approach, a similar debate for similar reasons (though perhaps with stronger positions) occurs between Nussbaum and Sen regarding the identification and selection of capabilities. According to Robeyns (2011), Nussbaum endorses a well-defined list of capabilities, one that should be enshrined in every country's constitution. Sen has been somewhat vague in responding to the question of how to select and weight capabilities; however, the secondary literature has put forth that Sen draws on his ideal of agency to argue that each group should itself select, weight, trade off, and sequence or otherwise aggregate capabilities as well as prioritize them in relation to other normative considerations, such as agency, efficiency, and stability.

was intended to mean human values more generally (and not the specific human values in the list presented here); the original wording was unfortunately ambiguous.

They continued:

Two caveats: Not all of the values that we review are fundamentally distinct from one another. Nonetheless, each value has its own language and conceptualizations within their respective fields, and thus warrants separate treatment here. Second, this list is not comprehensive. Perhaps no list could be, at least within the confines of a chapter. Peacefulness, compassion, love, warmth, creativity, humor, originality, vision, friendship, cooperation, collaboration, purposefulness, devotion, diplomacy, kindness, musicality, harmony—the list of other possible values could get very long very fast. Our particular list comprises many of the traditional values that hinge on the deontological and consequentialist moral orientations: Human welfare, ownership and property, privacy, freedom from bias, universal usability, trust, autonomy, informed consent, and accountability. In addition, we have chosen several nontraditional values within the [human-computer interaction] ... community: Identity, calmness, and environmental sustainability. Our goal here is not only to point to important areas of future inquiry, but also to illustrate how an overarching framework for human values and ethics in design can move one quickly and substantively into new territory. (p. 1187)

A few years later, Friedman et al. (2006a) revisited this list, with an emphasis on human values with ethical import that were often implicated in system design. We reproduce the table with that list of values and working definitions, omitting the column of references (see table 2.1). The pragmatic concerns remain: how to avoid reification of a certain set of values or world views, while at the same time positioning those bringing value sensitive design into their research and design processes to build upon each others' prior work. The tensions here may best be addressed through practice (see Borning & Muller [2012] for some suggestions).

*Beyond human values.* One last reflection on human values—what *people* consider important in their lives. This framing privileges the perspectives and values of human beings. After all, value sensitive design concerns the design process of technology that is carried out by human beings. Yet the technologies we design and build reach far beyond human beings to implicate other nonhuman entities. Here are four for consideration: nonhuman species, superorganisms, the Earth, and social robots. In sorting out how to account for nonhumans in value sensitive design, both homocentric (valuing nonhumans because of what they offer human beings) and biocentric

**Table 2.1**
Human Values (with Ethical Import) Often Implicated in System Design

| Human Value | Definition |
| --- | --- |
| Human welfare | Refers to people's physical, material, and psychological well-being |
| Ownership and property | Refers to a right to possess an object (or information), use it, manage it, derive income from it, and bequeath it |
| Privacy | Refers to a claim, an entitlement, or a right of an individual to determine what information about himself or herself can be communicated to others |
| Freedom from bias | Refers to systematic unfairness perpetrated on individuals or groups, including pre-existing social bias, technical bias, and emergent social bias |
| Universal usability | Refers to making all people successful users of information technology |
| Trust | Refers to expectations that exist between people who can experience good will, extend good will toward others, feel vulnerable, and experience betrayal |
| Autonomy | Refers to people's ability to decide, plan, and act in ways that they believe will help them to achieve their goals |
| Informed consent | Refers to garnering people's agreement, encompassing criteria of disclosure and comprehension (for "informed") and voluntariness, competence, and agreement (for "consent") |
| Accountability | Refers to the properties that ensures that the actions of a person, people, or institution may be traced uniquely to the person, people, or institution |
| Courtesy | Refers to treating people with politeness and consideration |
| Identity | Refers to people's understanding of who they are over time, embracing both continuity and discontinuity over time |
| Calmness | Refers to a peaceful and composed psychological state |
| Environmental sustainability | Refers to sustaining ecosystems such that they meet the needs of the present |

Source: Reprinted in part from Friedman et al. (2006a, p. 364–365).

(valuing all living things in and of themselves) orientations are likely relevant (Kahn, 1999). How to account meaningfully for the values of nonhumans within value sensitive design remains an open question.

## Interactional Stance

Value sensitive design takes an interactional stance on technology and human values. Unlike approaches that lean toward technological determinism or social determinism, interactional theories such as value sensitive design posit that human beings acting as individuals, organizations, or societies shape the tools and technologies they design and implement; in turn, those tools and technologies shape human experience and society (Friedman & Kahn, 2003).

One implication of the interactional stance is that "technology is neither good nor bad; nor is it neutral" (Kranzberg, 1986, p. 545). Thus, design matters. That is, values can be embodied, at least to some extent, within the features of a tool or technology. Electronic document readers, for example, can make text accessible to both blind and sighted people; information

systems that allow for legal names, nicknames, and preferred names might enable people to better represent their identities; multiplayer online games can be competitive or cooperative, thereby reflecting or resisting the values of certain groups of people.

At the same time, designers do not have complete control. Norms, practices, and incentives, perhaps originating from different stakeholders in a complex social ecology, can have a major influence on technology's effects. One group of stakeholders, for example, might use and appropriate a technology according to their values, thus achieving certain ends; while another group might use the same technology according to a different set of values, leading to different ends (Orlikowski, 2000). Framing effects, including persuasive marketing, around the introduction of a technology, opt-in or opt-out rules, and so forth, can be influential. In a different vein, some stakeholders may decide not to use a technology, perhaps to support a principled position or in keeping with a general disposition.

During the design phase of a value sensitive design project, after a period of discovery and analysis, the design team might similarly decide not to build a new technology or not to intervene. Taking no action—and perhaps waiting with vigilance—can be intentional and impactful. Or, after a period of investigation and design work, a design team might determine that rather than intervening with a new technology, the best path forward would be to return to a prior technical solution. Consider, for example, a brand of electronic voting machines that do not provide a reliable chain of custody. In this case, perhaps the team decides to intervene by recommending that the voting machines be decommissioned and replaced with the old mechanical paper-based system.

A further implication concerns anticipated and unanticipated effects that may arise when placing a technology in different settings. Since different groups of stakeholders are likely to adopt the technology in quite different ways, the effects of the technology are likely to be quite different. Accordingly, the interactional stance implies that the design team needs to be alert and ready for unintended consequences, which may arise narrowly with specific tools or individual practices or more broadly with infrastructure and social practice. In any case, unanticipated effects and impacts can be expected to emerge in a delicate interplay among technology, individuals, and societies.

A final implication is that the interactional stance frames the human-technology relationship as a dynamic process, working across relatively short and long periods of time. Thus, the initial use of a technology might be quite different from its long-term use. Education and training, technical customization, appropriation, workarounds: all of these use practices follow from the interactional stance. From this implication comes the importance of empirical investigations focused on the social context of use, along with technical investigations focused on technical features and mechanisms, pursued iteratively and integratively. This topic is discussed further in the sections on the tripartite methodology and the co-evolution of technology and social structure.

### The Tripartite Methodology: Conceptual, Empirical, and Technical Investigations

Think of an oil painting by Monet or Cézanne. From a distance it looks whole; but up close you see many layers of paint upon paint. Some paints have been applied with careful brushstrokes, others perhaps energetically with a palate knife or fingertips, conveying outlines or regions of color. The diverse techniques are employed one on top of the other, repeatedly, and in response to what has been laid down earlier. Together they create an artifact that could not have been generated by a single technique in isolation of the others. (Friedman et al., 2006a, p. 350)

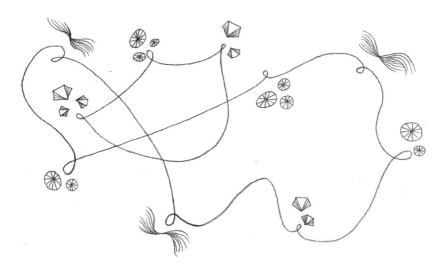

So, too, with value sensitive design. A technology emerges through an unfolding process, which is more than the sum of its parts. Value sensitive design employs an *iterative* methodology that *integrates* conceptual, empirical, and technical investigations.

The tripartite methodology of value sensitive design rests on the interactional stance. That is, values shape technology development, and, in various ways, values can be enmeshed in technology. Thus, technology in some ways reflects the values of the design team—the people responsible for design and implementation—either intentionally or not (Friedman & Kahn, 2003). Accordingly, the tripartite methodology of conceptual, empirical, and technical investigations seeks to position the design team to robustly address the value implications of sociotechnical design.

As the above description of painting conveys, the tripartite methodology structures particular design processes in an iterative and integrative manner, and in practice is best seen in holistic terms. Nevertheless, its parts are a good place to start; hence, we next briefly introduce the conceptual, empirical, and technical investigations.

*Conceptual investigations.* Conceptual investigations—which comprise analytic, theoretical, or philosophically informed explorations of the central issues and constructs under investigation—typically address questions of the following kind: who are the stakeholders? What is likely to be at stake for people and other nonhuman stakeholders? What theoretical commitments and choice of conceptual framework, if any, are made? If the design team makes a commitment to a particular ethical or cultural framework to support principled reasoning, how would it be articulated and integrated into the design process? What values are likely to be implicated? How will values be framed and characterized? What conceptual models, if any, for operationalizing a given value or values will be employed? How will results from an empirical or technical investigation be integrated into the conceptual framework of the project? What value-oriented criteria will be used to judge success of the design?

Value sensitive design projects commonly develop careful working conceptualizations of specific values. These conceptualizations clarify fundamental issues raised by the project at hand and provide a basis for comparing results across research teams. For example, in their analysis of trust in online system design, Friedman, Kahn, and Howe (2000b), drawing on Baier (1986), first offer a philosophically informed working conceptualization of trust. They propose that people trust when they are vulnerable to harm from others, yet believe those others would not harm them even though they could. In turn, trust depends on people's ability to make three types of assessments. One is about the harms they might incur. The second is about the goodwill others possess toward them that would keep those others from doing them harm. The third involves whether or not harms that do occur lie outside the parameters of the trust relationship. From such conceptualizations, Friedman et al. were able to define clearly what they meant by trust online. This definition is in some cases different from what other researchers have meant by the term—for example, the Computer Science and Telecommunications Board, in their thoughtful publication *Trust in Cyberspace* (Schneider, 1999), adopted the terms "trust" and "trustworthy" to describe systems that perform as expected along the dimensions of correctness, security, reliability, safety, and survivability. Such a definition, which equates "trust" with expectations for machine performance, differs in important ways from one that positions trust as fundamentally a relationship among people (sometimes mediated by machines).

The depth and robustness of an initial conceptual investigation can vary from relatively cursory armchair analyses to very thorough analytic work involving an interdisciplinary team that includes, for example, applied ethicists or legal scholars. In practice, conceptual investigations are often generative, leading to framing propositions. In subsequent project phases, initial propositions are likely to be refined or even substantially revised to respond to findings from other investigations.

*Empirical investigations.* Conceptual investigations can only go so far. Depending on the questions at hand, many analyses will need to be informed by empirical investigations of the human context in which the technology is situated. Empirical investigations—which might draw upon the entire range of quantitative and qualitative methods used in social science research—focus, for example, on questions such as: how do stakeholders apprehend individual values in the sociotechnical context? How do stakeholders prioritize competing values or otherwise envision resolution of value tensions? Are there differences between espoused practice (what people say) compared with actual practice (what people do)? Moreover, because the development of new technologies affects groups as well as individuals, questions emerge of how organizations appropriate value considerations in the design process. For example, regarding value considerations, what are organizations' motivations, methods of training and dissemination, reward structures, and economic incentives?

Value sensitive design projects have fruitfully employed such methods as observations, interviews, surveys, experimental manipulations, collection of relevant documents, and measurements of user behavior and human physiology. While some have critiqued value sensitive design for not being more directive about method (e.g., Le Dantec et al., 2009), we are hesitant to be overly prescriptive. Rather, the challenge is to select a method (or a constellation of integrated methods) that fits a particular project at a particular point in the design process. Within that framing, any reasonable method from the social sciences, as long as it is well chosen given the context, may be employed. That said, later in this book we shall discuss 17 methods that over the past two decades have been either invented or appropriated from social science or engineering specifically for value sensitive design.

*Technical investigations.* Value sensitive design adopts the position that technologies provide value suitabilities that follow from properties of the technology. That is, a given technology is more suitable for certain activities and more readily supports certain values, while rendering other activities and values more difficult to realize. Technical investigations—which focus on technology as the unit of analysis—address such questions as: What features of a technical infrastructure enable, hinder, or even foreclose certain kinds of designs for supporting human activity? How do policies, laws, or regulations create opportunities or constrain options for technological development?

In one form—retrospective analyses—technical investigations focus on how existing or historical technological properties and underlying mechanisms support or hinder human values. For example, some video-based collaborative work systems provide blurred views of office settings, while other systems provide clear images that reveal detailed information about who is present and what they are doing. Thus the two designs differentially adjudicate the value tension between an individual's *privacy* and the group's *awareness* of individual members' presence and activities.

In a second form—proactive design—technical investigations involve the design of systems to support values identified in a conceptual investigation. For example, Fuchs (1999) developed a notification service for a collaborative work system in which the underlying technical mechanisms implement a value hierarchy, whereby an individual's desire for privacy overrides other group members' desires for awareness.

*Integrative and iterative investigations.* No one type of investigation is sufficient on its own; rather, all three investigation types are needed to inform and shape and reshape each other. The first robust use of the tripartite methodology reported in the value sensitive design literature can be found in the investigation of informed consent and cookies in web browser security (see the Informed Consent Online section in chapter 4 for a discussion). This work employed a conceptual investigation of informed consent online, both retrospective and proactive technical investigations, an empirical evaluation of the technical work, and then refinement of the initial conceptual investigation based on the empirical results. The Method and Applications chapters that follow provide numerous examples of the diverse ways in which the three types of investigations can be combined, interact with each other, and provide mutually constitutive refinements.

A design process may begin with any of the three types of investigations.[3] Many projects begin with a conceptual investigation to frame the design space and to, for example, at a minimum identify the key stakeholders, values, and potential benefits and harms (Borning & Muller, 2012). Other value sensitive design projects have started with an empirical investigation: see the Human-Robot Interaction, Homeless Young People, and Privacy in Public sections in chapter 4. Still others have begun with a technical investigation: see the Security for Mobile Devices section in chapter 4 and the CodeCOOP group software system (Miller et al., 2007).

### Stakeholders

Given the aim to account for human values in a principled and systematic manner throughout the design process of technology, a critical question becomes: whose values are to be taken into account? Value sensitive design answers this question: those who are or will be significantly implicated by the technology. These simple words belie enormous complexity. How do you define "implicated?" And what makes an implication significant

---

3. We note that in one critique it was suggested value sensitive design requires the design team to begin with a conceptual investigation (Le Dantec et al., 2009); this was an error. To clarify, value sensitive design does not prescribe an order for the different types of investigations.

enough to warrant consideration in the design process? While such questions defy definitive responses, further theoretical constructs in value sensitive design point the way forward.

Value sensitive design adopted "stakeholder," a term with a long history, to refer to those people or entities who are or will be significantly implicated by a technology. In the 1990s, this term stood out in sharp contrast to the dominant language of "users" and "user-centered design," which focused attention almost entirely on the people interacting directly with a technology. The intent was to develop broader language and, thereby, to create space to reach beyond only users to consider systematically those affected by a given technology.

Stakeholder theory and analysis has been developed in varied fields, including management information systems (Mitchell, Agle, & Wood, 1997) and environmental management (Reed, 2008; Reed et al., 2009). Among many definitions, a now-classic definition of stakeholder is the following: "A stakeholder in an organization is (by definition) any group or individual who can affect or is affected by the achievement of the organization's objectives" (Freeman, 1984, cited by Mitchell et al., 1997, p. 856). However, given the pervasiveness of information technologies across all spheres of life, considering stakeholders in terms of an organization is limiting. Stakeholder analysis within human-computer interaction has addressed this limitation to some degree. Shneiderman and Rose (1996), for example, placed stakeholders within a framework for developing social impact statements of information technology design. They defined stakeholder as "anyone who

will be affected, directly or indirectly, by the new system like the end users, the software staff, and the organization's clients" (p. 92). Further, within participatory design, some have argued for stakeholder identification and analysis to extend beyond users (Muller, 1995).

Within value sensitive design, stakeholders are broadly conceived: they can be people, groups, neighborhoods, communities, organizations, institutions, or societies, and can also include past and future generations, non-human species, and other elements such as historic buildings or sacred mountaintops (see Reed, 2008). Value sensitive design asks designers to seek out a robust set of stakeholder groups and to legitimate those stakeholders who have a good deal at stake—that is, to provide an analytical or empirical rationale for their inclusion in a design process. Equally important can be the rationale provided for why certain groups or individuals might be set aside from the design process. Identifying and characterizing stakeholders may require extensive empirical work.

*Roles, not individuals (or other entities).* Stakeholders within value sensitive design are defined by and understood in relationship to their interaction with a technology or sociotechnical system. That is, stakeholders are considered by role, rather than by "person" or other "entity." A "role" pertains to a stakeholder's duties, contextual identity, or particular circumstances. For example, the same person at one point in time might be a user of a technology (e.g., speaking on a cell phone or driving in an autonomous vehicle), and at another point in time a bystander in regard to the same technical system (e.g., sitting in a café near someone else speaking on a cell phone or crossing the street in front of an autonomous car). Defining stakeholders in terms of roles positions designers to understand how the same "entity"[4] could hold multiple relationships to the same technology, as well as the potentially dynamic nature of an entity's relationship to a particular technology. As explicated in chapter 3, the potential for dynamic roles can provide unique opportunities for value elicitation as well as for engaging value tensions.

*Explicitly supported project values, designer values, and other stakeholder values.* Taking an overarching perspective on technology design, four broad categories of stakeholders and their respective values come to the fore: the project sponsors; the designers; and all other direct stakeholders (i.e., the

---

4. Note that the term "entity" is used here to account for nonhuman stakeholders such as an organization, nonhuman species, or sacred mountaintop.

users) and indirect stakeholders. Explicitly supported project values refer to the values articulated by project sponsors and clients, or to those values that are found within the project goals. These are the values that motivate the project and comprise the project's core commitments. Designers bring their own personal and professional values to their work, including professional ethical standards. These are referred to as designer values. In addition to the stakeholders just mentioned, there are also the stakeholders largely outside of the project—those who will in some way be implicated by the system, either directly or indirectly, now or in the future.

Within value sensitive design, successful design processes normally account for explicitly supported project values, designer values, and stakeholder values. At a minimum, in addition to surfacing other stakeholder values, designers are encouraged to make their own values, as well as the project values, explicit and transparent throughout the design process. Such transparency can help to surface areas where values among different stakeholders largely are aligned or where there may be tensions. In instances where tensions are identified among explicitly supported project values, designer values, and other stakeholder values, methods will be needed to mitigate those tensions. For example, in the design of a large-scale urban simulation for land use and transportation, Borning et al. (2005) encountered tensions among the explicitly supported project values of democratization of the urban planning process and representativeness of stakeholder perspectives; individual designers' values, which tended toward environmental sustainability; and other special interest group stakeholder values, which included economic development, among other goals. To help ensure an appropriate overall framing among these values, they developed a set of principles and a prioritization scheme for determining workflow. Approaches for addressing value tensions are discussed below.

*Direct and indirect stakeholder roles.* A fundamental distinction in role concerns the distinction between stakeholders who directly interact with a system—the *direct stakeholders*—and those *indirect stakeholders* who, although they never or rarely interact with the system as end users, are nevertheless affected by the system. One clarifying example is a medical record system that is designed for doctors, nurses, and insurance companies—the direct stakeholders—but is not intended to be used by the patients, the indirect stakeholders. Clearly, an individual patient obtains benefit or harm from the system, although he or she might never interact with it. Similarly, because medical record systems may affect the economics of health care, society at large might also be considered an indirect stakeholder.

Consider these further examples, which begin to illustrate how the distinction between direct and indirect stakeholders can clarify, expand, and enrich a possible design space: police officers (direct) with video cameras in their cars and bystanders (indirect) who happen to be video recorded; parents (indirect) who may be impacted by scheduling choices negotiated by an elementary school student (direct) and his teacher (direct) in a classroom calendaring system; snow leopards (direct) with GPS collars who are tracked by game wardens (direct) to be protected from poachers (indirect); and a college student's (direct) yet-to-be-born child (direct, albeit in the future) who might one day be curious about her parent's college photographs on Facebook. As noted above, with the distinction between direct and indirect stakeholders, it is possible to explore what happens when the same individual shifts between these roles. Consider again a police officer driving a patrol car equipped with a video recording application. When on duty, she would be in a direct stakeholder role; but when off-duty on an evening walk, should she happen to be recorded by a colleague's patrol car, she would be in an indirect stakeholder role.

In addition to direct and indirect stakeholder roles, it is often useful to consider stakeholders in terms of targeted and nontargeted roles (Nathan, Friedman, Klasjna, Kane, & Miller, 2008). A targeted role is the typical, expected role that a stakeholder might hold. A nontargeted role, on the other hand, is an atypical case. In a groupware system, for example, uncooperative employees who coordinate creative hacks to game the system would likely be in nontargeted roles. In this vein, and germane for security analyses, a common nontargeted role that often requires consideration is the malicious role when, for example, a once-trusted insider becomes a thief.

Given the close mapping between direct stakeholders and users as studied in user-centered design, a good deal is known and documented about direct stakeholder roles in the human-computer interaction literature. Less has been documented about indirect stakeholder roles, so we call out a few patterns here. The "bystander" noted above is one common type of indirect stakeholder role. This role occurs when a direct stakeholder in interaction with a technology impacts—either positively or negatively—another in close physical or digital proximity. For example, while commuting on public transport, one passenger, the bystander, is likely to be bothered by a second passenger (the direct stakeholder) who is holding a loud, intimate conversation via his mobile phone. In this situation it is difficult, if not impossible, for the bystander to maintain the role of being "left alone." On the other hand, in an emergency situation, the same bystander might benefit from the availability of another passenger's mobile phone and call to public emergency responders. In this example, we see that the widespread availability of mobile phones may at times undermine aspects of bystanders' privacy, while also offering a degree of safety.

Another common indirect stakeholder role is the "human data point." This role occurs when data about an indirect stakeholder is sensed and recorded in an information system that the stakeholder does not have a way to access directly. The example above of patient data in an electronic medical record is one example. Other examples include video recordings of citizens in a public space by police wearing body-worn cameras; video recordings of license plates at public street intersections by electronic vehicle systems; smart-city sensing and recording of water usage patterns by utility companies; and recording, retention, and analysis of search queries and results by search companies. Some people may expend considerable effort to identify and avoid the many situations where they may otherwise unwittingly (Vines et al., 2013) become a "human data point." This kind of indirect stakeholder role underlies the ability to provide good information about patterns of human behavior for improving computing and other services as well as underlies the surveillance society—by corporations and by government.[5] Identifying and documenting other types of indirect stakeholder roles remains an open line of inquiry.

With this language—namely the distinction between direct and indirect stakeholders and the notion of roles, both targeted and nontargeted—we can see how stakeholders hold varying relationships with technology. This said, any analysis will be limited by the human ability to foresee how technologies will be appropriated—and experience shows that it is difficult, if not impossible, to anticipate all uses and practices. Nevertheless, developing descriptive accounts of stakeholder-technology relationships through these distinctions provides a means for legitimating stakeholders.

---

5. Similar data point roles can be found in studies of ecosystems; for example, when a few wolves in a larger pack are collared with GPS trackers to investigate human-wolf behaviors.

The "watcher and the watched" empirical studies (Friedman, Kahn, Hagman, Severson, & Gill, 2006b), for example, considered the psychological welfare of both the direct stakeholders (the watcher) as well as the indirect stakeholders (the watched). The CodeCoop study (Miller et al., 2007) considered the design of groupware for software engineers who took on varying roles (code contributors vs. questioners vs. code re-users). The UrbanSim research (Davis, 2008) considered how indirect stakeholders (homeowners) might be positioned to become direct stakeholders by becoming active contributors in urban planning. These and other studies discussed in chapter 4 show approaches for legitimating and engaging stakeholders. Discussion of methods for working with stakeholders, including harms and benefits analyses, can be found in chapter 3.

*Pro-social stakeholder roles.* Typically, when conducting stakeholder analyses, the orientation is toward how that stakeholder might directly or indirectly benefit or be harmed by the technology. However, at times, stakeholders are implicated not by how the technology affects them, per se, but rather by the position the technology places them in vis-à-vis the possibility of helping others—what is known as "pro-social action." Pro-social action refers to when and why people act to help others, often seemingly voluntarily and without obvious benefit to themselves. The ethical, societal, and psychological aspects of pro-social actions and situations have been well studied in the moral philosophical as well as moral psychological literature (Bar-Tal, 1976; Eisenberg, Fabes, & Spinrad, 2007; Schroeder & Graziano, 2015). There is much to draw on here.

The pro-social role can apply to both indirect and direct stakeholders. Rector, Milne, Ladner, Friedman, and Kientz (2015) bring to the fore the pro-social bystander in their work exploring opportunities for exercise technologies for people who are blind or low-vision. In one scenario involving rigorous outdoor exercise, a blind or low-vision jogger is able to run freely and unescorted on a public track by using a head-mounted display and headphones to hear whether or not he is staying in his lane. They point out that should the blind or low-vision jogger encounter difficulties (e.g., veering off the track), other sighted joggers who happen to be running at the track might find themselves in a situation where they could step in to help. If so, what should sighted individuals in physical proximity to the blind or low-vision jogger do? What actions are they morally implicated to take to help, and how can they do so in a manner responsive to the wishes, dignity, and autonomy of the blind or low-vision jogger? In such situations know-ing if, when, and how to help can be complex and nuanced. An analogous pro-social direct stakeholder can be seen in work on OneBusAway (Bonnar, Campbell, Drapeau, Bennett & Borning, 2015). This work explored ways to encourage regular OneBusAway users—thus, direct stakeholders—to contribute information about the characteristics of bus stops (e.g., if there are covered areas) with the aim of providing accurate information for bus riders who are blind or low-vision. Germane to our discussion about pro-social stakeholder roles and relevant for design interventions, OneBusAway users by and large reported contributing this information as a service to others, without seeking compensation or enhancement to their personal reputation.

*Special populations.* When addressing the question of who will be impli-cated by a technology, we have found that, in addition to mainstream consumers or corporate workers, special populations often come to the forefront. By "special populations," we mean stakeholders who embody or represent a form of diversity that is normally considered outside of the mainstream. Often these stakeholder groups represent a minority or are somehow stigmatized. Or, these groups are somehow vulnerable because of a physical or psychosocial condition, or simply at the outer boundaries along some dimension. While the term "special population" is somewhat inelegant, we know of no better term that captures such varied populations as children, the elderly, victims of domestic violence, families living in pov-erty, high-performance athletes, celebrities, the current or formerly incar-cerated, indigenous peoples, people experiencing homelessness, religious minorities, non-technology users, and so forth. Clearly, a special popula-tion is a social construction. In some societies, it might be inappropriate to consider the elderly as a special population; in other sociotechnical contexts, it might be appropriate to consider women a special population. Although stakeholders from special populations might not initially appear salient, examining their interests and the potential technological impacts typically leads to a more complete understanding of how a greater range of people might be implicated by a new system. In addition, considering stakeholders from special populations may lead to more robustly designed systems. For example, a mobile application targeted toward a mainstream audience might be made more robust by considering how children and the elderly would use the application, since mainstream stakeholders could share the application from time to time with just these types of people.

*Some open questions.* A number of questions remain for the development and use of stakeholder theory and analysis in value sensitive design. First, while conceptual and empirical work can be used to identify stakeholders, their roles, and their relationships to each other and to technology, there is no guaranteed way to identify a complete list of stakeholders. Also, there is no guaranteed way to satisfactorily describe their relationships with each other and to technology. Indeed, given the complexity of human-technology relations, how could it be any other way? In practice, as the three value sensitive design investigations are applied, greater clarity and detail about stakeholder circumstances and roles will be obtained, and new stakeholders may emerge.

Second, and relatedly, it can be difficult to decide how to limit the list of stakeholders. When, for example, energy life-cycle and supply-chain analyses are brought into the consideration of new technologies, we can see that from a long-term, widespread perspective, in principle all of humanity is impacted by new technological development. Value sensitive design projects have not yet robustly considered technology in such broad terms as transnational or environmental justice frameworks. In practice, value sensitive design projects have largely considered the direct and indirect stakeholders that make up relatively local, or at least fairly narrowly bounded, contexts of use, although one important exception is work on multi-lifespan information system design (Friedman & Nathan, 2010; Yoo et al., 2013b). Third, a key question relates to how stakeholders are represented in the design process. While the methods presented below substantially address this question, this is an enduring question of design theory and method.

Finally, the work to date on stakeholders is groundwork for still larger challenges. Namely, while the considerations above can provide a rationale for legitimating stakeholders, in themselves these considerations do not provide a principled framework for whom or what to include in a design process and how to weigh differing stakeholder interests. When, for example, might the interests of an indirect stakeholder trump the interests of a direct stakeholder? Or, how should the potential harms and benefits experienced by indirect stakeholders be weighed against the potential benefits of direct stakeholders? How should nonhumans—such as other species, the Earth, or social robots—be considered in stakeholder analyses?

## Value Tensions

As the interactional account makes clear, human values do not exist in isolation. Rather, much like the threads in a spider web, values are situated in a delicate balance. Touching one value implicates others. Privacy, for example, often sits in relationship with security and trust; autonomy is often in relationship to identity, dignity, and community. What is important to one group of stakeholders may or may not be important to another group. Thus, one challenge for value sensitive design is how to frame a design process to engage constructively in this interconnectedness of human values and experience. Granted, at times it may be a useful pragmatic strategy to foreground a single value—say, privacy or community. However, whatever knowledge is gained from studying a single value largely in isolation eventually will need to be integrated with an understanding of that value in the complex interrelatedness of human life and activity.

*Design trade-offs, value conflicts, and value tensions—a question of design thinking.* Within value sensitive design, the interrelatedness of human values in the design process has been framed in various ways: initially, in terms of *design trade-offs*, then as *value conflicts*, and most recently as *value tensions*. Albeit nuanced, each of these terms frames a somewhat different

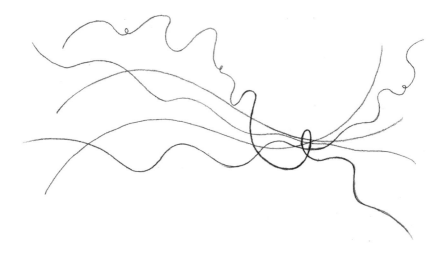

relationship among the relevant values and predisposes the designer to seek different sorts of solutions. The term "trade-off" conveys an approach in which designing for one value will diminish another value. Consider the values of privacy and security, which as noted above often sit in close relationship with each other. A design trade-off orientation casts the design situation as one in which either privacy (e.g., one is left alone) is well supported at the expense of security (e.g., one is watched to ensure protection), or vice versa. While in some cases resolution must necessarily take the form of a trade-off, framing the design situation in terms of a trade-off conceptually predisposes designers to seek solutions of this form. The term "value conflict," in contrast, acknowledges potential opposition among values, but leaves open whether their resolution must diminish one in order to support the other(s). When privacy and security goals come into conflict, design resolutions can seek solutions responsive to both. For example, an isolated local area network without wireless connectivity and disconnected from the Internet can provide both privacy and security. This is not to say that technical solutions such as this that support both values will always be possible; the isolated local area network, for example, might have impractical implications for a third value, that of access. Nevertheless, a value-conflict framing orients the designer to seek solutions that do not necessarily optimize one value at the expense of the other.

Finally, the term "value tension," like that of "value conflict," conveys the idea of values potentially in opposition but allows for solutions that balance each value in relation to the others, such that the adjudication of the tension holds each value intact. For example, a system design that judiciously allows some types of information in some contexts to be anonymous (supporting privacy) while requiring other types of information in other contexts to have known sources (supporting security through accountability) might realize such a balance. By and large, we have found the value tension framing to be the most expansive and to position the broadest design thinking.

*Value tensions: Locus and temporality.* Given a framing in terms of value tensions, we next observe that values can align or come into tension at various levels of human experience—within an individual; among individuals; between an individual and a group; among groups, institutions, nations, and societies; and among any number of other combinations. In the course of everyday life, many people experience what we might refer to as internal value conflicts—situations in which the person considers two or more things to be important, and yet how to achieve both or balance among them is not obvious. For our purposes, we are particularly interested in how technology intersects with these situations. Consider cell phones, with their now-familiar dilemmas. On the one hand, a person may value family and friends, wanting to be the sort of person who is readily accessible and responsive. On the other hand, that same person may value uninterrupted time to focus on projects, be they personal or work-related. Importantly, that internal tension exists independent of a particular technology, and individuals have long negotiated ways to balance among those competing values. A technology, such as cell phones, throws that tension into sharp relief as it supports one of the values (access) by enabling 24/7 connection while putting at risk preservation of the other value (to be left alone). Similar forms of value tensions can also exist among individuals. For example, parenting software to help adults track on their mobile phones the whereabouts and activities of teenagers may place an adult's values of child safety and parental responsibility in tension with a teenager's values of autonomy and independence. At stake is how to support a young person's maturation process while keeping that individual safe from irreparable harms (Czeskis et al., 2010).

Or, consider this example, which highlights value tensions between two groups. As documented in the social informatics literature, newspaper reporters value the ability to keep their working drafts hidden (privacy) until they are ready to share their drafts with their editors, while editors wish to have an awareness of what reporters are writing about and how those stories are progressing (access and accountability). In the context of these value tensions, a new-at-the-time computer system was introduced into a newspaper agency that gave editors access privileges to reporters' files without requesting permission or providing notice, thereby shifting organizational practice. In turn, once reporters learned of this system feature, some modified their writing practices to place drafts in obscurely named files, so as to reestablish their previous ability to hide working drafts.

Adding yet another layer of complexity, the balance among a person's, a group's, or a society's values may change over time in response to any number of factors, including maturation, personal situation, shifting sociopolitical contexts, societal evolution, or environmental conditions. Correspondingly, how that person, group, or society seeks to resolve value tensions may shift accordingly. For example, at one point in life, when a person is single, she might value spontaneity and potentially more risky behaviors; at a later point in life, with a spouse and children, she might value more structured, safer behaviors as part of taking responsibility for others. In a similar vein, an organization in start-up mode with few employees might value a more egalitarian, free-flowing structure governed by few rules or policies, which encourages all employees to contribute ideas to support the organization's rapid growth and productivity; as the organization becomes established and grows in size, such free-form activity might be funneled into a more orderly structure (perhaps with some hierarchy) with a greater number of policies and rules governing workflow, contributions, and new ideas. Or consider that a nation recovering from widespread conflict may limit freedom of expression as a means to achieve security with transitional justice in the near term; then, as the civil society stabilizes and the transitional justice system evolves, it may shift toward increased freedom of expression. More generally, when conditions shift, previous value tensions may resolve almost as a natural outcome of the shift, while new value tensions arising from the shift may surface.

*Value tensions in practice: Two strategies.* Granting that value tensions are part and parcel of the design process, how, then, might designers engage with such tensions in their design work? We take up this question with respect to specific techniques in chapter 3. Here we describe briefly two overarching strategies that we have found useful: where possible, focus on shared action, not reasons; and, when in significant doubt, where possible, pause the design process and wait.

Turning to the first, we make the observation that sometimes, even with strongly held conflicting values and beliefs, parties can agree on a course of action without agreeing on the reason for that action or having a shared worldview. For example, E. O. Wilson, in his book *The Creation: An Appeal to Save Life on Earth* (2006), urged that fundamentalist Christians who believe God has appointed them stewards of "all God's creatures on Earth," and evolutionary biologists who believe in preserving biodiversity for survival of life on Earth, come together around a shared course of action to preserve biodiversity from their very divergent perspectives. In terms of technology design, there are several practices that can be inferred. Consider that, at times, when working with diverse stakeholders, meaningful progress can be made by foregrounding discussion of the presence or absence of specific technical design features and sidestepping stakeholders' reasons for those preferences. That is, sometimes diverse stakeholders may be able to agree on the shape of a technical design and on specific technical features, but for very different reasons. For example, in designing a system to automatically optimize electricity consumption in a home by moving use of energy-intensive appliances to non-peak times (e.g., water heater, dishwasher), individuals strongly motivated by economic values and those strongly motivated by environmental ones might agree on a technical solution without having to come to consensus on their motivations or evaluation criteria for a good system—to save money or to save energy, respectively. To be clear, this does not mean that understanding stakeholder worldviews and reasons is not important in the design process. It is. But it does mean that at certain points in the design process, meaningful progress can be made by identifying the possibility for common action, should it exist, without also requiring shared worldviews. In fact, it may be just this understanding of the underlying reasons and worldviews that positions designers to identify one or more potential courses of action or sets of technical features that may be acceptable to individuals who hold such strongly conflicting views and values.

Considering the second strategy, we also acknowledge that at times, in the face of long-standing value tensions, constructive action may remain elusive. Designers may follow robust ideation processes to generate a wealth of "good" ideas that under scrutiny do not seem to resolve the value tensions to some reasonable level of satisfaction. In such situations, pause—a sort of suspended action—may be a beneficial design strategy (Friedman & Yoo, 2017). Such intentional pause gives additional time for ideas to arise, potentially previously not-yet-thought-of better ideas. Such pause also gives time for the technology or the sociopolitical context to shift, either or both of which might open up new opportunities or situations in which a way forward may become apparent. As with all design strategies, that of pause must be used with judgment and care.

The satisfactory resolution of value tensions at a particular point in time may require both empirical results on what direct and indirect stakeholders believe is important and analytic reasoning about potential stakeholder benefits and harms, reasoning which may explicitly draw upon a moral or ethical framework. How value tensions are adjudicated within value sensitive design is ultimately the responsibility of the designer.

## Co-evolving Technology and Social Structure

The interactional stance on technology and human experience points to a tight coupling between what is manifest technically and what is manifest socio-structurally. By socio-structural, we are referring to the structures human beings create to circumscribe their social lives—including but not limited to family structure, community organizations, work place organizations and managerial policies, religious institutions, schooling institutions, government organizations, and global agreements and institutions. Socio-structural elements may be explicit, as is the case with organizational charts, hierarchical management, and performance metrics in the workplace; or tacit, as may be the case with who plays the role of leader and who the followers within a group of friends. Consistent with the interactional stance, the socio-structural and the technical are intertwined in deep ways. Shaping one shapes the other, in an ongoing, delicate, dynamic balance. Email is a case in point. In organizations with strict hierarchies, email systems have evolved so that those individuals who are higher up in the hierarchy may send email messages to those below them, but those lower down in the workplace hierarchy may only send messages to their bosses and perhaps one or two levels above their bosses. In this way, the organizational structure shaped these email systems and, in turn, the technical structure of these email systems helps to construct and reinforce the organizational structure.

Taking this coupling of the technical and the socio-structural seriously leads to the observation that the design space for technological innovation encompasses not only the technical design space but also the corresponding socio-structural one. That is, when approaching a design problem, the theories, methods, and tools of value sensitive design can be applied both to the technical innovation as well as to the social structures in which the technology will be situated. The broader claim is that engaging both the technical and the socio-structural provides a more comprehensive design space—one with the possibility for solutions that might not be conceived of (or even possible) if approached from a technical or socio-structural perspective alone.

To provide a sense for what such co-evolution of technology and social structure might look like, consider two examples, one at the level of organizations and another at the level of law and regulation. The first concerns the development of a code repository and knowledge-base system in a large software company (Miller et al., 2007). Used in organizations worldwide, according to Grudin (1988), such knowledge-base systems are notorious for requiring a great deal of effort from a few people (who contribute content and answer questions) in order to provide benefit to a large number of other people (who reuse the content contributed by others and receive answers to their questions). These systems are also notorious for failing to be appropriated, in part due to inadequate incentive structures and inattention to issues related to reputation and privacy. To seek effective solutions here—in effect, to mitigate these particular and other identified value tensions—the research team not only identified a broad set of potential technical features (e.g., anonymous posts; "public" usage stats), but also potential management policies (e.g., contribution effort incorporated into performance evaluations). They then engaged stakeholders through surveys to garner their perspectives about both; thereby co-evolving the technical features of the knowledge-base system in coordination with the management policies governing and rewarding the system's use. Given the high cost to contributors for contributing (with relatively minimal benefit), design decisions—both technical and managerial—were taken that optimized the system from the contributors' perspectives. The system—the technology and the policies governing its use—was appropriated successfully by the unit for which it was designed. As further evidence of success, management decided to release the knowledge-base system broadly within the organization of over 30,000 software engineers.

The same strategy of co-evolving technology and social structure that we saw applied above at the organizational level can also be applied to narrower contexts, such as household computing, as well as broader contexts, such as law and regulation of technology innovation. To illustrate the latter, consider the development of a privacy addendum to an open-source license for a location-aware mobile device (Friedman et al., 2006c). Here, in order to preserve privacy commitments and protections in the technical design as the open-source code was appropriated and adapted by others, the original software developers sought to use legal measures to circumscribe future technical development to be within parameters that they deemed respected privacy (at least as they conceived of it). In terms of approach, the software team utilized methods and models for informed consent online and security threat analysis to develop a set of privacy parameters appropriate for the location-aware application. Then, a legal team used the privacy parameters to revise the original open-source license to incorporate specific privacy commitments, in effect yielding a new, more comprehensive open-source license—one that addressed privacy as well as intellectual property. The open-source, location-aware system was released under this new license. In turn, the new license that included the privacy addendum shaped (constrained) how other software developers could appropriate and adapt the code going forward, ensuring a continued commitment to the privacy parameters.

The main point here is this: conceptualizing the design space as both technical and socio-structural positions designers to engage both elements in seeking effective solutions. There are many ways to do so. Sometimes those solutions will be primarily of one sort or another—primarily technical or primarily socio-structural; that is fine. Other times, solutions will be an intricate blend of technical and socio-structural innovation—solutions that could not have been achieved with one dimension or the other in isolation.

## Multi-lifespan Design

Human societies face some significant problems that defy rapid solution.[6] The very structure of these problems and their solution spaces require

6. This section draws substantially from a prior publication (see Friedman & Nathan, 2010).

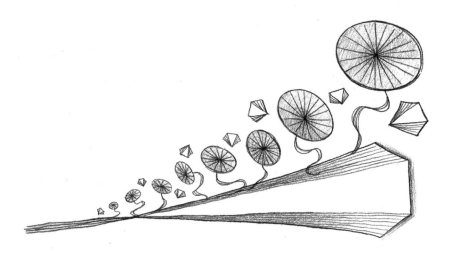

longer periods of time to unfold. Correspondingly, information systems that support those processes also develop over longer periods of time. Yet contemporary research and information-system design in industry is held to increasingly ambitious project deadlines, where design typically is conducted in three to six months and the system deployed for 18 months, then considered obsolete in five years; meanwhile, methods are honed to speed up the design process. Design research that seriously engages with longer-term design processes from diverse perspectives is sorely needed. To address this gap, multi-lifespan design, in a somewhat radical move, infuses the theoretical constructs of value sensitive design with just such a longer-term perspective.

Multi-lifespan design begins from the observation that certain categories of problems are unlikely to be solved within a single human lifespan (Friedman & Nathan, 2010). To date, three categories have been identified. The first entails healing from widespread or cyclical violence (e.g., genocide). The second entails tears in the social fabric (e.g., a social policy that significantly changes family and social structure within a generation, such as the one-child-per-family policy in China). The third entails natural timescales that move more slowly than a single human lifespan (e.g., regeneration of old-growth forests).

Approaching problems from a multi-lifespan design perspective opens up new opportunities, including the following.

*Preserving knowledge.* There may be information or knowledge that society possesses now, or could be collected in the near term, that could enable a greater range of possible solutions in the future. For example, in response to species extinction, the biologist E. O. Wilson and others have spearheaded efforts not only to protect habitat and endangered species but also to document the diversity of life on Earth (see the website Encyclopedia of Life: www.eol.org). Documenting biodiversity now does not replace species extinction, nor is it precisely clear now how such knowledge might be used in the future. What is clear is that if this knowledge—of species and their habitats—is not collected now, it will not be available to future generations when it might be of use.

*Supporting social structures and processes.* Information systems could be designed intentionally to help support social structure and processes that may be at-risk. Consider, for example, the implication of the widespread infection of HIV/AIDS in some regions of Africa on the social fabric of those communities. Many of these communities have experienced a large loss of life among those between 20 and 50 years old, leaving a gap in the social structure between the youth and elders. Moreover, during the next 10 to 20 years, many of these elders will die of old age, leaving a population primarily comprised of individuals under 40 years of age. With loss of life following this trajectory, much of the support roles, social networks, interdependencies, knowledge, extended family structure, caretaking, and other aspects of social life will be diminished or in some cases disappear entirely. The question arises: what can be done now, while some segments of those populations are still alive, to help identify and, where appropriate, create surrogate social structures to meet some of these needs?

*Remembering and forgetting.* In situations where personal or social harms have occurred, a tension exists between mechanisms for healing in which memories of harms may fade over time, and the increasingly widespread practice of recording human communication and activity. While no straightforward solution exists for how to balance these two activities of "forgetting" and "remembering," we can surface at least three relevant dimensions in information design: what communications and activities are recorded, how easily those are accessed and by whom, and the saliency of those recordings. Consider these dimensions in light of the documents from criminal tribunals and more informal courts for genocide, such as those for the genocides in Rwanda and the former Yugoslavia. On the one hand, those societies need to heal and move forward. Neighbors need to find a way to live peaceably with neighbors. On the other hand, there is a desire to know and remember what occurred, in part to ensure that such atrocities do not occur again and to protect against revisionist histories.

*Trust, security, and privacy.* The balance among trust, security, and privacy may be amenable to a longer-term design approach. According to Baier (1986), we trust when we are vulnerable to harm from others, yet believe those others would not harm us even though they could. Moreover, once breached, trust takes time to be reestablished. When we no longer trust others not to harm us, we often fall back on security as a means to protect ourselves from harm. In the current information climate, system design runs from security breach, to patch, to security breach, to patch again in what appears at times to be an unending cycle. Often the thing that we are seeking to protect is our privacy: who has access to our information, under what circumstances, and for what purposes or uses. Design for the short term tends to focus on preventing harms with tools such as firewalls and encryption, in what we might call a security worldview. A shift to the multi-lifespan perspective brings time into the design space so that trust has more opportunities to be established, built upon, and strengthened incrementally, as well as maintained. Designing with this goal in mind may create opportunities for a qualitatively different balance among trust, security, and privacy.

*Inclusivity and access.* In information system design, we typically seek solutions to issues of inclusivity and access within the constraints imposed by existing infrastructure and common practices. A multi-lifespan perspective positions us to envision more satisfying solutions. In the physical world, the progress made on wheelchair-accessible buildings and sidewalks points the way. One dimension includes the possibility of envisioning an information infrastructure that more readily supports access; a second dimension includes social policy to ensure implementation of that infrastructure (akin to the laws in some countries that require handicap access to buildings). Granted, the difficult question of variation among human capabilities remains.

The opportunities highlighted above provide guidance for framing multi-lifespan projects and identifying activities that can shape and enlarge the design space.

As a first project from this multi-lifespan design approach, we have engaged with information systems in support of transitional justice with the Voices from the Rwanda Tribunal project, a collection of video interviews with personnel from the International Criminal Tribunal for Rwanda (Nathan et al., 2011; Nilsen, Grey, & Friedman, 2012; Yoo et al., 2013b; Friedman, Nathan, & Yoo, 2016; Yoo et al., 2016; Friedman & Yoo, 2017; Yoo et al., 2018). This project explicitly leverages multi-lifespan opportunities for preserving knowledge, supporting social structures and processes, and remembering and forgetting. Moreover, it demonstrates how developing multi-lifespan design knowledge and methods will require sustained commitment to a design situation, both within that context and within scholarly communities. Correspondingly, such research endeavors will require appropriate evaluation criteria, reviewing standards, publication streams, and funding models consistent with longer-term investigations.

**Progress, Not Perfection**

We close this chapter on theory with one final construct, related to design practice: progress, not perfection.

*Progress, not perfection* arises in response to the typical design situation. Designing and implementing robust technical systems while also foreseeing their value implications is challenging, not least because, despite thousands of years of philosophical inquiry, the ideal conceptualization of human values has yet to be obtained. For designers and engineers who

operate under resource limitations and technological complexity, yet want to do the "right" thing, engaging human values in technical design can become daunting.

Confronted with the challenge of addressing human values in the design process, value sensitive design offers theory and method for making progress and for lowering real and imagined barriers. The current exposition of value sensitive design moves design practice in important directions. It moves designers toward the conceptualizations needed to identify shortcomings in current design processes and to seek remedies that promote human well-being. It moves designers toward the language needed to discuss the often immense social consequences of technical innovation with the public at large. And it moves designers toward considering human values as a design criterion—along with traditional criteria of reliability, efficiency, and correctness—by which systems may be judged poor and designers negligent. As with the traditional criteria for evaluating technical systems, we need not require perfection, but commitment to practice. And through practice, progress.

# 3   Method

The *Oxford English Dictionary* (2011) defines "method" as follows:

*Method (n).* A special form of procedure or characteristic set of procedures employed (more or less systematically) in an intellectual discipline or field of study as a mode of investigation and inquiry, or of teaching and exposition.

This definition foregrounds several qualities of method in value sensitive design. First, value sensitive design methods in their descriptive forms provide guidance on how to engage in a particular kind of research or design inquiry. Thus, methods help designers focus their attention on critical elements of the design situation, positioning them to obtain design insights. In their descriptive forms, methods and their outcomes can be scrutinized and compared with other methods. But methods also unfold as human activity. As such, the execution of a method may correspond more or less closely to its descriptive form. Thus, the use of a method always involves a kind of skillful performance that is learned. An expert will likely use a method differently than a novice.

A second quality of value sensitive design methods is that they are informed by the theoretical constructs of value sensitive design. Thus, to use a method well requires being faithful to value sensitive design theory. Here "being faithful" does not refer to some kind of easily recognized conformance; instead, it refers to a genuine engagement with theory. For example, a theoretical commitment in value sensitive design is to identify and legitimate the direct and indirect stakeholders in a design project. Accordingly, to do so, many different empirical and analytic methods might be employed, depending on the design situation. As methods are employed, new knowledge is generated that, in turn, informs theory—precipitating clarifications, extensions, revisions, adaptations, and even new dimensions. In so doing, theory and method engage in an ongoing dialog, each a tool to shape and reshape the other.

A third quality concerns the practical use of methods within value sensitive design. Value sensitive design methods are intended to be integrated with other methods and processes in technical design. Relatedly, value sensitive design methods are intended to be open to adaptation and evolution, so that their use is responsive to the elements of the design situation.

Over the past 20 years, a wide variety of methods that codify and operationalize how researchers, designers, and engineers can engage with values in technical design have been invented and used in value sensitive design projects. A good many of these methods have come from the social sciences; from fields such as anthropology and moral and social psychology (e.g., semi-structured interviews); and from approaches to design such as participatory design (e.g., Future Workshops). Despite the strength of existing methods from these established fields, at times, Friedman or her colleagues found themselves in the midst of research and design projects facing a challenge without a clear method for going forward. In those instances, the general strategy was to adapt existing methods or invent new ones that were particularly suited to engaging values in the technical context.

In this chapter, we provide an overview of 17 methods in value sensitive design and then turn to a broader discussion of value sensitive design practice. Specifically, we focus only on methods that have been invented for the investigation of values in technology (e.g., value dams and flows, Envisioning Cards) or methods that have undergone substantial adaptation or development (e.g., value-oriented semi-structured interviews, value sketches). Moreover, we do not discuss other important methods from design, philosophy, social science, and biology that have been employed in more standard ways. The application of such methods as card-sorting tasks, diary studies, experience sampling, Future Workshops, observation, physiological measures, and other common methods in value sensitive design projects is a substantial topic of its own.

## Seventeen Methods

Table 3.1 provides brief descriptions of each of the 17 methods, including their main purpose, an overview of method, and list of key references to papers. We then describe each of the methods more fully. Details on the

Table 3.1

Summary of 17 Value Sensitive Design Methods

| Method | Overview and Key References |
| --- | --- |
| **1. Stakeholder analysis**<br>*Purpose*: Stakeholder identification and legitimation | Identification of individuals, groups, organizations, institutions, and societies that might reasonably be affected by the technology under investigation, and in what ways. Two overarching stakeholder categories: (1) those who interact directly with the technology (direct stakeholders); and (2) those indirectly affected by the technology (indirect stakeholders).<br>See Friedman et al. (2006b); Nathan et al. (2008); Czeskis et al. (2010); and Watkins et al. (2013a). |
| **2. Stakeholder tokens**<br>*Purpose:* Stakeholder identification and interaction | Playful and versatile toolkit for identifying stakeholders and their interactions. Stakeholder tokens facilitate identifying stakeholders, distinguishing core from peripheral stakeholders, surfacing excluded stakeholders, and articulating relationships among stakeholders.<br>See Yoo (2018). |
| **3. Value source analysis**<br>*Purpose*: Identify value sources | Distinguish among the explicitly supported project values, designers' personal and professional values, and values held by other direct and indirect stakeholders.<br>See Borning et al. (2005). |
| **4. Co-evolve technology and social structure**<br>*Purpose*: Expand design space | Expanding the design space to include social structures integrated with technology may yield new solutions not possible when considering the technology alone. As appropriate, engage with the design of both technology and social structure as part of the solution space. Social structures may include policy, law, regulations, organizational practices, social norms, and other factors.<br>See Friedman et al. (2006c); and Miller et al. (2007a). |
| **5. Value scenario**<br>*Purpose*: Values representation and elicitation | Narratives, comprising stories of use, intended to surface human and technical aspects of technology and context. Value scenarios emphasize implications for direct and indirect stakeholders, related key values, widespread use, indirect impacts, longer-term use, and similar systemic effects.<br>See Nathan et al. (2007); Nathan et al. (2008); Czeskis et al. (2010); Woelfer et al. (2011); and Yoo et al. (2013a). |

**Table 3.1** (continued)

| Method | Overview and Key References |
|---|---|
| **6. Value sketch**<br>*Purpose*: Values representation and elicitation | Sketching activities as a way to tap into stakeholders' nonverbal understandings, views, and values about a technology. See Friedman et al. (2002b); and Woelfer et al. (2011). |
| **7. Value-oriented semi-structured interview**<br>*Purpose*: Values elicitation | Semi-structured interview questions as a way to tap into stakeholders' understandings, views, and values about a technology. Questions typically emphasize stakeholders' evaluative judgments (e.g., all right or not all right) about a technology as well as reasons (e.g., why?). Additional considerations introduced by the stakeholder are pursued. See Friedman (1997); Borning et al. (2005); Kahn et al. (2006); Freier (2008); and Czeskis et al. (2010). |
| **8. Scalable assessments of information dimensions**<br>*Purpose*: Values elicitation | Sets of questions constructed to tease apart the impact of pervasiveness, proximity, granularity of information, and other scalable dimensions. Can be used in interview, survey, and other formats. See Friedman (1997); Friedman et al. (2006b); and Munson et al. (2011). |
| **9. Value-oriented coding manual**<br>*Purpose*: Values analysis | Hierarchically structured categories for coding qualitative responses to, for example, the value-representation and -elicitation methods. Coding categories are generated from the data and a conceptualization of the domain. Each category contains a label, definition, and typically three sample responses from empirical data. Can be applied to oral, written, behavioral, visual, and other types of data. See Kahn et al. (2003); and Friedman et al. (2005a). |
| **10. Value-oriented mock-up, prototype, or field deployment**<br>*Purpose*: Values representation and elicitation | Development, analysis, and co-design of mock-ups, prototypes, and field deployments to scaffold the investigation of value implications of yet-to-be-built or widely adopted technologies. Mock-ups, prototypes, or field deployments emphasize implications for direct and indirect stakeholders, value tensions, and technology situated in human contexts. See Freier (2008); Woelfer & Hendry (2009); Denning et al. (2010); Czeskis et al. (2010); and Yoo et al. (2013a). |

**Table 3.1** (continued)

| Method | Overview and Key References |
|---|---|
| **11. Ethnographically informed inquiry on values and technology**<br>*Purpose*: Values, technology, and social structure framework and analysis | Framework and approach for data collection and analysis to uncover the complex relationships among values, technology, and social structure as those relationships unfold. Typically involves in-depth engagement in situated contexts over longer periods of time. See Nathan (2012). |
| **12. Model for informed consent online**<br>*Purpose*: Design principles and values analysis | Model with corresponding design principles for considering informed consent in online contexts. The construct of "informed" encompasses disclosure and comprehension; that of "consent" encompasses voluntariness, competence, and agreement. Furthermore, implementations of informed consent must not pose an undue burden to stakeholders. See Friedman et al. (2000a); Millett, Friedman, & Felten (2001); Friedman et al. (2002a); Friedman et al. (2005b); and Friedman et al. (2006c). |
| **13. Value dams and flows**<br>*Purpose*: Values analysis | Analytic method to reduce the solution space and resolve value tensions among design choices. First, design options that even a small percentage of stakeholders strongly object to are removed from the design space—the value dams. Then, of the remaining design options, those that a good percentage of stakeholders find appealing are foregrounded in the design—the value flows. Can be applied to the design of both technology and social structure. See Miller et al. (2007a); Czeskis et al. (2010); and Denning et al. (2010). |
| **14. Value sensitive action-reflection model**<br>*Purpose*: Values representation and elicitation | Reflective process for introducing value sensitive prompts into a co-design activity. Prompts can be designer or stakeholder generated. See Yoo et al. (2013a). |
| **15. Multi-lifespan timeline**<br>*Purpose:* Priming longer-term and multi-generational design thinking | Priming activity for longer-term design thinking. Multi-lifespan timelines prompt individuals to situate themselves in a longer time frame relative to the present, with attention to both societal and technological change. See Yoo et al. (2016). |

**Table 3.1** (continued)

| Method | Overview and Key References |
| --- | --- |
| **16. Multi-lifespan co-design**<br>*Purpose:* Longer-term design thinking and envisioning | Co-design activities and processes that emphasize longer-term anticipatory futures with implications for multiple and future generations.<br>See Yoo et al. (2016). |
| **17. Envisioning Cards**<br>*Purpose*: Versatile value sensitive design toolkit for industry and educational practice | Versatile value sensitive envisioning toolkit. Comprised of a set of 32 cards, the Envisioning Cards build on four criteria—stakeholders, time, values, and pervasiveness. Each card contains on one side a title and an evocative image related to the card theme; on the flip side, the envisioning criterion, card theme, and a focused design activity. Envisioning Cards can be used for ideation, co-design, heuristic critique, evaluation, and other purposes.<br>See Friedman, Nathan, Kane, & Lin (2011); Kaptein, Eckles, & Davis (2011); Friedman & Hendry (2012); and Yoo et al. (2013a). |

development and application of each method can be found in the cited work, which is presented in suggested reading order. Though these methods are presented in a stand-alone fashion for descriptive purposes, it is important to note that they are intended to be integrated into a robust value sensitive design process, one that employs the tripartite methodology. Further, the use of methods is shaped by the design situation and the particular skills and goals of the researchers or designers.

## 1.  Direct and Indirect Stakeholder Analysis

In the information field, stakeholder analyses are commonly employed by organizations to clarify project scope by systematically identifying individuals and groups that might reasonably be affected by the technology under investigation (Bødker, Kensing, & Simonsen, 2004; Mitchell, Agle, & Wood, 1997). In value sensitive design, stakeholder analysis is broadened to include not only individuals and groups but also institutions and societies. The emphasis is placed on identifying and legitimating stakeholders, including enumerating the ways in which stakeholders might be affected, along with documenting potential benefits, harms, and tensions. To focus the analysis, two overarching stakeholder categories are employed: (1)

direct stakeholders, those who interact directly with the technology; and (2) indirect stakeholders, those who do not directly interact with the technology but may nonetheless be affected. Depending on the technology, it may be possible to readily identify most, if not all, of the direct stakeholders. Indirect effects can be widespread and diffuse; accordingly, one challenge is to identify those indirect stakeholders who might be significantly impacted, either positively or negatively, by the technology.

Foundational Studies

• *Privacy in public.* Stakeholder analyses employed to shape the design of a research study on privacy in public, with an emphasis on indirect stakeholders, known as "the watcher and the watched" (Friedman et al., 2006b).

• *Reflections on direct and indirect stakeholders.* Discussion and reflection on the conceptual categories of direct and indirect stakeholders as well as limitations (Nathan et al., 2008).

• *Shifting between direct and indirect stakeholder roles—parent-teen mobile phone safety applications.* To surface differing stakeholder perspectives about a parent-teen mobile phone application for monitoring teens, study participants first take on the role of a direct stakeholder, for example, parent of a teen who uses the application, and then switch to that of an indirect stakeholder, for example, parent of a teen whose friend's parent uses the application (Czeskis et al., 2010).

• *Bus drivers as indirect stakeholders—mobile application to support public transit riders.* Stakeholder analyses used to surface bus drivers as key indirect stakeholders in a mobile phone application for transit riders (Watkins, Borning, Rutherford, Ferris, & Gill, 2013a).

## 2.  Stakeholder Tokens

Role-playing toolkits in which tangible, human-like tokens are used to represent people and other actors—in a family, a workshop, a community, a society at large—and their interactions have a long-standing history in education, counseling, community development, simulation, and human-computer interaction (DeLoache & Marzolf, 1995; Cantoni, Botturi, Faré, & Bolchini 2009; Sanders, 2009). Stakeholder tokens extend this tradition to explicitly aid the identification of stakeholders (see figure 3.1). The method asks participants to list all relevant stakeholders, or as many as they can, and label a token for each stakeholder group. This process helps to surface a more comprehensive set of stakeholders, including those that are typically

excluded from consideration. After the stakeholder groups have been identified, participants are asked to place the labeled tokens on a large, blank
piece of paper and to draw the relationship among the stakeholders. For
example, some participants might place stakeholders they view as "core"
in the center of the piece of paper and stakeholders they view as "peripheral" along the edges of the page. Reflecting the affective relations among
stakeholder groups, some participants might place tokens facing each other
and draw ears or hearts to indicate stakeholder groups that communicate
well and support each other; conversely, they might place tokens pointing
away from each other and draw broken lines to indicate conflict or tension
among different stakeholder groups. The playful and open-ended form of
the method allows participants to explore a diversity of stakeholders and
express the relationships and feelings participants perceive among those
stakeholder groups.

Foundational Study

• *Stakeholder tokens elements and process*. Stakeholder tokens as a designer
toolkit for supporting stakeholder identification and interactions; includes
a description of the physical materials in the toolkit and steps for use (Yoo,
2018).

### 3.  Value Source Analysis

As discussed in chapter 2, clarity and transparency about the source of values that implicate a system design can be critical. Explicitly supported *project values* refer to an agreed-upon set of values to guide system development
throughout the design process and can also serve as evaluation criteria.
Typically, these project values are subject to a principled analysis negotiated through public processes, and/or tied to funding sources. In contrast,
*designer values* refer to the personal or professional values each designer
brings to research and design work. There may or may not be a strong alignment between a designer's personal values and those identified to be explicitly supported by the system. One would hope that the explicitly supported
project values will also be shared by the designer, but often there will be
relevant designer values that are not explicitly supported project values.
Teasing apart these sets is a useful heuristic for reminding designers that
every relevant value they hold does not necessarily need to be explicitly
supported by that particular project. Even so, when the divergence between

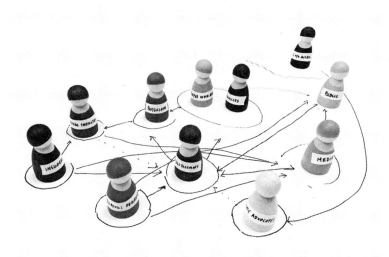

**Figure 3.1**
Generic wooden peg dolls were introduced as stakeholder tokens during the medical aid-in-dying project. Participants were asked to generate a list of all the stakeholders, including those who were excluded; label the tokens; and visualize the interactions among those tokens on a large piece of paper. Image courtesy of Daisy Yoo.

designer and project values is significant, then additional methods to man-age those differences may be warranted. Thirdly, and building on the stake-holder analyses (see above), *stakeholder values* refer to the values of different stakeholder groups that need to be taken into account. Here, too, there may be a divergence among the values held by different stakeholder groups. This method involves systematically identifying and distinguishing among the values to be explicitly supported by the project, the values held personally or professionally by designers, and the values held by direct and indirect stakeholders. Surfacing such differences or tensions among the values from these different sources can point to important places to seek to balance or resolve these differences. For example, in the development of a large-scale simulation for land use and transportation (Borning et al., 2005), the designers' values tended toward supporting the environment, while the project's explicitly supported value of representativeness pointed toward an evenhanded treatment of environmental values alongside of others, such as economic development. To ensure the project's explicitly supported val-ues were adequately addressed, specific periodic design reviews were put in place.

Foundational Study

• *Urban simulation for land use and transportation modeling.* Distinguished among those values explicitly supported as part of the project's goals and objectives, designers' personal values, and the often strongly held conflict-ing values of stakeholders in the design of a large-scale computer simula-tion for land use and transportation planning (Borning et al., 2005).

## 4.   Co-evolution of Technology and Social Structure

Most technical design considers technology in relative isolation, with a static view on policy, law, and other social structures. Expanding the design space to include not only technology but also the design of social structures may yield new solutions not possible when considering either alone. As appropriate, the design process engages reciprocally with and, in this sense, co-evolves technology and social structure. Social structures are viewed broadly and may include policy, law, regulations, organizational practices, social norms, and others. For example, in the design of a knowledge-base and code repository system in a large software organization (Miller et al., 2007), a two-pronged design approach was employed to achieve a suc-cessful balance among the values of reputation, privacy, and awareness:

one prong emphasized technical features of the knowledge-base system, such as opportunities for anonymous posts and feedback on frequency of use, while a second prong emphasized managerial policies for the system, including how, if at all, contributors would be rewarded during annual performance reviews. Importantly, the technical features and managerial policies worked in concert to address concerns about reputation for both contributors and question-askers.

Foundational Studies

• *Managerial policy and technology—knowledge-base system.* Working with a large software corporation, developed a knowledge-base and code repository groupware system in tandem with organizational policies for incentivizing employees' contributions to the system (Miller et al., 2007).

• *Software license and technology—privacy in an open-source, location-aware system.* Working with a large technology corporation, developed a legal addendum to an open-source license that preserves user privacy attributes for a mobile phone location-aware system (Friedman et al., 2006c).

## 5.  Value Scenario

Scenarios have long been used effectively in user-centered design to focus on and communicate about discrete features of a technology and the immediate context of use (Carroll, 1999, 2000). Value scenarios extend this tradition to surface additional important humanistic and societal considerations of technology and context. Specifically, the narratives are intended to emphasize (1) implications for direct and indirect stakeholders, (2) key values, (3) widespread use, (4) indirect impacts, (5) longer-term use, and (6) systemic effects. In any given application, some elements may be emphasized more than others. Depending on the context of use, a value scenario can act both as a values-representation and as a values-elicitation method. For example, and as explicated in greater detail below, Czeskis et al. (2010), in their role as researchers, wrote value scenarios around parenting technologies for teens as a means to explore a design space prior to conducting research with stakeholders. In contrast, Woelfer, Iverson, Hendry, Friedman, and Gill (2011) asked homeless young people to write value scenarios about mobile phones and safety as a means to elicit what the youth considered important in their lives.

Foundational Studies

• *Elements of a value scenario.* Value scenarios as a designer tool that build upon but are distinct from traditional scenario-based design; includes two exemplar value scenarios, one about avoiding crime when navigating a city and the other about social robots (Nathan, Klasnja, & Friedman, 2007).

• *Designer-generated value scenarios as a conceptualization tool—parent-teen mobile phone safety applications.* Value scenarios employed to situate a proposed new technology for parenting teens and explore a design space prior to developing a user study (Czeskis et al., 2010).

• *Stakeholder-generated value scenarios as an envisioning tool—homeless young people and safety.* Value scenarios employed with stakeholders to envision situations in which homeless young people could use a mobile phone to improve their safety (Woelfer et al., 2011).

• *Value scenarios repurposed as design prompts—co-design and mobile phone safety.* Previously written value scenarios employed to prompt reflection in a co-design activity focused on using mobile phones to improve safety for homeless young people (Yoo, Huldtgren, Woelfer, Hendry, & Friedman, 2013a).

## 6.  Value Sketch

Sketches, collage, and other visual expressions provide a means to tap into nonverbal understandings (Crilly, Blackwell, & Clarkson, 2006; Lynch, 1960). With value sketches, the emphasis is on understandings, views, and values about a technology. Through drawings, participants can "show" rather than "tell" what is important to them in relation to a particular technology in a particular context. Value sketches can also be helpful in understanding how a technology is situated in place or in explicating how particular values are implicated by technical functioning. For example, the value sketches in figure 3.2 show users' understandings of a "secure connection" on the web, which they use to make decisions about what information to submit electronically. Similar to value scenarios, value sketches can act as both a values-representation and a values-elicitation method.

Foundational Studies

• *Sketching processes—web browser security.* Study participants drew sketches to express their understandings of a secure web browser connection and to situate a discussion about security and privacy in web-based interactions (Friedman et al., 2002b).

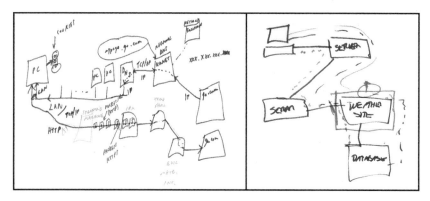

**Figure 3.2**
The drawing on the left shows a conception of a secure connection in terms of encryption while the information is in "transit." The drawing on the right shows a conception of a secure connection in terms of a secure boundary (box) around a specific "place" on the web. Reprinted from Friedman et al. (2002b).

• *Sketching experience of place—homeless young people and safety.* As part of a larger study on mobile phones and safety, to surface perceptions of where and when homeless young people might feel unsafe as well as to situate value scenarios grounded in place, study participants sketched their perceptions of safe and unsafe areas for homeless young people on a local map (Woelfer et al., 2011).

## 7. Value-Oriented Semi-structured Interview

Semi-structured interviews provide a means to tap into stakeholders' understandings, views, and values (Kahn, 1999; Piaget, 1929/1960). Interview questions can be honed to elicit information about values and value tensions in relation to technology. Typical questions emphasize stakeholders' evaluative judgments about a technology (e.g., "Is it all right or not all right that technology X has feature Y or behavior Z?") as well as rationale (e.g., "Why or why not?"). Value tensions can be explored in a variety of ways. One entails introducing alternative resolutions of the tension and inquiring which resolution (if any) resonates with the stakeholder's perspective (e.g., "Some people like X about the system for Y reason. Other people like A about the system for B reason. Are your views more similar to one person or the other? Why?"). The semi-structured nature of the interview provides an opportunity to pursue topics in depth as well as engage new considerations the stakeholder introduces into the conversation.

Foundational Studies

• *US adolescents—online privacy and electronic property*. Interviews employed to elicit adolescents' views and values of privacy and property as they apply to electronic information—reading others' computer files and copying software (Friedman, 1997).

• *US urban planners—urban simulation for land use and transportation modeling*. Interviews employed to elicit urban planners' and modelers' reflections on the relationship between values and policies important to land use and the technical features in the large-scale UrbanSim simulation (Borning et al., 2005).

• *US preschool children—robotic dogs*. Interviews employed to elicit preschool children's conceptions as well as social and moral judgments about a robotic dog (Kahn et al., 2006).

• *US children—personified agent*. Interviews employed to elicit children's conceptions of self-reflective personified agents (e.g., avatars) as warranting moral consideration (Freier, 2008).

• *Swedish and US adults—privacy in public*. Interviews employed to elicit adults' reflections on the use of web cameras in a public plaza, particularly on their conceptions of privacy in public; first conducted in the United States (Friedman et al., 2006b) and then in a comparative study in Sweden (Friedman et al., 2008c).

• *US adolescents and their parents—mobile phones for safety*. Interviews employed to elicit teenagers' and their parents' views and values on mobile technologies to support parental awareness and notification of teenager activities and location (Czeskis et al., 2010).

## 8.   Scalable Assessments of Information Dimensions

Assessments of the importance of a value or the severity of a harm may depend on a number of scalable dimensions, such as granularity of information, proximity, and pervasiveness. This value-elicitation method takes such scalable dimensions into account by structuring questions to explicitly tease apart their impact (e.g., "For public records, ... how comfortable would you be with searching public records by state? By city? By zip code? By neighborhood name? By home address? By last name only? By first and last name?" [Munson et al., 2011]). Assessment of scale can be used in a wide range of formats, including interviews, surveys, value scenarios, and value sketches.

Foundational Studies

• *Pervasiveness—copying commercial software.* Investigated the effect of fewer or greater number of copies on adolescents' views and values on copying commercial software for personal use, to give to friends, and to sell to others (Friedman, 1997).

• *Pervasiveness and proximity—privacy in public.* Investigated the impact of pervasiveness of and proximity to a technology on participants' views and values about web cameras in a public plaza (Friedman et al., 2006b).

• *Location—public records online.* Investigated the impact of granularity of location information on participants' views and values about online public records for real estate sales and for political campaign contributions (Munson et al., 2011).

## 9.  Value-Oriented Coding Manual

Coding manuals provide one systematic means for coding and then analyzing qualitative responses to value-representation and -elicitation methods, such as the value scenario (e.g., narrative), value sketches (e.g., visual), and semi-structured interview (e.g., discourse) methods described above. Typically, the coding categories are generated from the data and a conceptualization of the domain. Each category contains a label, definition, and as a rule of thumb up to three sample responses from the data. Depending on the research or design project, the coding schemes may capture technical as well as values and other social aspects of the data. For example, a coding manual for a project on privacy in public (Friedman et al., 2005a) included categories about technology as well as about values such as privacy and property. A few examples follow below.

• *Technology.* An appeal based on existing technologies (e.g., "Anybody could put a camera out here and film people") or on technological augmentations of the physical world, time, or biology (e.g., "Not only are your actions viewable to anyone here, they'd be viewable to anyone there").

• *Privacy.* An appeal based on a claim, an entitlement, or a right of individuals to determine what information about themselves is communicated to others, including private content (e.g., "Because it's your personal thoughts and feelings"); legitimate use (e.g., "There's absolutely no reason for anybody to need to know"); maintain anonymity (e.g., "It's perfectly fine if we're not capturing people, individual people"); and control (e.g., "It depends on how closely you guard it").

• *Property.* An appeal based on a concept of tangible property (e.g., "They could have a right to do that since it's university property") and intangible property (e.g., "My image, if I'm being looked at, is a different, I feel a different property right").

Foundational Studies
• *Interview data—privacy in public.* Coding manual (36 pages) for analyzing direct and indirect stakeholder views, values, and tensions around privacy in relation to web cameras in a public plaza (Friedman, Kahn, Hagman, & Severson, 2005a).
• *Chatroom data—robotic dogs.* Coding manual (61 pages) for analyzing robotic dog owners' online chatroom discourse from the perspective of social robots, moral judgments, and human experience (Kahn, Friedman, Freier, & Severson, 2003).
• *Discussion forum data—Telegarden.* Coding manual (49 pages) for analyzing online discussion forum data from Telegarden participants with an emphasis on human experience of technologically mediated nature (Kahn, Friedman, & Alexander, 2005).
• *Sketch data—web browser security.* Coding manual (10 pages) for analyzing study participants' sketches and dialog explaining security for web browsers (Friedman et al., 2002b).

**10.   Value-Oriented Mock-up, Prototype, or Field Deployment**
Mock-ups, prototypes, and field deployments can be employed to scaffold the investigation of value implications of technologies that have yet to be built or widely adopted. To do so, these established methods specifically are adapted to emphasize implications for direct and indirect stakeholders, value tensions, and technology situated in human contexts. With these and other potential adaptations, these methods can be introduced into development, analysis, and co-design processes to aid with values representation and elicitation. For example, in a project investigating early-stage concepts for keeping homeless young people safe with mobile phones, participants—homeless young people, service providers, and police—were prompted to sketch and create prototypes of possible solutions with paper, clay, and other craft materials (Yoo et al. 2013a). See figures 3.3, 3.4, and 3.5 for examples.

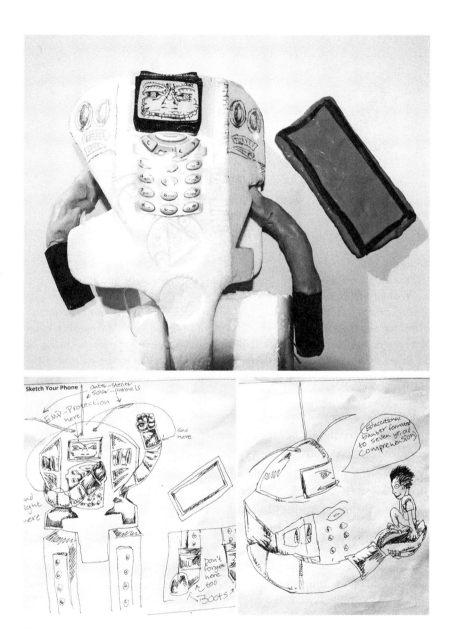

**Figure 3.3**
A solution: a robot, named "Failed Delusions," prototype and two sketches (Homeless Young People). Failed Delusions holds a symbiotic relationship with its owner, a homeless young person; is able to fly; provides warnings of impending law enforcement; and offers sophisticated communication functions.

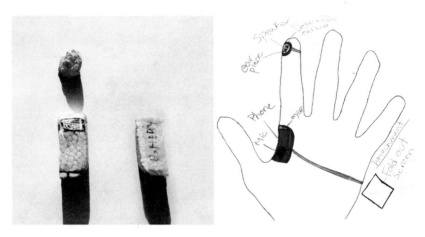

**Figure 3.4**
A solution: a wearable phone, named "Hassle Free," prototype and sketch (Homeless Young People). Hassle Free is designed to discreetly augment a homeless young person's body so that it can detect falls and other bodily harms and automatically call for assistance. It is made of light-weight materials, with a controller located between the thumb and index finger, a small ear piece attached to the tip of the index finger, and a foldout screen that can be attached to the outside of the user's hand.

Foundational Studies

• *Mock-ups—security for health and parenting applications.* Lo-fi mock-ups employed in one study to convey to patients with implantable cardiac devices a diverse set of potential security solutions for their devices (Denning et al., 2010), and in another study to convey to parents and teens a range of technical features to balance security, privacy, and notification considerations in a parent-teen mobile phone security application (Czeskis et al., 2010).

• *Video prototypes—information systems for homeless young people.* Three short videos (1:30–3:30 minutes) of physical prototypes for presenting paper brochures, each emphasizing a different value (respect, autonomy, and trust), were used to elicit stakeholder views on a design space (Woelfer & Hendry, 2009).

• *Prototypes—co-design for mobile phone safety.* In a co-design activity, participants employed paper and clay prototypes to express their ideas for using mobile phones to improve safety for homeless young people (Yoo et al., 2013a).

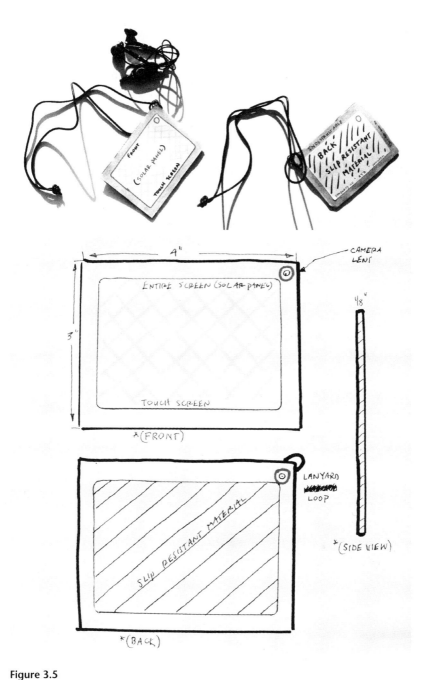

**Figure 3.5**
A solution: a wearable phone, named "INDESTRUCTIBLE," prototype and sketch (Police Officers). INDESTRUCTIBLE includes a camera and screen designed to support rich interactions between a homeless young person and health professionals or service providers. It is waterproof and extremely durable for harsh outdoor environments, pliable so that it can be fastened to the body, and offers such features as theft protection and solar charging.

• *Wizard of Oz prototype—personified agent.* Children interact with a personified agent implemented by wizard-of-oz techniques in the context of a tic-tac-toe game to elicit the children's views on personified agents as potentially warranting moral personhood (Freier, 2008).

• *Working prototype—household indicators for urban simulation.* Design, development, and evaluation of a working prototype for a user interface and system to explore the impact of region-wide land use and transportation policies on households (Davis, 2008).

• *Field deployment—privacy in public.* Field deployment of webcams in a public place, with images seen on large displays in university faculty and staff offices as part of a longer-term study (Friedman, Freier, Kahn, Lin, & Sodeman, 2008b) and as part of a controlled experiment (Friedman et al., 2006b).

## 11.   Ethnographically Informed Inquiry on Values and Technology

Ethnographically informed research focused at the intersection of technology and human activity (Nardi & O'Day, 1999; Orlikowski, 2000) can be employed to probe the complex relationships among values, technology, and social structure, particularly as those relationships unfold over time. Such work makes a particular commitment to identifying and clarifying values and value tensions; the endeavor is dynamic, involving in-depth engagement in situated contexts over longer durations. The emphasis might be on a particular community or social structure as that community and its members appropriate and adapt to existing technologies, as well as how community members in the course of those processes shape those technologies. Points of interest often occur at the boundaries, where strongly held individual or community values may come into tension with behaviors or experiences facilitated by the technology. For example, in the ethnographically informed study of an emerging ecovillage (Nathan, 2012), digital information technologies, such as email, at times conflicted with community values around equitable access to information for those less technologically savvy or living on limited incomes with limited access to the Internet.

Foundational Study

• *Environmental sustainability, information technology, and intentional communities.* Ethnographic exploration of two eco-villages, one well-established and the other in early phases of development, to gain insight into the tensions among commitments to environmental sustainability and other core values with the use and dependence on information technology (Nathan, 2012).

## 12.  Model for Informed Consent Online

One mechanism for protecting human values is to provide stakeholders with an opportunity to agree to the use of a technology that impacts their lives in important ways. The model for informed consent online provides design principles and a value-analysis method for considering informed consent in online contexts. The construct of "informed" encompasses disclosure and comprehension; that of "consent," voluntariness, competence, and agreement. Furthermore, implementations of informed consent must not pose an undue burden to stakeholders. Among other applications, this model is relevant for much of the current work on usable security and privacy, pointing toward the importance of "informing through interaction" and the need for just-in-time management of privacy and security options with low burdens of use.

Foundational Studies

• *Elements of model.* Description of the model for informed consent online, including eight design principles for guiding implementation (Friedman et al., 2000a).

• *Evaluation criteria for existing technology—cookies, web browser security, and machine-generated ads in Gmail.* Informed-consent model employed to surface limitations in the handling of cookies in then state-of-the-art (circa 1995–1999) web browsers, despite industry efforts to provide better information and controls (Millett, Friedman, & Felten, 2001); and to counter challenges of misrepresentation when Google first introduced machine-generated ads in Gmail, its email application (Friedman, Lin, & Miller, 2005b).

• *Design criteria for guiding new technical features—cookies and web browser security.* Informed-consent model used to design and develop two technical features—ready-to-hand information and just-in-time cookie management—to address some of the limitations in state-of-the art web browsers' handling of cookies; implemented and deployed as a Mozilla plug-in (Friedman et al., 2002a).

• *Design criteria for guiding law and policy—privacy protections for location-aware applications.* Informed-consent online model employed in conjunction with a traditional security threat analysis model to surface elements for a privacy license for an open-source location-aware application (Friedman et al., 2006c).

## 13. Value Dams and Flows

At key junctures in a design process, there is often a need to reduce the solution space and resolve value tensions among design choices. Value dams and flows provide one analytic method for doing so. First, design options that even a small percentage of stakeholders strongly object to—the value dams—are removed from the design space. How to identify a suitable threshold percentage for determining value dams is an open research question; current research has used a heuristic on the order of 7–10%. Then, of the remaining design options, those that a good percentage of stakeholders find appealing—the value flows—are foregrounded in the design. This method, as with other methods, can be applied to the design of both technology and social structure. For example, in the design of a knowledge-base and code repository for a large software organization, the value dams and flows method was used to refine feature selection in the technical system as well as organizational policy for regulating use of the system (Miller et al., 2007).

Foundational Studies

• *Balancing privacy, anonymity, and reputation—industry groupware system.* Value dams and flows method employed to identify a set of technical features and organizational policies that positively balanced concerns for privacy, anonymity, and reputation (Miller et al., 2007).

• *Discerning objectionable and acceptable solutions—security for implantable cardiac devices.* Value dams and flows method employed to identify and put aside technical security approaches that patients with implantable cardiac devices found objectionable (Denning et al., 2010).

• *Deciding not to collect data—parent-teen mobile phone safety application.* Value dams and flows employed to identify the conditions under which certain data about teens should not be collected or, alternatively, collected but shared only in emergencies (Czeskis et al., 2010).

## 14. Value Sensitive Action-Reflection Model

In co-design and similar types of activities, a common challenge is to position stakeholders to generate creative ideas or to reflect on their ideas

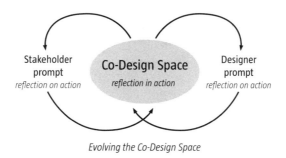

*Evolving the Co-Design Space*

**Figure 3.6**
Value sensitive action-reflection model. Stakeholder and designer prompts are introduced to expand the co-design space and to prompt co-designers to reflect on their evolving design.

(Sanders & Westerlund, 2011). The value sensitive action-reflection model addresses this challenge with a structured, reflective, and iterative process in which value sensitive prompts are introduced (see figure 3.6). The prompts, which can be created by either designers or other direct and indirect stakeholders, are intended to lead participants to reconsider their designs from a values perspective at various points in the co-design activity. For example, co-design participants might be given a value scenario and instructed to "revise your current design solution, if needed, to account for the scenario."

Foundational Study
• *Designer and stakeholder prompts—co-design and mobile phone safety*. A stakeholder prompt (e.g., stakeholder-generated value scenario) and a designer prompt (e.g., Envisioning Cards) were used to stimulate iterative design in a co-design process with homeless young people, service providers, and police officers (Yoo et al., 2013a).

**15.  Multi-lifespan Timeline**
Most people have a relatively easy time thinking about what will happen next week or next month, or what happened last month or last year. But when the time frame is longer—say 20, 50, or 100 years—many people draw a blank. A multi-lifespan timeline was developed to help stimulate and anchor longer-term design thinking for both designers and participants within a frame of technological and societal change. Figure 3.7 shows a multi-lifespan timeline that stretches 100 years into the past and 100

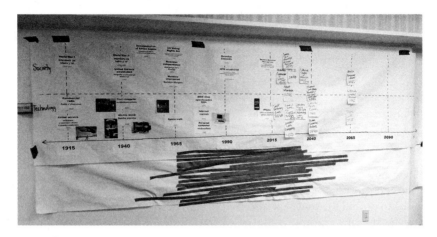

**Figure 3.7**
A large-scale timeline (36 × 160 in.) that was presented to participants in 2015 during the Voices from the Rwanda Tribunal project. Participants first added pieces of blue tape representing their lifespans on the timeline and then added past and anticipated future events.

years into the future—about three generations looking backward and forward. The top half of the timeline represents events that participants view as largely societal (e.g., the end of apartheid in South Africa); the bottom half represents technological developments, again from the perspective of participants (e.g., the first moon landing of the Apollo 11). These two categories are not intended to be disjoint; as participants recognize interdependencies they may choose to place events in the middle, reflecting both societal and technological dimensions. In preparation for using the method, the timeline is populated with 10 to 15 events from the previous 100 years. Specifically, the method asks participants to situate their personal lifespan (expected) on the timeline using a piece of tape that represents roughly 75 years. Then participants brainstorm previous societal and technological events from the past 100 years, writing these on sticky notes and adding them to the timeline. Finally, participants turn to the next 100 years, imagining potential societal and technological events, writing these on sticky notes, and also adding these to the timeline. In this manner, participants construct a visual representation of past societal and technological change, anticipate futures, and place themselves within that changing landscape.

Foundational Study
• *Transitional justice—Rwandans and others from the African Great Lakes region living in the diaspora in the United States.* Multi-lifespan timeline employed to prime longer-term design thinking prior to envisioning future information systems to support transitional justice in the aftermath of the 1994 genocide in Rwanda (Yoo et al., 2016).

## 16. Multi-lifespan Co-design
The human-computer interaction community has a long history of co-design that comes from participatory design (Muller & Kuhn, 1993; Bødker, Ehn, Sjögren, & Sundblad, 2000; Spinuzzi, 2005). Co-design provides a means for participants to work alongside experienced designers to contribute ideas through constructing solutions (Sanders, Brandt, & Binder, 2010). Leveraging all the strengths of traditional co-design, multi-lifespan co-design extends the established practice by explicitly positioning participants to anticipate farther-out futures, on the order of 20 or 35 years— roughly the length of a generation (see figure 3.8 for examples). Specific prompts within the co-design activity provide design constraints for longer timeframes (e.g., envision an information system for use 20 years from now) and consideration of stakeholders in the future (e.g., your future self in 20 years; when your children become your age). Longer-term considerations on settings and society are also brought to the fore (e.g., regrowth of forests; emergence of transitional justice systems and reconciliation after widespread violence). Taken together, these longer-term design constraints invite participants to envision generational change for individuals, families, organizations, and society writ large, and to conduct their design investigations mindful of the landscape of that change.

Foundational Study
• *Transitional ju stice—Rwandans and others from the African Great Lakes region living in the diaspora in the United States.* Multi-lifespan co-design employed to prompt envisioning specific information systems 20 years in the future that would support peace-building, healing, and transitional justice in the aftermath of the 1994 genocide in Rwanda (Yoo et al., 2016).

## 17. Envisioning Cards
The Envisioning Cards (Friedman, Nathan, Kane, & Lin, 2011) are a practical and versatile toolkit to bring value sensitive design theory and method

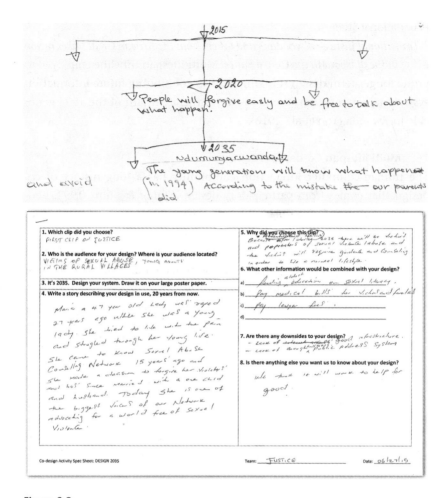

**Figure 3.8**
Multi-lifespan co-design spec sheets and evidence of multi-lifespan thinking observed during the Voices from the Rwanda Tribunal project. Working in groups of three to four, participants generated sketches and stories about an information system for transitional justice that would be used 20 years from now. The sketch (top) shows a gradual unfolding of the Rwandan unity and reconciliation process ("Ndi Umunyarwanda") with clear indication of the years 2015, 2020, and 2035. The story in the spec sheet (bottom) illustrates a survivor of rape taking steps toward healing over a span of 20 years.

into industry and educational practice. Comprising a set of 32 cards, the cards build on four criteria: stakeholders, time, values, and pervasiveness. As shown in figure 3.9, each card contains on one side a title and an evocative image related to the card theme. The examples (and envisioning criteria) include: Non-targeted Use (stakeholders), Sustained Friendships (time), Value Tensions (values), and Crossing National Boundaries (pervasiveness). On the flip side, there is the envisioning criterion and identifying color, title, card theme, and a focused design activity. Envisioning Cards can be used for ideation, co-design, heuristic critique, evaluation, and other purposes.

Foundational Studies
• *The Env isioning Cards.* The Envisioning Card toolkit: www.envisioningcards .com.
• *Ideation—co-design and mobile phone safety.* Envisioning Cards employed to scaffold non-designers' active participation in a co-design process, including focused iterative design (Friedman & Hendry, 2012; Yoo et al., 2013a).
• *Value implications—persuasion profiling.* Envisioning Cards employed in a professional workshop setting to anticipate the uses, benefits, and harms of persuasion profiling (Kaptein, Eckles, & Davis, 2011; Friedman & Hendry, 2012).
• *Heuristic value analysis—cloud computing.* Envisioning Cards employed as an analytic heuristic tool to surface critical issues for potential cloud computing solutions (Friedman & Hendry, 2012).

**Methods in Action**

The methods are versatile. In one way or another, they all foreground human values in the research, design, and engineering process. Here we seek to provide some pragmatic guidance for their use. To begin, the same method can be used in a variety of ways—for different types of investigations (e.g., conceptual, empirical), with diverse stakeholder groups (e.g., direct, indirect), and to support multiple purposes (e.g., to elicit stakeholder values, as design guidelines, as evaluation criteria). Moreover, methods can be integrated in a sequence in the course of moving through a research, design, or development process in either a research or industry environment. Of course, many of the methods here might also be employed within other methodological frameworks.

**Figure 3.9**
Four sample Envisioning Cards, 3.5 × 5 in., showing front and back sides.

We turn now to explicate some of this versatility. Our treatment is by no means exhaustive. We begin with some strategies for getting started and heuristics for conducting different types of investigations. Then we provide a detailed illustration of the use of one method—value scenarios—across a range of contexts, stakeholders, purposes, and goals as a way to explicate the robustness and integration of the methods more generally. We conclude with a brief discussion of skillful practice and the creative application of the methods.

### Some Methodological Strategies and Heuristics

Applying value sensitive design can seem daunting.[1] After all, there is much to consider. Which methods? When in the design process? In what sequence? How to get started? How to talk with stakeholders and technologists about values in technical systems? How to balance values in tension? As with any complex practice, no simple algorithm or checklist will suffice to guide effective practice. That said, a set of methodological strategies and heuristics gleaned from existing value sensitive design projects point the way. Toward that aim, in this section we provide some practical suggestions for skillful practice.

**1. Getting Started**   Any of these core aspects—a value, technology, policy, or context of use—readily motivates value sensitive design. We suggest starting with the aspect that is most central to your work and interests. In one of the application studies that follow, Woelfer, Hendry, and colleagues, for example, began with a population (homeless young people) and a value (safety) of central interest, and moved from there to implications for mobile phone design. In the case of computer security, Denning, Kohno and colleagues began with a technology (implantable cardiac devices) and a situated context of use (cardiac patients in their lived lives); upon consideration of those two, values issues quickly came to the fore.

**2. Clarify Explicitly Supported Project Values and Designer Stance**   At the onset of the project, spend some time reflecting on and identifying the explicitly supported project values. As noted above, these values may be subject to a principled analysis, negotiated through public processes, and/

1. This section draws substantially from a prior publication (see Friedman et al., 2006).

or tied to funding sources. With the explicitly supported project values in hand, then turn to articulate the researcher or designer stance—that is, as suggested by Borning and Muller (2012), make visible the background and perspectives of the individuals who are carrying out the work. For example, in their work in Rwanda with the Voices from the Rwanda Tribunal project, Yoo et al. (2013b) write about themselves:

Our project originated with researchers at universities in the United States and Canada and was developed further with Rwandan practitioners specializing in peace-building and healing communities. As with the collection of the testbed interviews, this work is independent of the Rwandan government, the [International Criminal Tribunal for Rwanda], … and the United Nations. The United States and Canadian members of our team are comprised of [human-computer interaction] … researchers and designers; law, human rights, and conflict resolution scholars and practitioners; technologists; and videographers. In addition to domain area expertise, these team members bring familiarity with a multi-lifespan information system design framing and the Voices from the Rwanda Tribunal project. Several of these project team members have worked previously in Rwanda and elsewhere in Central and East Africa. The Rwandan members of our team are comprised of counselors and interpreters experienced in post-conflict healing. They bring expertise in working with survivors and perpetrators of widespread violence and recovery from trauma, particularly in the Rwandan context. Our Rwandan partner organization is Healing and Rebuilding Our Communities [HROC], a Quaker based organization. HROC regularly runs workshops in Rwanda, Burundi, and elsewhere in the Great Lakes Region that bring together perpetrators and survivors to rebuild their communities. The research reported here while situated with respect to community, place, participant composition, and receptiveness within the HROC workshop structure was independent of the HROC regular trauma healing and reconciliation workshops. (p. 2529)

**3. Framing Technical Work**   Early in a project, it is usually helpful to frame the design situation from a technical point of view. This framing is intended to surface technical elements that hold potential to be shaped through conceptual and empirical investigations. Such work puts in place a foundation for later integration and iteration within the tripartite methodology.

Framing technical work follows from the interactional stance. It is important to understand what aspects of the design situation can be addressed by technical means and what aspects are open to socio-structural interventions. Where, in short, does the design team have the mandate, control, or power to intervene? Relatedly, where and how will technical solutions require cooperation and collaboration from others, such as employers, government, parents, and so on? In some situations, it will be possible to co-evolve the technical and policy environments. For example, in the Code-COOP project (Miller et al., 2007), technical features of a knowledge-base and code repository along with performance incentives from management were designed in tandem to optimize for system adoption and appropriation. In other situations, technical solutions will require cooperation with other stakeholders (e.g., a workplace technology that is accessible for adults with disabilities still requires employers to hire such people).

Within a sociotechnical context, technical investigations focus on the technology itself—its layers and structure, communication protocols, functionality, capacity to scale, vulnerabilities and strengths, and so forth. Technical experts, therefore, are often called upon. In doing their work on security for wireless implantable medical devices, computer security experts Denning and Kohno collaborated with medical device safety and effectiveness experts Maisel and Reynolds to design empirical investigations with both patients (Denning et al., 2010) and medical device providers (Denning et al., 2014).

The focus of a technical investigation can be retrospective or it can be proactive. With the former, the emphasis is on understanding the value implications of an existing technology, and with the latter, it is on investigating new technological possibilities. For example, in their exploration of informed consent for cookies in web browsers, Friedman and her colleagues first conducted a retrospective analysis of web browser settings and features relevant to cookies from 1995 to 1999 (Millett et al., 2001). Based on that analysis, they designed a plug-in for the Mozilla browser to address some of the limitations identified in the retrospective study (Friedman et al., 2002a). Typically, in our experience, proactive work benefits from examining how related technologies have progressed, what proximate and distal causes have led to sociotechnical failures, and what assumptions are not likely to hold in the future with particular attention to inflection points.

**4. Identify Direct and Indirect Stakeholders**   Direct and indirect stakeholders can be identified using both conceptual and empirical methods. Typically, it is helpful to conduct an initial conceptual investigation that systematically identifies direct and indirect stakeholders, then to confirm and/or revise those results based on empirical inquiry.

Many considerations go into a robust stakeholder analysis. We will briefly discuss three. First, as stakeholder groups and subgroups are identified, it is helpful to develop clear definitions, recognizing that an individual may be a member of multiple groups. Addressing difficult edge cases for placing individuals within a stakeholder group often improves the analysis. For example, in the UrbanSim project, an individual who works as an urban planner and lives in the area is both a direct stakeholder (e.g., through the person's direct use of the simulation to evaluate proposed transportation plans) and an indirect stakeholder (e.g., by virtue of living in the community for which the transportation plans will be implemented). Second, because technologies often have far-reaching effects, it is at times difficult to discern the most germane indirect stakeholder groups. As a heuristic, generate as many indirect stakeholder groups as possible and then give priority to indirect stakeholders who are strongly affected, particularly if there is a moral issue involved, or to large groups that are somewhat affected. Third, among the many important challenges for meaningful involvement of stakeholders, one stems from differences in power relations (Floyd, Mehl, Reisin, Schmidt, & Wolf, 1989; Muller, 2003). For example, in organizational settings, there might be low-level employees who are either direct or indirect stakeholders and who have little control over the design or use of a system (e.g., workers on an assembly line). Opportunities for participation will need to be carefully constructed so as to provide real possibilities to contribute ideas and concerns in as risk-free a manner as possible. In such instances, explicitly supported project values can go some distance toward legitimating the inclusion of and accounting for the perspectives of less powerful stakeholders.

**5. Identify Benefits and Harms for Stakeholders**  Having identified the key stakeholders in a particular design context, systematically identify the potential benefits and harms for each group. Given an interactional stance on technology and human activity, a broad perspective on benefits and harms at individual, societal, and environmental levels can be helpful. Both conceptual and empirical investigations can be employed here. Moreover, when conducting empirical investigations, attend to issues of technical, cognitive, and physical competency of stakeholders. In such cases, care must be taken to ensure that stakeholders' interests are represented in the design process, either by representatives from the affected groups them-selves or, if this is not possible, by advocates.

**6. Identify and Elicit Potential Values**  As the methods above suggest, there are numerous ways to identify values that are potentially relevant for a given technical design. Some of these methods involve conceptual investi-gations that draw on analytic strategies or philosophical arguments; others involve empirical investigations involving values discovery and elicitation from direct and indirect stakeholders. One analytic strategy entails map-ping benefits and harms onto corresponding values. Specifically, with a list of benefits and harms in hand, researchers and designers are in a strong position to recognize corresponding values. At times the mapping is immediate—for example, a harm that is characterized as invasion of privacy maps onto the value of privacy. At other times the mapping is less direct, if not multifaceted. For example, with human-robot interaction, companion-ship may be one benefit; such a benefit potentially implicates not only the value of psychological welfare, but also those of accountability, identity, and moral personhood. In some cases, the corresponding values will be obvious, but not always.

Table 2.1 in chapter 2 provides a list of human values with ethical import often implicated in information system design. As discussed within that section, there are pros and cons to providing an explicit list of values that are frequently implicated (Borning & Muller, 2012). On the one hand, such a list may help to orient researchers and designers more quickly to values of import and help to legitimate accounting for human values in the design process—particularly in settings for which such investigations are atypical. On the other hand, at best such lists are incomplete, and at worst such lists can be misused to reify the consideration of a certain set of values over others that might be equally or more important. Empirically based values-representation and -elicitation methods provide a complement to conceptual means of identifying values. Here any number of the methods—stakeholder-generated value scenarios, value sketches, value-oriented semi-structured interview, value sensitive action-reflection model—can be used individually or in combination.

**7. Develop Working Definitions of Key Values**  As key values are identified from conceptual or empirical sources, develop careful working definitions for each. Here it is helpful to turn to the relevant literature. In particular, the philosophical literature can help provide criteria for what constitutes a particular value and, thereby, guide how to assess it empirically. For example, the existing literature helped provide criteria for the model of informed consent online described above. The adjective "working" is important here: generally the working definition should be a few sentences—a book-length discussion of a value will be more difficult to use in providing useful guidance in the value sensitive design process.

**8. Identify Potential Value Tensions**   Values rarely exist in isolation. Rather, they often sit together in a delicate balance and, at times, come into conflict. Moreover, the tensions among two or more values in one culture might be experienced quite differently in another. Once key values have been identified and carefully defined, a next step might entail examining potential conflicts or tensions among the key values. For the purposes of design, value tensions usually should not be conceived of as "either/or" situations, but rather as constraints on the design space. Admittedly, at times designs that support one value directly hinder support for another. In those instances, a good deal of discussion among the stakeholders may be warranted to identify the space of workable solutions. Some value tensions found in the human-computer interaction literature include accountability versus privacy (Miller et al., 2007), trust versus safety (Czeskis et al., 2010), environmental sustainability versus economic development (Borning et al., 2005), privacy versus access (Munson et al., 2011), and control versus autonomy (Kaptein et al., 2011).

**9. Heuristics for Interviewing Stakeholders**   As part of an empirical investigation, it can be useful to interview direct and indirect stakeholders to better understand their judgments about a context of use, an existing technology, or a proposed design. A semi-structured interview often offers a good balance between addressing the questions of interest and gathering new and unexpected insights. In these interviews, the following two heuristics can prove useful.

First, in probing stakeholders' reasons for their judgments, the simple question "Why?" can go a good distance. For example, seniors evaluating a ubiquitous computing video surveillance system might respond negatively to the system. When asked "Why?" a response might be: "I don't mind my family knowing that other people are visiting me, so they don't worry that

I'm alone—I just don't want them to know who is visiting." The researcher can probe again: "Why don't you want them to know?" An answer might be: "I might have a new friend I don't want them to know about. It's not their business." Here the first "why" question elicits information about a value tension (the family's desire to know about the senior's well-being, which the senior also values; and the senior's desire to control some information); the second "why" question elicits further information about the value of privacy for the senior.

Second, ask about values not only directly, but indirectly, based on criteria specified in the conceptual investigation. For example, suppose an interview methodology is being employed to investigate participants' views about value "X" (e.g., trust, privacy, or respect), perhaps in the context of a particular technology. One option is to ask directly about the value. "What is X?" "How do you think about X?" There is merit to this direct approach. Certainly, it gives participants the opportunity to define the value in their own terms. That said, participants likely have nuanced ideas and concepts about a given value that they may not be able to express abstractly. To enrich value elicitation and articulation, alternative approaches that position participants to reason in concrete situations provide useful complements. As is common in social cognitive research (see Kahn [1999], chap. 5, for a discussion of methods), participants could be interviewed about a specific hypothetical situation, a common everyday event, a task just performed, or a behavior just engaged. With these more indirect approaches, participants are positioned to draw on their concrete experiences to surface and reflect on their understandings and views of a particular value in relation to a particular technology.

**10. Heuristics for Technical Work**   Technical work begins with good engineering practice. Recall that value sensitive design is intended to be used in concert with, rather than to supplant, other good technical practices; hence, bring engineering best practices to bear. We call attention to one in particular: worst-case analyses. Because of the potential for significant harms—for example, to human dignity and justice—value sensitive design practices should anticipate and address worst-case scenarios throughout the technical design process.

Within engineering practice and technical work, value tensions are common. To address them, many viable strategies are available, as discussed above. Methodologically, we have often found it less useful to ask stakeholders to explicitly balance two values in the abstract (e.g., "set a slider to indicate your preferred balance between reputation and trust"). Rather, we have found it more useful to ask stakeholders to focus on a specific technical feature and how it implicates a particular value (e.g., for the feature of *anonymous replies* and the value of *trust*, "On a scale of 1 to 5, how strongly do you agree with this statement: I would be less inclined to trust an anonymous reply to a question."). With stakeholder data in hand about the relation between technical features and particular values, it is possible to employ the value dams and flows method (see above) to first narrow the design space (value dams) and then prioritize which remaining features to include (value flows). Integrating an empirical and a technical investigation, this two-pronged strategy was employed in the CodeCOOP project to design a knowledge-base and code repository (Miller et al., 2007).

In shaping technical design, we have also found it useful to attend to the mental models of both direct and indirect stakeholders, again with particular attention to value implications. In other words, help stakeholders develop robust mental models for reasoning about how a system works and for diagnosing unexpected outcomes that might implicate agency, community, identity, privacy, or other relevant values. For example, Friedman et al. (2002b) showed that some users interpreted the "key" or "padlock" icon used in web browsers for a secure connection to mean a "secure place" (see figure 3.2). An "armored car" icon connoting "security-in-transit," on the other hand, might have helped these users develop a more robust mental model of a secure connection and thereby enabled users to take actions to protect their data accordingly.

Design the technical system and associated processes so that taken together they are positioned to respond to change as the system is deployed, appropriated, and gains traction in the world. Stakeholder groups are likely to appropriate a deployed system in unexpected ways, and unanticipated values and value tensions are likely to emerge. Thus, when possible, design flexibility into the underlying technical architecture so that it can be responsive. In UrbanSim, for example, Freeman-Benson and Borning (2003) used agile programming techniques to design an architecture that could more readily accommodate new land use, transportation, and environmental indicators and models.

We conclude with two related heuristics that are germane for computing and information systems, where we have done most of our work. These heuristics stem from the structure, malleability, and adaptability of digital technology.

Approach computing and information systems in terms of layers and their interdependencies. The lower-level layers of an architecture place constraints and give affordances for what will be easy, difficult but doable, or impossible to implement at the levels of interaction. For example, consider two cell phone architectures and their respective implications for building in privacy protections. In one—a *broadcast* architecture—the cell phone announces its presence to all nearby receivers; privacy-enhancing solutions for this architecture will need to do considerable work to contain or protect the signals that are automatically broadcast. In the second—a *receiver* architecture—the cell phone listens to those devices around it and then determines (perhaps with a person's input) which device, if any, to communicate with; privacy-enhancing solutions for this architecture will be much easier to implement (e.g., ignoring or not responding to received signals) and likely easier to make transparent to the user and monitor for accountability.

Further, control at the lower levels of an architecture is of great importance for many reasons, including investigating different interaction design options for supporting desired values and responding to unanticipated impacts as systems are appropriated. As one case, Millett and colleagues encountered the need for lower level control in their early work on informed consent, cookies, and Internet protocols, concluding "that browsers (and other software) should not be designed to volunteer information without putting in place some override mechanism" (2001, p. 51). Ubiquitous computing, augmented reality, Internet of Things, and smart grids with sensors that collect and then disseminate information at large have only intensified these concerns. Thus, consider building technical hooks at the lower levels that are accessible from the upper levels for accessing and observing data, destroying or keeping redundant copies of data, and turning technical features on and off.

The notion of layers and hooks may be relevant to other types of technologies. For example, Stuart Brand provides a similar construction around layers, characterizing the order of civilization with "the fast layers [that] innovate" built on top of "the slow layers [that] stabilize" such that "the whole combines learning with continuity" (1999, p. 37). Moreover, as we look toward the future with the emergence of meta-materials and other innovations, information and computing technologies are merging in fundamental ways with physical materials, biology, and infrastructure. Should this trend continue, the structure, malleability, and adaptability of digital technology may become more pervasive and these heuristics more broadly applicable.

### One Method in Action: Value Scenarios Across Contexts

Having provided descriptions of a number of methodological strategies and heuristics, we now turn to a detailed illustration of the use of one method—value scenarios—across a range of contexts, stakeholders, and purposes as a way to explicate the robustness and integration of the methods more generally. Importantly, value sensitive design methods are often used together to achieve research and design goals. Thus, in the process of illustrating value scenarios, other methods such as the value sensitive action-reflection model, value sketches, and Envisioning Cards are also discussed.

*Same method, different types of investigation.* The same method can be used in support of different types of investigation. As one illustration, value scenarios have been used in conceptual, empirical, and technical investigations as follows. In their conceptual analyses of parenting technologies with teenagers, Czeskis et al. (2010) used value scenarios early in their work to explore the research and design space and to surface potential tensions among various stakeholders. Specifically, they generated approximately 20 value scenarios, each one focused on a different constellation of elements that followed from their conceptual work. Below is one scenario, excerpted from Czeskis et al. (2010), that provides a vision for how a mobile phone tracking and context-monitoring application might influence the lives of direct stakeholders (teens and their parents) as well as indirect ones (the teen's friends and those friends' parents). In the scenario, while providing some comfort for parents and a particular sense of connection, values such as trust and respect appear to be eroded, since the technology easily allows parents to watch their teens unnoticed. At its broadest level, the scenario points to the possibility for far-reaching changes in societal expectations and norms around what constitutes good parenting.

## Value Scenario: One Dad's Dilemma

**Mobile parenting technology.** PhoneTracker is a hypothetical mobile phone application and website designed to help parents keep track of their teens. Once installed on a mobile phone, parents can use the application to surreptitiously turn on the phone's microphone or to read text messages on the teen's phone at any time (by logging into a webpage).

**Scenario.** Paul puts a great store of trust in his 14-year old son Ben. He's been raising Ben in a suburb of San Jose, California since Ben's Mom passed away six years ago. They talk to each other a lot: share baseball, play music, take canoe trips. Although they are very close, things have changed a bit since Ben entered high school a few months ago. Ben hangs out with friends more, communicates less, and generally spends less time around the house. Paul misses the connection with Ben but figures this is normal for a teen. After all, teens need their privacy and space from their parents.

At Paul's work, talk of "life with teens" is common conversation. Several of Paul's coworkers have been telling tales: they suspect their teens of experimenting with drugs, notice alcohol on their teens' breath, and reckless driving. Last week, Betty bragged about a mobile phone app her husband had secretly installed on their daughter's cell phone: PhoneTracker. Now Betty knows where her daughter is hanging out, with whom, and what they're talking about. From reading text messages on her daughter's cell phone, Betty got a tip that the party planned for Saturday night would be pretty rough. So Betty planned a family gathering for Saturday night and "nipped that one in the bud." In no uncertain terms, Betty told Paul that in this day and age, any parent who isn't using a tool like PhoneTracker to keep tabs on their teens is being a negligent parent. Downright irresponsible. And, irresponsible not only with respect to their teen but also with the other teens involved. At first Paul is appalled that Betty is "spying" on her daughter. But over time, pressured by Betty's stories as well as her comments that he is oblivious and naive, Paul begins to question his own judgment as a parent. He secretly installs Phone-Tracker on Ben's phone.

Over the next several months, Paul checks Ben's activities regularly. Paul notices no discontinuities between Ben's stories and what PhoneTracker reports. Paul also develops a good sense of whom Ben hangs out with, where they go, and how they spend their time. It's a funny but comforting sort of communication. To his surprise, Paul also learns a great deal about Ben's best friend Jon. Things Jon's parents probably don't know. Paul wonders about that—is he spying on Jon too? Is he obligated to tell Jon's parents? How would he feel if Jon's parents were watching Ben in this way?

Then the whole thing fell apart. One evening, while Paul was checking Ben's activities on PhoneTracker's website, Ben came up behind him. Ben saw what his father was looking at. Ben went ballistic—storming out of the house, shouting that Paul does not trust him. The next day, Ben threw his phone away and clams up. He's mad and sullen. Somehow, Paul's and Ben's relationship is never quite the same. (Czeskis et al. [2010], p. 4)

In contrast to the conceptual use of designer-generated value scenarios (Czeskis et al., 2010), as part of an empirical investigation, Woelfer et al. (2011) placed value scenarios in the hands of homeless young people and the service providers and police officers with whom they interact regularly. Specifically, to elicit ideas for how a mobile phone could help homeless young people stay safe, Woelfer and her colleagues instructed participants to write their own value scenarios addressing safety with this prompt:

Homeless youth and young adults may face special challenges in keeping safe from harm. Please write a story about how a cell phone could help to keep a homeless youth or young adult safe. There are no right answers. The story can be as long or short as you like. It can be about a real situation or about a fictional situation. (p. 1710)

This prompt resulted in value scenarios that, taken together, revealed key considerations for the design of mobile phones for improving safety, including situation (e.g., reaction to a hostile event, accident), purpose (e.g., warn others of an impending event, document an event), mobile phone technology (e.g., functionality such as making calls or recording audio), and locus of welfare (e.g., self or other-directed). For example, one homeless young man wrote about the use of mobile phones to document police abuse:

I would use devices in my cell phone to record law enforcement, when they choose to harass me.

A homeless young woman called attention to the benefits of having a mobile phone (functional or not) and wrote:

I feel when hitching rides, with a cell phone you can be kept safe. If you're walking down the road with your thumb out and a cell phone to your ear a 'weirdo' is less likely to pick you up.

Not all of the value scenarios pointed to benefits from mobile phones. For instance, another homeless young man foregrounded the reality of living on the streets and highlighted the potential for increased vulnerabilities and risk to safety:

I don't think cell phones keep people safe because if you call the cops for seeing a crime you might get beat up later for snitching.

Yoo, Huldtgren, Woelfer, Hendry, and Friedman (2013a) extended this empirical work with homeless young people to a technical co-design activity that employed value scenarios as a key design prompt. Specifically, in the context of the value sensitive action-reflection model, Yoo and her colleagues asked homeless young people and those with whom they interact regularly to design (including physically constructing a prototype) a mobile phone that would help to keep homeless young people safe. Participants were given the following instruction:

Homeless youth and young adults may face special challenges in keeping safe from harm. Please make a prototype of a cell phone that might help keep a homeless youth or young adult safe. There are no right answers.

Continuing with the value sensitive action-reflection model, once participants had an initial design and prototype in hand, they were given a sample of 11 stakeholder-generated value scenarios from the Woelfer et al. (2011) study above, repurposed to use as stakeholder prompts. Participants were instructed to select one value scenario and to consider their prototypes in light of the situation described in the scenario. Then they completed a specification sheet to record any changes they would make to their prototypes or to explain why no changes were needed to accommodate the situation conveyed in the value scenario.

*Same method, different stakeholder groups.* While it seems readily apparent that the same method can be used with the different stakeholder groups, it is nonetheless worth noting. In the detailed example above regarding value scenarios, Woelfer et al. (2011) used value scenarios with four stakeholder groups: homeless young people, service providers, police officers, and community members; and Yoo et al. (2013a) with three of those four stakeholder groups: homeless young people, service providers, and police officers.

*Same method, different purposes.* It is also the case that the same method can be used for different purposes in the research and design process. Depending on the method, purposes might include:

- communicating with a client
- representing values relevant to a particular technical design
- eliciting values from diverse stakeholder groups, both direct and indirect
- legitimating value considerations to key decision makers
- prompting value considerations in a prototyping context
- selecting among various technical options in a design process
- evaluating the quality of a proposed technical design
- providing assessment criteria for a deployed technology.

Returning to the detailed discussion of value scenarios above, Czeskis et al. (2010) used value scenarios to guide their initial conceptual analysis of values relevant to a particular technical design, that of mobile parenting technologies for teens; Woelfer et al. (2011) used value scenarios as a values-elicitation method with diverse stakeholder groups including homeless young people, service providers, police officers, and community members; and Yoo et al. (2013a) used value scenarios as a value sensitive design prompt in a co-design activity as part of the value sensitive action-reflection model.

*Same purpose, different methods.* At times, well-chosen methods used in combination may yield more meaningful results than a single method in isolation. In fact, any mixed method approach typically would be based on a similar rationale. Recall that above, in their work with homeless young people and those with whom they regularly interact, Woelfer et al. (2011) were interested in eliciting participants' understandings of safety for homeless young people and the potential for mobile phones to improve those situations. To do so, they employed value scenarios as a means to tap into participants' stories about safety or lack of safety and employed value sketches to tap into participants' knowledge for safe and less-safe places within the neighborhood. As a second example, and working with similar populations, Yoo et al. (2013a) used stakeholder-generated value scenarios (from the Woelfer et al. [2011] study) as structured prompts in a co-design process that, in turn, was part of a value sensitive action-reflection model. Moreover, as part of that model, Envisioning Cards were also employed as designer-generated structured prompts in the same co-design prototyping process. Thus, to achieve the goal of eliciting participants' ideation for using mobile phones to improve safety for homeless young people, value scenarios, Envisioning Cards, value-oriented prototyping, and the value sensitive action-reflection model were used in combination.

*Same stakeholder group, different methods.* A corollary following from the discussion of "same purpose, different methods" entails the observation "same stakeholder group, different methods." Specifically, the stakeholder groups in Woelfer et al. (2011) each engaged with value scenarios and value sketches; those in Yoo et al. (2013a) used value scenarios, Envisioning Cards, value-oriented prototypes, and the value sensitive action-reflection model.

## Developing Value Sensitive Design Methods

The methods presented in this chapter have been developed in order to address specific needs designers and researchers encountered when working on projects. When bringing values into a design process, common needs include eliciting values from stakeholders; representing and foregrounding values in sociotechnical situations; analyzing the relationships among values; addressing value tensions; and so forth. The methods shown in table 3.1 address these and related needs.

How, if at all, are these methods distinctive? Simply put, they have been shaped by the theoretical constructs of value sensitive design. The methods in table 3.1 are not a definitive set. Instead, they can be considered examples within a large space of possible value sensitive design methods. Accordingly, by examining how these methods have been created and used, it is possible to understand the broader space of methodological innovation in value sensitive design. The opportunities for innovation are many, and much remains to be done.

To meaningfully extend or create new methods, it is often helpful to begin with the theoretical constructs. The constructs are essential to the methods. To illustrate, consider this question: how might the common user-centered design method of personas be modified in light of value sensitive design? Personas are fictional characters, often based on market research, that represent a particular demographic or a characteristic user (Pruitt & Grudin, 2003). Personas typically have motivations, along with aspirations, needs, and goals, and they partake in characteristic activity scenarios with technologies. Personas can serve various purposes. They can help market researchers, designers, and engineers communicate. In addition, they can assist designers to construct an empathetic relationship with potential users, allowing designers to move beyond their own vantage point to the motivations and goals of an idealized user, the persona.

The invention of a *value persona*, as a new method, might go in several directions. Following the distinction between direct and indirect stakeholders, personas might be constructed to represent both users with goals for interacting with a technology along with personas that are affected by a technology but do not interact with it. While a father (indirect stakeholder) might not directly interact with his adolescent son's (direct stakeholder) social media accounts, he might be affected by his son's changing moods.

Value personas might be potentially useful for both stakeholders. Similarly, following the constructs of values and value tensions, the personas might also include key values, working definitions, and the most salient value tensions, possibly between personas or within a persona. Continuing with our father and son personas, key values for the father might be maturation, trust, and safety; key values for the son might be maturation, trust, autonomy, and social acceptance among peers (e.g., the coolness factor). Value tensions might take several forms. Within a persona, the father might feel tensions between enabling his son's maturation and concern for his son's safety; the son might feel tensions between seeking trust with his father and social acceptance among peers. Between personas, value tensions might exist between the father's concern for his son's safety and the son's value of personal autonomy. In this example, value personas take on a distinct character by reflecting some of the theoretical constructs, in this case of direct and indirect stakeholders, values, and value tensions.

More generally, one way toward methodological innovation is to consider how the theoretical constructs of value sensitive design might be used to rework common methods. *Personas* to *value personas* illustrates one of many possible transformations.

### Working with Versatility

Given such wealth and versatility of method, which method(s) should a researcher or designer use when, and for what purposes? Volumes could be written here. While skillful practice defies easy description, one reasonable answer is: whichever method or methods in combination make good sense for the particular context, technology, and human values.

With that in mind and an eye on brevity, we offer the following seven heuristics for the overall research and design process; as with other suggestions in this section, this set is not exhaustive.

1. Adopt and extend the methods for your own purposes. Build from what is presented here in ways that are meaningful for the sociotechnical setting—the context, technology, and values.

2. Recall the interactional stance of value sensitive design. The application of these methods follows from that stance; seek an iterative and integrative use of method as the design process unfolds over time.

3. As one means to identify and avoid blind spots, conduct a conceptual investigation to identify key stakeholders (direct and indirect), benefits and harms, values, and value tensions relatively early in the process.

4. If new values of import surface during the design process, engage them. As appropriate, draw on the existing literature to develop criteria for defining these values.

5. Use a variety of empirical values-elicitation methods, rather than relying on a single one.

6. Continue to elicit stakeholder values throughout the design process to support problem definition, shape and refine design solutions, and inform the evaluation of the evolving system.

7. There are almost always unanticipated consequences to newly designed and deployed technologies. Thus, if possible, continue the value sensitive evaluation process through the deployment phase and plan to make changes to the system and the implementation if new issues of import surface.

The 17 methods, heuristics, and examples we have discussed here, as well as others not explicitly taken up, go a good distance toward providing tools for engaging substantively with human values in the technical design process. To these, we add other important methods from design, philosophy, social science, and biology that can be employed in more standard ways to the same end. That said, there is every expectation that, in the course of conducting new research and design work in new contexts, with new technologies that implicate human values in nuanced and potentially new ways, other methods used alone or in combination will be needed. In response, researchers, designers, and engineers will bring their imaginations and creativity to bear, yielding further methods and insights. Through such activity, the corpus of value sensitive design methods and the variation of their use in combination will expand, providing an ever-richer toolset.

# 4 Applications

By intent, the theory and methods of value sensitive design could be applied to the design of any technology. Neither the theoretical constructs nor the methods are technology-specific. That said, the vast majority of work to date applying this approach has been in information system design broadly conceived, and more recently in engineering. This work spans the spectrum of human activity: it includes work with *individuals*—involving physiological responses to large displays, human interaction with robotic pets, and security for implantable cardiac devices; *small groups*—involving interactions of homeless young people with mobile phones and parenting technology for use with teens; *organizations*—involving software knowledge and code repositories for a large software company and real-time information systems for public transit; *public space*—involving public records online and privacy in public spaces; *social policy*—involving large-scale urban simulation for land use and transportation planning, waste water treatment plants, and open-source privacy licenses; and *global issues*—involving information systems in support of transitional justice.

In this chapter, we focus on 10 application domains. As a collection, perhaps the most noteworthy feature of these application domains is their contextual diversity, as shown in table 4.1. In choosing this set we have sought to include projects conducted by researchers from diverse fields (e.g., civil engineering, computer science, design, information, and philosophy) that employ a diversity of value sensitive design methods (e.g., Envisioning Cards, stakeholder analyses, value-oriented semi-structured interviews, value sketches); engage a diversity of stakeholders (e.g., cardiac patients, homeless young people, bus drivers, the general public) and a diversity of technologies (e.g., web browser security, parenting technologies, urban simulation, waste water treatment); and represent the historical development

**Table 4.1**

Application Domain by Author, Key Values, and Key Technologies

| Application | Authors(s) | Key Values | Key Technologies |
|---|---|---|---|
| 1 Informed Consent Online | Batya Friedman | Informed Consent—Privacy—Security | Web browsers—Mobile apps—Open source |
| 2 Security for Mobile Devices | Alexei Czeskis, Tamara Denning, Tadayoshi Kohno | Personal Relationships—Safety—Security—Self-image—Social Development | Implantable cardiac devices—Mobile parenting technology |
| 3 Persuasive Technology | Janet Davis | Accountability—Autonomy—Identity—Informed Consent—Privacy—Reputation—Trust | Groupware—Targeted advertising—Health applications |
| 4 Human-Robot Interaction | Nathan Freier | Accountability—Autonomy—Human Dignity—Psychological Well-being—Social Development—Trust | Robotic dogs—Avatars—Humanoid social robots |
| 5 Computers and Disabilities | Shiri Azenkot, Katherine Deibel, Alan Borning | Access—Community Empowerment—Fairness—Freedom—Human Welfare—Identity—Independence—Normalcy—Privacy—Safety—Self-respect—Social Acceptance | Public transit apps for deaf-blind riders—Computer-based reading support systems |
| 6 Homeless Young People | Jill Palzkill Woelfer, David G. Hendry | Caring—Economic Development—Independence—Ownership—Relationship Building—Respect—Safety—Self-worth—Trust | Paper-based information services—Community technology center—Personal digital devices |
| 7 Privacy in Public | Batya Friedman | Access—Accountability—Informed Consent—Privacy in Public—Social Expectations—Transparency | Cameras in public spaces (USA and Sweden)—Online public records |

**Table 4.1** (continued)

| Application | Authors(s) | Key Values | Key Technologies |
|---|---|---|---|
| 8 Land Use, Transportation, and Environment | Alan Borning, Kari Watkins | Access—Economic Development—Enjoyment—Fairness—Health—Safety—Sustainability | Simulation to support urban planning—Public transit information systems |
| 9 Engineering Design Practice | Jeroen van den Hoven, Ibo van de Poel | Environmental Care—Health—Responsible Innovation—Safety—Sustainability—Trust—Well-being | Waste water treatment plants—Customs compliance systems |
| 10 Envisioning Criteria | Lisa Nathan | Any | Any |

of value sensitive design, including the early projects on informed consent online as well as more recent work on implantable cardiac devices and envisioning criteria. Yet within these varied application domains, several common themes emerge, including the careful characterization of the values at stake; an interactional stance whereby values are investigated as interplay among technologies and individuals, groups, or societies; and the use of innovative methods during the design process.

In order to convey the diversity of voices working within a value sensitive design approach, each application section that follows has been written by some of the leading researchers in that domain. For each application domain, the researchers and designers have drawn upon and, in many cases, extended value sensitive design to meet the particular challenges of that domain. Each section first provides an introduction that explicates critical value issues, tensions, and concerns as they manifest within that domain; then discusses briefly two or three key projects, highlighting aspects of applying value sensitive design; and concludes with reflections on the domain and contributions to value sensitive design.

### Informed Consent Online

Author: Batya Friedman

Computing and information technologies increasingly observe and mediate human action. Typically, the technology does so under the direction of corporations and governments. These technologies often collect vast amounts of information about those activities and actors, as well as potentially bystanders, institutions, and governments. Yet all too frequently, the people acting with and through the technology have little knowledge about what information is being collected, by whom, for what purposes, in relation to what other information, and for what duration. Think of this as vast, pervasive, surreptitious data collection. Moreover, even if those interacting with the technology have such knowledge, they often have few meaningful opportunities to consent to or decline participation. That is, to live in the modern world, engage in social life, pursue education, conduct business, or contribute to civic society in one way or another requires action mediated by computing and information technology. To avoid such mediated action is tantamount to withdrawing from participation in many aspects of social, civic, and civil life.

One way to modulate the impact of this kind of surreptitious data collection is through secure technology working in the background to essentially encrypt or mask the data from unvalidated observers. Such solutions place the burden on largely automated technical mechanisms, with the technologist as adjudicator. Another way is through informed consent, in which direct and indirect stakeholders, based on their knowledge of how the system works, choose whether or not to participate. Such solutions leave the decision making primarily in the hands of these stakeholders. In this section, we focus on the latter approach of informed consent and, in one project, examine how the two approaches might complement each other.

Two constructs form the basis of informed consent (see, for example, National Commission for the Protection of Human Subjects of Biomedical and Behavioral Research [1978]; and for online contexts, Friedman et al. [2000a]). Here, we follow closely the concise definitions used in Millett et al. (2001). The construct of "informed" encompasses *disclosure* and *comprehension*. "Disclosure" refers to providing accurate information about the benefits and harms that might reasonably be expected from the action under consideration. If that action involves collecting information about an individual, then the following should be made explicit: (1) what information will be collected; (2) who will have access to it; (3) how long it will be archived; (4) what it will be used for; and (5) whether—and, if so, how—the identity of the individual will be protected. "Comprehension" refers to the individual's accurate interpretation of what is being disclosed. Because online interactions lack the benefit of face-to-face interactions that can help ensure comprehension though dialogue, special efforts on the part of designers may be necessary to analyze what users need to understand about a particular disclosure and to utilize strategies to increase the likelihood that comprehension will be realized.

The second construct of "consent" encompasses *voluntariness, competence*, and *agreement*. "Voluntariness" refers to ensuring that the action is not controlled or coerced. Coercion is an extreme form of influence that controls by compulsion, threat, or prevention (e.g., an overt threat of violence), and thereby violates the component of voluntariness. Furthermore, certain forms of manipulation can undermine voluntariness, particularly when it alters the individuals' choices or perception of choices by some means other than reason (see the discussion of persuasive technology by Davis below). A less obvious form of coercion can occur when there is only one reasonable way for individuals to receive certain needed services or information. "Competence" refers to possessing the mental, emotional, and physical capabilities needed to be capable of giving informed consent. Web designers of sites targeted for children and adolescents, for example, will need to be especially cognizant of the component of competence. Finally, "agreement" refers to a reasonably clear opportunity to accept or decline to participate. In online interactions, opportunities to accept or decline should be visible and readily accessible rather than buried under layers of menus or hidden in obscure locations. Moreover, the aspect of ongoing agreement or the ability to withdraw consent may have relevance for online interactions. After all, people's goals and situations in life may change over time; correspondingly, what they may wish to consent or not consent to may also change over time. For example, users could be provided with the opportunity to withdraw their data from a recommendation system at any time. As a society, we have a good deal of experience with implicit consent: by virtue of entering into a situation the individual agrees to the activities that are known to occur in that context. Implicit consent holds when the other criteria discussed above have also been met.

From the perspective of a value sensitive design retrospective, the informed consent online projects—particularly those around cookies and web browser security—in addition to their content area, represent the first explication of the full tripartite methodology of conceptual, empirical, and technical investigations. In this early explication, the investigations are applied in a somewhat linear fashion. From a methodological perspective, these projects are described here for two reasons: first, to show the early thinking and work with the tripartite methodology; and second, to provide a clear example of each of the investigations and how the three types of investigations can dovetail to achieve a larger, more complete research and design goal.

### Informed Consent Online: Specific Projects

The first project we describe is of both historical and current interest: *historical*, from a value sensitive design perspective, in that it represents the first published piece of work to employ robustly the tripartite methodology; and *current*, from a topical perspective, in that the design challenges for informed consent online continue to be a pressing topic today. As a case in point, in the United States in February 2014, the Office of the National Coordinator for Health Information Technology (ONC) launched a new challenge to create an online notice of privacy practices (Pritts, 2014). In work conducted from roughly 1999 to 2002, we examined informed consent online in the context of cookies and web browser security. We began with a conceptual investigation to develop a model for informed consent for online interactions (Friedman et al., 2000a). This work drew heavily on the Belmont Report (National Commission for the Protection of Human Subjects of Biomedical and Behavioral Research, 1978) for work with human subjects and yielded the constructs above, with adaptations for nonresearch contexts and the online environment. With a model for informed consent online in hand, we next turned to analyzing existing technical features in the two most common web browsers at the time, Netscape Navigator and Internet Explorer, considering all major versions from 1995 to 1999 in light of the model (Millett et al., 2001). Results of this technical investigation of existing technology showed that despite the addition of numerous technical features (e.g., options to decline a cookie, or accept some but not all cookies), the out-of-the-box experience for users remained unchanged: all cookies were enabled and hidden from the user. Continuing with this work (Friedman et al., 2002a), the next question became: using the model for informed consent online (results from the conceptual investigation) as design guidelines, could we do better? That is, could we redesign the web browser to do a better job of handling cookies with respect to informed consent? This technical investigation took the form of designing a plug-in for the Mozilla browser and included two new types of technical mechanisms: a "cookie watcher" in the periphery that made visible whenever a cookie was set and indicated if that cookie was from a third party; and second, a just-in-time management mechanism that enabled users to review and manage individual cookies at their discretion (see figure 4.1). A formative evaluation with users investigated the extent to which these new technical features improved the user experience of informed consent with respect to cookies. The results of this empirical investigation, by and large, were positive. One finding highlighted the burden for providing explicit informed consent in instance after instance, resulting in a modification to the model of informed consent online. Thus results from the empirical investigation led to further refinements in the conceptual investigation. Another finding highlighted a user desire to be informed when and why a

**Figure 4.1**

A screenshot of the Mozilla browser with the plug-in showing the peripheral awareness "cookie watcher" on the left-hand side of the browser window and the "just-in-time" cookie management mechanism as a pop-up in the middle of the screen. In the cookie watcher, a red background indicates a third party cookie.

website wished to use (as opposed to set) a cookie. Further technical investigation in response to this finding pointed to limitations in the HTTP protocol for realizing this and other important aspects of informed consent online.

A key design challenge for informed consent online emerged in the cookies and web browser security work above as well as other research (Cranor, 2000): how to inform without undue burden to the user. After all, the user has come to the system to achieve some goal, and while providing informed consent may be important, it is by and large a distraction from the task at hand. Informing through interaction is one approach toward providing a solution (Friedman et al., 2005b). The general idea is to design systems in such a manner that, through interaction with the system, users are informed of the right sort of information at the right time so they can make informed decisions; moreover, users' active choice to continue interacting with the system constitutes implied consent. To provide a flavor for informing through interaction, consider the representation of a secure connection in web browsers. Historically, web browsers represented a secure connection with either a key or padlock icon (i.e., a whole key or closed padlock indicated the connection was secure—the https protocol; a broken key or open padlock indicated the connection was not secure—the http protocol). Our empirical study of users' understanding about secure connections in web browsers (Friedman et al., 2002b) showed that at least some users understood a secure connection to refer to a secure place (e.g., the website where data was being sent) rather than to security of information in transit (for an example, see the value sketch in figure 3.2). This finding led us to conclude that an alternative icon for representing a secure connection may be warranted, one that would more readily lead users to construct a more accurate mental model. While we did not specify or test specific alternatives at that time, the icon of an armored car that would convey the idea of security in transit seems an intriguing possibility.

A third research project investigated the question: could open-source software licenses be extended to account for other values in addition to freedom, access, and intellectual property? We conducted this work in the context of an open-source location-aware application running on a mobile phone, with privacy the value of interest (Friedman et al., 2006c). Our first step was to generate a set of privacy parameters that could eventually be translated into the legal language of a software license. The strategy we employed combined results from the informed consent online model with those from a traditional security threat analysis. Results from the informed consent analysis provided detailed insight into what information to disclose, how to disclose it, when and what type of agreement to obtain, and what assessments (e.g., of competence and voluntariness) would be reasonably beyond reach. In contrast, results from the threat analysis pointed to vulnerabilities and means to remedy them. While there was some overlap between the results from both models, each yielded important unique insights. For example, the informed consent online model provided specific guidance about what type of information needed to be disclosed and under what conditions. In contrast, the security threat analysis brought attention to the vulnerability of special populations, such as victims of domestic violence who can be placed at greater risk should their location be discovered; and surfaced the possibility of deleting links or removing data as a means to minimize the duration of time for which a threat was "active." Some recommendations from the models were deemed impractical given the current state of the art (e.g., to determine if a person at the other end of an Internet connection would be competent to give consent). The privacy parameters formed the basis for a legal license written by legal staff. This portion of the license is known as the privacy addendum. The location-aware mobile phone application was released under an open-source license that contained the privacy addendum along with legal language to ensure open access.

### Informed Consent Online: Contributions

The late 1990s and early 2000s saw public discomfort and debate over privacy concerns relating to cookies in web browsers—enough that organizations developing web browser software devoted significant resources to adding new features to mitigate concerns. Now, as we approach 2020, we see similar issues around social media, augmented reality, and Internet of Things technologies, as well as online delivery of health information and other key information services. While the specific technologies have changed, the relevance of this early work persists, pointing to the need to inform users of the right sort of information at the right time, without undue burden. Good solutions remain elusive. At least one way to move the field forward would be to develop a set of new ideas that improve upon informing through interaction and scaffold users' construction of meaningful mental models—models that would position users to make good choices for the collection, dissemination, and use of information about themselves. Importantly, while some of these challenges can be addressed through better technical design, some may require policy and regulation to ensure that viable opportunities for choice are preserved.

Fundamental to value sensitive design is the tripartite methodology, in which conceptual, technical, and empirical investigations are employed in an integrative and iterative manner in the service of accounting for human values throughout the design process. Historically, the work on informed consent online for cookies and web browsers provided the first clear proof of concept of this methodology in the published literature. As described above, the work began with a conceptual investigation (of informed consent online), then a technical investigation of existing technology (web browsers), a technical investigation of the redesign of the then-current technology (the open-source Mozilla browser) guided by the conceptual investigation (the model of informed consent online), followed by an empirical investigation of the resulting technical design (of the redesigned web browser), that in turn led to refinements to the conceptual investigation (of the model for informed consent online).

In addition to providing a proof of concept for the tripartite methodology, this research contributed the model for informed consent online as well as demonstrated the use of value-oriented criteria (i.e., the model for informed consent online) for purposes of both evaluation (of existing technology) and design guidelines (for new technical design). Key to value sensitive design is the claim that value sensitive methods can be used in concert with (rather than supplant) other well-founded technical and nontechnical methods. This kind of complementarity of method was illustrated with the work on an open-source privacy addendum in which a more robust solution was obtained through combining results from a more traditional threat analysis with that from the model of informed consent online. From a value sensitive design perspective, numerous open questions remain. Some encompass how to do informed consent online well. Challenges of undue burden on the user, informing through interaction, and constructing useful mental models fall within this purview. Other questions entail how to achieve the goals of informed consent online through combination with other solution strategies such as policy, regulation, threat analyses, computer security, and so forth. The idea here is that better solutions may be constructed by looking beyond informed consent itself to engage a broader range of tools and techniques.

## Security for Mobile Devices

Authors: Alexei Czeskis, Tamara Denning, and Tadayoshi Kohno

Traditionally, computer security—a field focused on ensuring that computer systems behave as expected even in the presence of miscreants—has focused on purely computational mechanisms: for example, how to create an algorithm for encrypting data on a hard drive or how to design input-sanitization techniques to protect a website against cross-site scripting attacks. While the security goals for these traditional systems are fairly well defined—security practitioners predominantly agree on what it means for a hard drive to be encrypted or for a website to follow best practices—the security landscape is changing as technologies become more pervasive and personal: technologies are starting to serve as surrogate nannies for our children and being implanted within our very bodies. It is not immediately clear what security criteria users want for their personal, pervasive devices. Indeed, while various mechanisms may improve some aspects of security, they may also grate against other fundamental values that are important to stakeholders. There are many references describing examples where users accidentally misuse or intentionally circumvent security measures with poor usability—Gaw, Felten, and Fernandez-Kelly (2006) and Whitten and Tygar (1999), to name just a couple—however, the question of how security systems interact with human values goes beyond the topic of usability to issues such as self-image, interpersonal relationships, autonomy, and culture.

Consider, for example, wireless implantable pacemakers and defibrillators, which are both widely deployed and intimately personal. These are nonstandard computing devices that have been demonstrated to have wireless security vulnerabilities (Halperin, Kohno, Heydt-Benjamin, Fu, & Maisel, 2008; Maisel & Kohno, 2010; Gollakota, Hassanieh, Ransford, Katabi, & Fu, 2011). Even though the current risk to patients is extremely low—due in part to the difficulty in exploiting the vulnerabilities—the presence of such vulnerabilities has led security researchers to explore a variety of security solutions (Gollakota et al., 2011; Rushanan, Rubin, Kune, & Swanson, 2014; Rasmussen, Castelluccia, Heydt-Benjamin, & Capkun, 2009). Some obvious solutions, such as protecting the medical device with a password that only the prescribing doctor knows, are not appropriate because such security measures can be in direct conflict with critical safety goals: medical personnel may need immediate communication access to the device in case of an emergency such as a car accident. Researchers have thus proposed a spectrum of solutions, ranging from tattooing a patient with the device's password to requiring the patient to wear a separate, external device—such as a wristband—solely for the purpose of increasing security (Cherukuri, Venkatasubramanian, & Gupta, 2003; Denning, Fu, & Kohno, 2008; Gupta, Mukherjee, & Venkatasubramanian, 2006; Rasmussen et al., 2009; Schecter, 2010; Rushanan, Rubin, Kune, & Swanson, 2014). Value sensitive design can be a useful approach for helping to develop technical solutions that are responsive to key stakeholders and their values. While password tattoos might be secure and usable, would patients want them or not, and why? Would an external "security wristband" impact a patient's self-image?

As a second example, consider the numerous technologies currently available on the market that are meant to aid with parenting. One class of technologies, such as Net Nanny (https://www.netnanny.com) and PC Tattletale (https://www.pctattletale.com), empower parents with the ability to monitor their children's web, email, and online social networking activity. Another technology, DriveCam, allows parents to install a camera in their teen's car in order to record videos of any potentially dangerous driving behaviors ("Teen driver safety system": Lytx, n.d.). For younger children, parents can buy GPS tracking wristbands or jackets ("GPS tracking device for kids": BrickHouse Security, n.d.; White, 2007). Computer security clearly plays a key role in these systems: for example, the data from the Drive-Cam video camera must traverse the DriveCam corporate network and the general Internet before reaching the teen's parents, and thus might benefit from encryption; similarly, one would hope that a toddler's GPS location is not available to everyone. However, even bigger issues are at stake: how do today's and tomorrow's systems affect the relationships between parents and teens? How do these technologies affect a child's maturation? What information should be shared among children, parents, and other parties like law enforcement or the government? Drawing on the results of research investigating these and related questions, we can begin to develop suitable security solutions. We have been turning to value sensitive design in our research to make progress on these questions.

## Security for Mobile Devices: Specific Projects

We now provide examples where we used value sensitive design to help design security systems for two very different application areas. Our first project addresses the specific challenges with implantable medical devices mentioned above. Our second project is more forward-looking, attempting to understand and tackle the challenges with future parent-teen safety technologies.

We undertook a project using the value sensitive design framework in order to investigate the personal, social, and logistical issues surrounding the use of implantable cardiac devices and potential security system designs (Denning et al., 2010). As an exploratory study, we conducted value-oriented semi-structured interviews with 13 patients with implanted pacemakers or implantable cardioverter defibrillators; the interview included both general questions intended to surface patient values surrounding their implanted devices and more specific questions about eight potential implantable device security systems (Denning et al., 2010). The security systems selected for the study are neither complete nor perfect designs; they were chosen to represent a spectrum of design and interaction properties (see figure 4.2). Values that emerged as being important to patients included: security; safety; privacy; aesthetics; psychological welfare; convenience; cultural and historical associations; self-image and public persona; and autonomy and notification. We also gathered feedback on the properties of our presented systems in order to inform the design of future security systems for wireless implantable medical devices.

Turning to our second project, we began by anticipating the harnessing of mobile devices as a useful and ubiquitous medium for parenting (Czeskis et al., 2010). We expect these technologies to have significant implications for parent-teen relationships, affecting domains such as privacy, trust, and maturation. For example, how would teens respond to their parents' constantly knowing their location, what they are doing, with whom they are speaking, or their current mood? How will parents respond to having so much insight into the lives of their teens? How will teens feel when they find out their friends are using a technology that reports their conversations to their friends' parents? Will these feelings cause teens to actively subvert these technologies and subsequently cause rifts in families? Traditional computer security techniques can help alleviate some concerns—for example, encrypting communications can help prevent information from

**Figure 4.2**
Physical mock-ups that were presented to participants during the implantable medical device project. These mock-ups were intended both to make system designs more concrete for participants and to provide an easy visual way to recall and refer to systems. The mock-ups were intentionally rough in nature in order to suggest unpolished, flexible system designs. Six of the eight mock-ups are shown here, in order from left to right, by row (starting at the top left): a medical alert bracelet with a device password imprinted on it; a tattoo of a device password encoded in a 2D barcode format; the same password tattoo in ink visible only under ultraviolet light; computationally active security wristbands; example pacemakers and implantable cardiac defibrillators, to indicate that security solutions could be built directly into implantable medical devices; and a restricted-access external device to be used by medical personnel in order to activate wireless capabilities on an implantable medical device. Photo credit: Nell Carden Grey.

accidentally falling into the hands of third parties. However, as with medical devices, conventional security techniques do not tell us how to address the broader human context and value challenges associated with these new technologies.

We utilized the theory and methods of value sensitive design to help understand value challenges that might emerge with future mobile parenting technologies. First, we developed value scenarios to explore the potential benefits, harms, and challenges (see the value scenario "One Dad's Dilemma" in chapter 3). We then conducted value-oriented semi-structured interviews with 18 participants (nine teens and their parents; Czeskis et al., 2010). We note that these parent-teen dyads volunteered to participate in the study and presumably have reasonably good relationships with each other. As we had hypothesized, results showed that teens and their parents were concerned about the privacy issues surrounding mobile parenting technologies. However, participants' opinions differed significantly depending upon the type of information being shared. For example, participants were much more concerned about the sensing and reporting of teens' internal states (e.g., mood) than the reporting of external environments (e.g., location). Furthermore, the situation (e.g., emergency vs. nonemergency) in which the data was released made a major difference, as did whether or not the teen was notified that the sensing was taking place. Additionally, we expected that teens would be more conservative in sharing information about their daily activities with their parents than their parents would like; however, the results did not support this expectation, reflecting instead a high level of agreement between parents and teens about the amount of information that should be shared. In fact, in the situations where parents and teens in our study did disagree, the teen tended to be willing to provide more information than the parent wanted. Finally, informed by our value scenarios and interview results, we were able to synthesize and identify key technical goals and challenges—such as strongly protecting the privacy of a teen's contextual information during ordinary situations, but immediately making that information available to others as appropriate in an emergency—and corresponding architectural levers for these technologies.

## Security for Mobile Devices: Contributions

Quite often, given a range of technical security and privacy techniques or further potential technical research directions, computer security researchers and practitioners do not know which technique or direction to choose. This challenge arises because there is in actuality no such thing as a "perfect," "ideal," or "right" level of security and privacy; security and privacy are often in tension both with each other and with other values, and those values and tensions may not be immediately clear. Consequently, technologies and practices around information systems must not only balance security and privacy but also other equally important but very different values, such as autonomy and trust. The above examples illustrate how value sensitive design can be used to enhance and supplement traditional system-design methodologies in the security domain and identify key value tensions and directions for overcoming them.

The research described above also provided methodological contributions to value sensitive design. We mention two here. In the course of analyzing the interview results from our implantable medical device study (Denning et al., 2010), we developed a variation of the value dams and flows method (see method 13 in chapter 3); this variation was used to choose which subset of system designs among the eight presented would be needed to provide maximal satisfaction among our participants. We began by identifying the system option that was least offensive to the largest number of participants. We then supplemented that system selection with the system that was liked by the largest number of nonoverlapping participants—that is, participants who did not express liking the system design already chosen. We continued adding systems in this manner until the portfolio contained at least one system that each of the participants had indicated liking. In another application of this method, one might stop adding systems once some predetermined maximum number of systems has been reached. Second, for our research on parent-teen safety technologies (Czeskis et al., 2010), we developed a new empirical strategy for having interview participants envision their roles as both direct and indirect stakeholders. For example, teen participants provided their privacy preferences as users of the parenting technology (a direct stakeholder; see Alice in figure 4.3). They would then provide their privacy preferences as the friend of a user of the parenting technology (an indirect stakeholder; see Alice in figure 4.4).

**Figure 4.3**
Direct stakeholder role: Illustration of the type of mobile phone safety system participants were asked to envision. Teen Alice has a smartphone that recognizes certain aspects of her context and then sends that information to her parent under certain conditions.

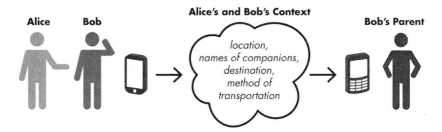

**Figure 4.4**
Indirect stakeholder role: Illustration of the same mobile phone safety system. Teen Alice, as an indirect stakeholder, has a friend teen Bob who has a smartphone that reports a part of his context to his parent. Whenever Alice is with Bob, Bob's parent will be able to know various information about Alice.

## Persuasive Technology

Author: Janet Davis

In the words of B. J. Fogg, persuasive technology is meant "to change what we think and do" (Fogg, 2003). While adopting new technology often changes our behavior, persuasive technology is designed with the *intent* to change behavior as its primary goal. Persuasive technology is often informed by psychological research, such as models of goal setting (Consolvo, McDonald, & Landay, 2009), behavior change (Consolvo et al., 2009), and influence strategies (Kaptein, Lacroix, & Saini, 2010). Although persuasive technology can be used to sell products, most research reported in the human-computer interaction and related literature has emphasized values of social import as the end of persuasion, notably health (e.g., the Mobile Health 2010 conference) and environmental sustainability (for a review, see Zapico, Turpeinen, & Brandt [2009]; for a critique, see Brynjars-dottir et al. [2012]). Specific applications related to these values include promoting physical activity (e.g., Consolvo et al., 2009; Kaptein et al., 2010) and environmentally sustainable transportation habits (e.g., Froehlich et al., 2009; Gabrielli & Maimone, 2013). Persuasive technologies raise concerns not only about ends, but also about means: the values implicated by introducing persuasive technology at all, and by employing particular strategies for persuasion.

Persuasive technology calls into question the value of *autonomy* (Davis, 2009): "people's ability to decide, plan, and act in ways that they believe will help them achieve their goals" (Friedman et al., 2006a, p. 364). Who chooses the behavior to change? Problems can arise when designers impose their behavioral goals on those who encounter the technology, particularly when designers' goals are at odds with the values or interests of the intended audience. Ethical designers must take care not to violate users' autonomy through deception (Berdichevsky & Neuenschwander, 1999; Fogg, 2003), coercion (Fogg, 2003), or psychological manipulation (Fogg, 2003). But persuasive technology can also support autonomy, such as when users adopt technology to achieve their own goals for behavior change (Davis, 2011, Oinas-Kukkonen, 2010). In either case, informed consent is key (Davis, 2009; Millett et al., 2001; see the discussion of informed consent online by Friedman above in this chapter): users should clearly understand the designers' "motivations, methods, and intended outcomes" (Berdichevsky & Neuenschwander, 1999) and must be free to choose whether to engage with the technology. Particularly vulnerable to persuasive technology are groups such as children, who are unable to give informed consent and may not recognize attempts to persuade them.

At the same time, supporting the ends of persuasion may conflict with autonomy and informed consent. Indeed, Berdichevsky and Neuen-schwander (1999) write: "The creators of a persuasive technology should disclose their motivations, methods, and intended outcomes, *except when such disclosure would significantly undermine an otherwise ethical goal*" (emphasis added). For example, prenatal care is unequivocally good for the health and survival of mothers and their babies. Some paternalism would seem morally justified in deploying systems that persuade pregnant women who would eschew prenatal care to instead take advantage of it (e.g., Ramachandran et al., 2010). As another example, immunization benefits not so much the individual receiving the immunization, as the "herd immunity" of the population at large. Many governments have policies that aim to coerce parents to immunize their children. Under these policies, it would seem acceptable to expose parents involuntarily to technologies that aim to persuade them to immunize their children. Spahn (2012) offers a way to navigate this ethical strait: He argues that respect for autonomy demands not factual consent, but rather ideal rational consensus. That is, the ethical persuasive technology designer chooses those ends and means to which an ideal actor, open to rational arguments and unencumbered by irrational desires, would agree. Considering the examples above, one might argue for relaxed standards of informed consent when the intended behavior is prescribed by those who are obligated to act in others' best interests (e.g., health care professionals), or by laws and policies enacted for the good of society as a whole.

Two further key values are *accountability* and *identity*. As with decision-support systems (Johnson & Mulvey, 1995), persuasive technologies cannot be held accountable for the outcomes of their use (Fogg, 2003; Davis, 2009); rather, accountability lies with designers, users, and other decision makers. Finally, behavior is intimately tied with identity. Our identities—for example, as "green consumers" or "healthy eaters"—influence our behaviors independently of our habits and attitudes (Sparks & Shepherd, 1992). Our identities resist change, as we act to bring our behaviors and situations into agreement with our self-concepts, but we nonetheless adapt our identities to resolve persistent discrepancies and to accommodate new roles and self-concepts (Burke, 2006). Even changes in our everyday activities—as promoted by many persuasive technologies—can lead to identity change (Burke, 2006).

Beyond the values that motivate the use of persuasive technology, and those inherently implicated by its use, we must also consider values implicated by the particular strategies that persuasive technologies employ (Davis, 2009). Because many persuasive strategies involve tracking and reporting user behavior—for example via self-monitoring, tailoring, and social comparison (Fogg, 2003)—Berdechevsky and Neuenschwander

(1999) include *privacy* prominently in their ethical principles for persuasive technology. However, not all persuasive technologies involve tracking or reporting behavior—for example, a mobile application might promote public transportation use by providing information to the user rather than by collecting information from the user—so privacy will be of concern for many but not all persuasive technologies. Future work should further explore values implicated by particular persuasive strategies. For example, the following project concerns *reputation* both as a persuasive strategy and as a value that can be supported or undermined.

### Persuasive Technology: Specific Projects

Value sensitive design can contribute to the design of effective and ethical persuasive technology. In particular, value sensitive design may help the design team and stakeholders involved in the design process identify value sensitive strategies for promoting the desired behavior, and at the same time identify value tensions and harms (both real and perceived) that may inhibit the desired behavior or undermine important values. Davis (2009) compared two groupware systems intended to promote knowledge sharing across organizational boundaries: BlueReach, designed from the perspective of persuasive technology (Brodie et al., 2007), and CodeCOOP, designed using value sensitive design theory and methodology (Miller et al., 2007a). While both considered the value of *reputation*, the persuasive technology perspective considers reputation primarily as a strategy to promote knowledge sharing: publicly sharing useful information enhances one's reputation (Brodie et al., 2007). In contrast, the value sensitive design perspective led Miller et al. (2007) to consider potential harms to reputation (e.g., from asking a silly question) that might impede the desired behavior. Moreover, Miller et al. considered a richer field of values from the start of the design process, including not only reputation but also privacy, trust, and awareness. Early empirical investigations let the designers assess and mitigate these value tensions before building the CodeCOOP system, thereby leading to a successful deployment (Miller et al., 2007). Singley et al. conducted empirical investigations of barriers to BlueReach's use only after a less-than-successful deployment; only then did harms to reputation emerge as a significant concern that stopped people from using the system (Singley, Lai, Kuang, & Tang, 2008). Value sensitive design's tripartite methodology guided Miller et al. to address users' perceptions of harms early in the design process, and thus sidestep a significant barrier to the desired behavior.

Value sensitive design can also help designers envision futures of novel technologies. A technique for increasing the effectiveness of persuasive technology is persuasion profiling (Fogg, 2006; Kaptein et al., 2010; Kaptein, 2015): estimating the effects of particular influence strategies on individuals based on their past responses to influence attempts. Such estimates can be used to select an influence strategy (e.g., an appeal to consensus or authority [Cialdini, 2001]) that is most likely to lead the individual to comply with, rather than resist, the target behavior. Persuasion profiling most obviously applies to online targeted advertising: with persuasion profiles, not only the products advertised but the content of the ads can be tailored to appeal to the individual (Kaptein & Eckles, 2010). For example, an advertisement for a book could either say it is a bestseller or cite editorial reviews, depending on whether the individual is more susceptible to appeals to consensus or to authority. Persuasion profiling can be implemented by tracking users' behavior using web browser cookies; thus this approach raises further concerns regarding *informed consent*, both for collecting data and for displaying ads (Kaptein et al., 2011; Millett et al., 2001). Social science findings suggest that influence strategies become less effective once their use is made salient. That is, when people know they are the target of an influence strategy, they are less likely to change their behavior. Disclosure of persuasion profiling could undermine its effectiveness (Kaptein et al., 2011). This effect suggests a deep tension between more effective persuasion (at least of this kind) and informed consent.

If advertising were the only application of persuasion profiling, we might resolve this tension by arguing that informed consent is of far greater moral weight than selling products. However, exploring persuasive technology through the Envisioning Cards (Friedman et al., 2011; see also the Envisioning Cards method in chapter 3) drew attention to applications beyond advertising (Kaptein et al., 2011). For example, persuasion profiling could enhance the effectiveness of an application to promote physical activity, adapting its persuasive messages over time to favor those that most consistently preceded the desired behaviors. Individuals might even choose to share their persuasion profiles with friends or family who could support them in their goals, thus invoking the value of *trust*, defined as "expectations ... between people who can experience goodwill, extend goodwill toward others, feel vulnerable, and experience betrayal" (Friedman et al., 2006b). Finally, of special concern is the profiling of children, who are particularly vulnerable to influence and unable to give informed consent. Some might nonetheless encourage parents to use persuasion profiling technologies to influence their children to do what is good for them (e.g., to lead obese children to change their eating habits). After all, parents have always used knowledge of their children's personalities to more effectively teach and protect them. But even this laudable use of persuasive technology could have undesirable repercussions: such manipulation could harm children's growing autonomy and trust in their parents (Kaptein et al., 2011). Moving beyond the analysis of Kaptein et al., trade-offs between conflicting values may look very different in different cultures. Where personal autonomy and interpersonal trust carry significant weight in an individualist culture, as discussed above, a collectivist culture might emphasize respect, obedience, and conformity.

### Persuasive Technology: Contributions

Thus, while persuasive technology has potential to do good—and indeed, most persuasive technology research has focused on this potential—the endeavor of changing behavior poses deep, inherent concerns about human values. While ethical principles and guidelines have long been proposed (Berdichevsky & Neuenschwander, 1999; Fogg, 2003), value sensitive design helps trace points of uneasiness to their foundations: values such as autonomy and informed consent. Future conceptual investigations should continue to explicate the roles and relationships of the values discussed here in the context of persuasive technology. However, study of the ethics and values of persuasive technology must go beyond the conceptual. Future work should, for example, apply empirical methods to explore where stakeholders draw the line between acceptable and unacceptable persuasive technologies. Page and Kray (2010) interviewed focus groups about the acceptability of various persuasive technology scenarios; a value sensitive design approach would construct such scenarios according to a thorough conceptualization of the values at hand, and thus provide more robust and generalizable findings. A value sensitive design approach would also more intentionally identify the range of stakeholders to interview and probe more deeply into reasons for stakeholders' judgments (see the discussion of privacy in public by Friedman below). Furthermore, design projects should investigate the integration of value sensitive design methods and persuasive technology principles throughout the development cycle. Such projects would employ not only conceptual and empirical but also technical investigations to address values implicated by the ends and means of persuasion.

## Human-Robot Interaction

Author: Nathan Freier

Human-robot interaction (HRI) is a rapidly maturing field (for a survey, see Goodrich & Schultz [2007]), one that is particularly concerned with the ways in which robots can be designed to (1) engage socially with their human counterparts and (2) behave as smart tools extending the capabilities of their human users. This dichotomy between robots as social actors and robots as tools for human users extends to the heuristics employed by researchers and designers to determine what counts as a robot. In terms of technology, the field tends to focus on autonomous or semi-autonomous hardware systems with onboard software control systems, but does, at times, include purely software systems such as graphical avatars. In terms of form, robots can include everything from human replicas to nonanthropomorphic platforms with physical actuators designed to manipulate the robots' environments.

Among many other topics, the field addresses the broad "issues of social responsibility in HRI, focusing on the unique features of robotic interaction that call for responsible action … value-specific domains [include] autonomy, accountability, trust, and/or human dignity" (Freier, Billard, Ishiguro, & Nourbakhsh, 2010, p. 11). One primary focus of this discussion includes the ethical use of robots in the military, a topic with significant gravitas that has garnered attention in recent years (Arkin, 2008; Sharkey, 2007). A second central issue of ethical import stems from the dissonance between the apparent social capabilities of some robotic systems and the lack of those systems' established moral standing in the world. In explicating this issue, Kahn et al. (2007) present a set of benchmarks intended to provide the field with metrics by which to measure the authenticity of human-robot relationships, and ultimately to articulate the experiences that make humans uniquely human. The nine benchmarks proposed are autonomy, imitation, intrinsic moral value, moral accountability, privacy, reciprocity, conventionality, creativity, and authenticity of relation. This initial set of nine is proposed as a starting point from which a much larger body of benchmarks can progress with the goal of creating standardized frameworks for evaluating and comparing social and moral interactions that humans may have with robots.

In this exploration of authentic human-robot relationships, children and their relationships to autonomous, social robots comprise a unique and important area of inquiry. Researchers have investigated the value of psychological well-being in the context of interactions between children and robots. Psychological well-being is operationalized in different ways for each of the projects, but all maintain the importance of considering children's healthy development as a core driver for assessing and guiding robot design.

### Human-Robot Interaction: Specific Projects

To develop an understanding of children's conceptions about and interactions with a social robot, researchers conducted a series of projects with Sony's robotic dog, AIBO (Kahn et al., 2006; Melson, Kahn, Beck, & Friedman, 2009a; Melson et al., 2009b). In each of these projects, researchers observed the children interacting with both the robotic dog (see figure 4.5) and with either a stuffed toy dog or a live dog for comparison, and conducted value-oriented semi-structured interviews during the children's interactions. The results suggested that children conceive of the robotic dog in ways that cross material, biological, psychological, social, and moral categories. These findings prompted the researchers to raise the concern that children would expect genuine reciprocal interaction with the robot, but would experience only an impoverished form of that reciprocity in return.

**Figure 4.5**
Young children interacting with a robotic dog.

The implication is that children may come of age conceiving of a robotic dog or other robotic, social playmate as a social other, while the inherent materiality of the robot would limit children's fully realized concept of what a social other requires of a reciprocal relationship: a shared sense of moral, autonomous standing.

The materiality of the robot is not the only factor in shaping the human-robot relationship. The interaction design of physical social robots as well as virtual social robots (or graphical avatars) can have significant implications for how children and subsequently adults form relationships with technologies in their lives. For example, Freier (2008) showed that 8- to 9-year-old children are significantly more likely to attribute moral standing to a graphical avatar that makes claims to its own rights (90% of children) than, in contrast, to the same avatar that does not make those claims (47% of children). In other words, in designing a social technology, the choices that the designers make in shaping how the technology responds to ethical challenges are likely to have significant implications for how children conceive of that technology as a moral agent, and thus how children construct their relational understanding of the technology.

The humanoid form of social robots is particularly compelling from a values perspective. The anthropomorphic features of these robots further blur the line between machine and social other, thus increasing the likelihood of children's overattribution of social and moral standing to the technology. Kahn et al. (2008b, 2012), for example, showed that when children (9–15 years old) observe a humanoid robot being controlled seemingly against its will (i.e., put into a closet against the robot's stated objections), the children ascribe moral attributions to the humanoid robot (e.g., deserves fair treatment, should not be harmed psychologically). Though children were aware that the robot was a technology, most children were unwilling to judge it appropriate to treat the robot unfairly or to act in a way that appeared to cause psychological harm.

## Human-Robot Interaction: Contributions

The methods for investigating these and related questions in the field of HRI are varied and still in development. There are, for example, concerns with how one assesses the psychological impact of interactions with humanoid robots that are treated in ways intended to put participants in morally ambiguous situations. Wizard-of-oz study designs, which sometimes include a form of deception and are thus ethically challenging, provide a compelling methodology for investigating value issues in HRI. As with many other fields, there is an ongoing debate as to whether behavior or reported thought is a more telling source of data for fully understanding the human-robot relationship; this is a particularly challenging problem when investigating the value implications of such relationships.

Even in the face of such methodological challenges, by taking a value sensitive approach to understanding human-robot interaction early on in the maturation of the HRI field, researchers are able to provide design guidance that holistically accounts for the potential ethical implications of future robot-interaction design. The HRI field has an abundance of applications that implicate human values. Given the interactions that children will have with robots and the use of robots in the military, as well as values implicated by HRI such as accountability, autonomy, dignity, identity, and trust, the field of HRI will continue to benefit from value sensitive research into the very fundamental question that interactions with robots pose: who are we as humans? And how are we different from the machines we build in our own likeness?

## Computers and Disabilities

Authors: Shiri Azenkot, Katherine Deibel, and Alan Borning

All humans differ in their abilities to one extent or another. A substantial number of people, however, have a disability that could significantly limit their participation in work, school, civic life, recreation, or other activities. Such disabilities can be broadly grouped into physical (e.g., difficulty in walking), sensory (e.g., deafness, blindness, or low vision), cognitive or mental (e.g., memory loss or learning disabilities), or some combination of these. One or more technologies may allow a person with a disability to remove or partially work around the barriers to participation. Some of these technologies (e.g., eyeglasses) are so widespread and familiar as to often disappear into the background. Others are low-tech but typically viewed as a distinct tool for people with a disability (e.g., wheelchairs and white canes). Still others make use of cutting-edge medical or computer technology (e.g., prosthetic limbs and predictive speech synthesis).

Alongside this diversity of technologies are multiple competing theories of disability (Clough & Corbett, 2000; Matthews, 2009), each of which has different value commitments. Two of the most prominent are the medical model and the social model. Under the former, a disability is viewed as a problem or error that needs treating or repair, while the latter argues that the problems and challenges experienced by a person with a disability come from the inaccessible design of products and the environment, not the person or the disability. Values implicated by these competing views include access, autonomy, community, empowerment, fairness, freedom, human welfare, identity, normalcy, privacy, self-respect, and social acceptance. This list also hints at some of the value tensions that arise from these competing views. For example, one tension between access and fairness concerns whether a given technology or practice (e.g., receiving extra time on tests in schools) is necessary to ensure access or whether it gives an unfair advantage to the person using it (Lovett, 2010). Other tensions include those between identity and normalcy, between individual benefits and societal costs, and between privacy and requesting accommodations. Despite these strong connections between assistive technologies and human values, researchers have only recently begun to apply value sensitive design in a principled fashion to these questions. We now describe two specific projects, pointing out some key values and value tensions, and conclude with some open questions and directions for future work.

## Computers and Disabilities: Specific Projects

The first project focuses on using technology to improve the experience of public transit riders who are blind (people with severe vision loss) or deaf-blind (people with severe vision and hearing loss). People must travel to places such as work, shopping, and doctors' offices to lead productive and independent lives. People with severe visual impairments usually cannot drive, so they often rely on public transit to travel independently. Azenkot et al. (2011) conducted interviews with six blind and seven deaf-blind adults to identify the specific challenges they faced when using public transit and the human values that were important to them. Independence was overwhelmingly identified as the key value. In addition, safety was important to about half the participants. Current access technologies do not support many secondary values shared by participants, including affordability (since they often require specialized hardware) and comfort (participants had to carry several devices that each served one or few functions).

Participants stated that the most effective way to support independence and safety is with easy access to the information they need, such as route and schedule information, and details about their bus stops. The connection with independence is clear: for example, if blind or deaf-blind riders can easily access automated real-time arrival information for a bus on their mobile phones, they don't need to seek out a nearby person or phone someone at a call center to find this out. For safety, some participants stated that knowing more about their surroundings (e.g., about obstacles or potential dangers from traffic) enhanced their safety, while others stated that projecting an air of confidence (rather than looking lost or being heard phoning for help) made them less vulnerable to attacks or harassment.

To help address these needs, Azenkot et al. (2011) developed GoBraille, a system that provides real-time bus arrival times and information about bus stops using a refreshable Braille display. While a minority of blind people read Braille, interviews revealed that it has important advantages: it is less distracting (i.e., leaves hearing available for sensing the environment), better for retaining information, and more private. Braille is also the primary means of accessing digital information for deaf-blind people.

GoBraille is built on a framework that connects an easily carried Braille display with a built-in keyboard to a mainstream smartphone using a Wi-Fi connection. Thus, it enables a user to access most of the features of a smartphone (GPS, 3G, compass, and more) in Braille, as well as speech. Two versions of GoBraille were developed and evaluated: one for blind people and one for deaf-blind people. User studies with 10 blind participants indicated that, for all participants, GoBraille enhanced the key value of independence. For participants who were concerned about safety, GoBraille enhanced their sense of safety as well. Azenkot et al. evaluated the version of GoBraille for deaf-blind people, which included a much more minimalist interface, through a co-design process with a deaf-blind person.

A second project focuses on a different sort of disability, namely reading disabilities. Deibel (2011) investigated value sensitive design's applicability to disabilities and technologies in her doctoral work on understanding the multiple factors that influence the adoption and usage of assistive technologies by adults with reading disabilities (RDs) such as dyslexia. For people with RDs, the act of reading is a labored, slow process, despite their possessing adequate intelligence, education, and sensory abilities. Computer-based reading support for people with RDs is currently offered primarily through text-to-speech systems, but the usage of such technologies by adults with RDs appears to be rare (Deibel, 2011; Elkind, Black, & Murray, 1996). In conceptual investigations, recognizing the likelihood that new assistive reading technologies would also fail to be adopted into regular use, Deibel utilized value sensitive design to develop a value-stakeholder framework that characterizes the sociocultural, technical, and contextual factors that influence the adoption and usage of assistive technologies by adults with RDs. A key element of this framework is that many adults with RDs choose to take advantage of the invisible nature of their disabilities and opt to not disclose their disabilities to others. This decision to hide is driven in part by past negative experiences such as being ridiculed by peers or accused of laziness by teachers and other authority figures (Deibel, 2011; Edwards, 1994; Matthews, 2009). Upon reaching adulthood, many adults with RDs unsurprisingly choose to keep their disability private and will make tactical decisions, such as not requesting accommodations at university or choosing jobs with minimal amounts of reading, to appear as normal as possible to others. Importantly, this hiding severely impacts technology adoption, since the diffusion of new technologies is driven largely by communication channels and awareness of those technologies. Synthesizing insights from the literature on reading disabilities, disability studies, and technology adoption, Deibel characterized the motivation for and effects of hiding one's disability as a series of interactions among values of literacy, normalcy (wanting to appear "normal"), identity, privacy, and community, as shown in figure 4.6.

Deibel went on to validate this framework with two empirical investigations. One involved value-oriented semi-structured interviews with 10 adults with RDs in which the participants discussed their literacy practices, usage of technologies, and the role that having an RD has played in their lives. Informed by the value-stakeholder framework, the interview questions were developed to explore the impact of having an RD on the participant's life and sense of self, although many of the participants engaged in such discussions without prompting from the interviewer. Thus, the participants echoed the desire to not let their RD status define their identities and described the deliberate efforts they make to control disclosure to others. For example, when asked if he would use an assistive technology that would signify he has an RD, one participant stated: "I wouldn't mind using it at home, but I would never use it for work. I actually think it's detrimental

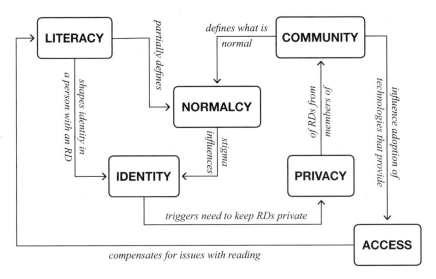

**Figure 4.6**
One example of the value interactions identified by Deibel (2011). The motivation and consequences of hiding one's reading disability are shown via interactions and connections among identified values.

to tell my employers I'm dyslexic ... people just end up treating you differently." This and other similar comments suggest that assistive technology for adults with RDs needs to go beyond just supporting the reading process and should support the values of normalcy and privacy, thereby aiding the user in managing the extent of disability disclosure.

Deibel also conducted a second empirical investigation in which she analyzed threads involving RDs from online discussion boards. Here, she found that the relative anonymity of the Internet allowed individuals with RDs to openly discuss their disabilities both with others with RDs as well as people without them. Deibel then used the value-stakeholder framework to propose design guidelines (see table 4.2) for assistive reading technologies and also proposed an extensible software application that would promote reading assistance to all types of readers, not just those with reading disabilities.

### Computers and Disabilities: Contributions
These projects hint at the diversity of values implicated by the range of disabilities and technologies. For the work on supporting blind and deaf-blind

**Table 4.2**

Value-Informed Recommendations for Designing Assistive Reading Technologies for Adults with Reading Disabilities (from Deibel, 2011).

| | Design Recommendation | Values Implicated |
|---|---|---|
| 1 | Support the reading process and reading tasks | Literacy |
| 2 | Support the acquisition of rich digital texts | Access, empowerment, fairness |
| 3 | Provide multiple forms of accommodations | Access, choice, fairness |
| 4 | Typography matters | Choice, fairness, literacy, normalcy |
| 5 | Recognize and control disclosure due to technology usage | Choice, identity, normalcy, privacy |
| 6 | Support and adapt to multiple usage contexts | Community, literacy, privacy |
| 7 | Include support for fairness arbitration and usage negotiations | Access, fairness, privacy |
| 8 | Bring expert knowledge to the end user | Access, choice, empowerment, fairness |
| 9 | Mitigate purchase and usage costs | Access, fairness |
| 10 | Design for all readers | Fairness, literacy, normalcy |

transit riders, independence was paramount, with safety also a concern for some. There are some value tensions that emerge in this work (for example, regarding supporting blind or deaf-blind riders versus the overall cost of developing and deploying the technology), but in comparison with other value sensitive design projects, these tensions were not particularly strong—few would disagree with the overall goal of supporting independence for this population. In contrast, the work on supporting adults with reading disabilities uncovered many significant value tensions, for example between perceptions of normalcy on the one hand, and community and support on the other. Even what these technologies are called exposes value tensions. For example, some people view the term "assistive technology" as paternalistic and prefer the term "access technology." Yet for reading disabilities, "assistive technology" is the preferred term for many (there is nothing inaccessible about the printed page—it is just very hard to read); the term "access technology" biases the potential solution space strongly toward text-to-speech software, which in many cases is both a less-desirable solution (e.g., because of privacy considerations) and also one that, in effect, says "give up—you won't be able to read the printed word."

In terms of contributions to value sensitive design methodology, the primary direct stakeholders in Deibel's work posed several challenges for conducting research of a participatory nature. Given that many adults with RDs choose to hide their disability from others, these individuals tend not to see themselves as a community, nor to work together collectively toward shared goals. Even individually, most are unlikely to discuss problems they experience and work toward solutions unless some aspect of their privacy is ensured. This also contributes to a more general understanding about which value-elicitation methods may be most effective in the presence of certain types of value tensions and concerns. In particular, for a group for which hiding some attribute is a central issue, empirical methods that preserve anonymity or that distance the participant from the person collecting the data are likely to be useful. In Deibel's research, it was the analysis of posts in an online discussion forum; other such methods might include anonymous surveys or interviews conducted via online chat, so that stakeholders and researchers do not have to meet or physically interact with each other.

## Homeless Young People

Authors: Jill Palzkill Woelfer and David G. Hendry

Homelessness among young people (ages 13 to 30) is a serious problem, with upward of 3 million young people experiencing homelessness each year in the United States (Whitbeck, 2009). Young people become homeless for many interrelated reasons. Among the common ones are intergenerational poverty, severe family conflict often connected with substance abuse, mental health disorders, an LGBT (lesbian, gay, bisexual, or transgender) orientation, being unable to afford shelter after "aging out" of foster care or other social services, and abuse and neglect by caregivers (Barry, Ensign, & Lippek, 2002). Homeless young people often suffer from the effects of trauma. They are generally distrustful of adults and such institutions as schools, courts, and social services because of repeated failures by those institutions and longstanding disappointments. Mental illness, especially depression and syndromes related to trauma, is also very common, as are the interrelated causes and effects of homelessness. To humanize this brief clinical introduction: a young man who grows up in a crack-addicted, drug-dealing home may need to leave with his younger sibling for safety; a young woman who comes out as a lesbian may be pushed out of home by her parents because of specific religious beliefs; or the parents of a family living in poverty may drop a teenager off at a gas station, saying "sorry, we can't look after you any longer."

When on the street, a young person's survival depends on developing knowledge and skills for street life. Being isolated can be dangerous; making connections with other street youth can provide a measure of resiliency (Kidd & Davidson, 2007; Kidd & Shahar, 2008; Rice, Milburn, & Monro, 2011). In American society, to meet basic needs, young people often come to rely on community-based, grassroots service agencies, which provide food, temporary shelter, health care, and refuge from the street. In addition, service agencies can offer programs for developing life skills, including healthy eating and cooking, effective interpersonal communication, searching for and keeping jobs, and so forth. Service agencies, most importantly, provide young people with opportunities for meeting caring adults, for doing activities that engender feelings of self-worth, and for working with case managers with expertise for navigating government and non-profit social services. It is thought that community-based service agencies that are targeted to young people and focused on building healthy adult-youth relationships often provide a critical step for escaping homelessness (Slesnick, Dashora, Letcher, Erdem, & Serovich, 2009).

Community-based service agencies conduct their work within a web of stakeholders and value tensions. In our work from 2007 to 2012 and continuing to the present in various ways, we found that service agencies are embedded within a neighborhood and have connections to other governmental and professional institutions. Similar to a stateswoman who is duty-bound to citizens or parents who are responsible for their children, staff members of service agencies take on responsibility for the welfare of young people. Yet we also found that young people who are experiencing homelessness often resist the guidance and rules that come from such assumed responsibility. As a result, homeless young people sometimes express their independence, like many young people, in ways that can be harmful to themselves or others. Herein lies a value tension between service agencies and young people: concern for welfare, which may be seen as paternalistic, is in tension with young people's desire for independence, which may lead to circumstances of vulnerability. Related to this tension, service agency staff members are knowledgeable of the street and tolerant of it, but only as a means for moving young people toward more dominant social norms. In a different vein, community stakeholders such as business owners and homeowners may resent the existence of service agencies because they might attract homeless young people to a neighborhood, leading to less safety, reduced property values, and fewer shoppers. Outside service agencies, homeless young people can be stigmatized by their physical appearance and by their presence in public settings, leading to additional forms of vulnerability and making it even more difficult to escape homelessness (Woelfer & Hendry, 2009).

### Homeless Young People: Specific Projects

We have worked with a number of colleagues and in collaboration with a service agency that is part of an alliance of nine service agencies located in Seattle, Washington. In this work, we have pursued research, design, and service projects, asking a twofold question: what is at stake as digital media and personal digital technology diffuse into communities of homeless young people, and how, if at all, might information systems help improve the welfare of young people and help them escape homelessness?

In early work, we investigated the information ecology of a community of homeless young people and the alliance of service agencies that support them (Woelfer, Yeung, Erdmann, & Hendry, 2008; Woelfer & Hendry, 2009). Value sensitive design prompted a focus on stakeholder values—what our service agency collaborators considered to be important—rather than operational improvements only, such as improved usability or greater operational control of documents. Over 250 brochures and flyers from four service agencies were collected. These materials covered such topics as art, drugs/alcohol, employment, events, food, health, IV drug use, special LGBT services, legal issues, pet care, relationships/safety, reproductive health, and shelter/housing. However, these materials were typically haphazardly organized and poorly presented on bulletin boards and folding tables located in the entranceways of service agencies, thereby creating a mismatch with the service agencies' values of caring, respect, and trust. Even more, the materials appeared to be overwhelming. Simply put, not only did these materials represent aspects of young people's lives, often problematic ones, they also represented all the challenges that would need to be overcome. In design-based research, responding to this mismatch, we developed prototypes for illustrating how this information could be presented in alternative forms, consistent with the values of the service agency (see figure 4.7). Short videos of the prototypes in action were created and then used to elicit feedback from agency stakeholders. The video prototypes catalyzed conversations about current information resources—arrangement and presentation—and led the service agency to reconsider how its brochures and flyers were presented. In this way, a future possibility was made concrete and enabled consideration of current practice in new terms. Extending the value scenario method, these prototypes illustrate how values can be deliberately placed into concrete artifacts and portrayed through video, which in turn can be used to frame conversations with stakeholders, to elicit feedback about values, and to explore future possibilities for design.

In a second project focused on design and service, we worked along with service agency staff and two young men in transition out of homelessness to create a community technology center and curriculum for homeless young people (Hendry et al., 2011; Woelfer & Hendry, 2010). The goal of the curriculum, called New Tech for Youth Sessions (NTYS), was to position youth to learn digital media skills and, importantly, to engender feelings of self-worth. The key issue was to address the tension between preserving the values of the service agency drop-in—interpersonal communication, calmness, refuge, and safety—and giving young people online access, which was thought by drop-in staff to hold the risks of social isolation, unproductive time, or even harmful or subversive uses. To address these tensions, consideration was given to the physical space of the drop-in, and we decided to create a small area for a printer and file server, augmented with a pool of eight laptop computers stored in a portable charging cart for flexible use and security. Then, by a participatory process involving homeless young people and drop-in staff, we developed a curriculum comprising (1) guidelines for conversation and working together; (2) a supporting social structure of homeless young people, peers who are in transition out of homelessness, and instructors; (3) incentives for completing the class; and (4) learning activities geared toward seeking employment. By teaching about 100 youth in about 20 classes, we found that homeless young people desire to use digital media in all its forms and are often quite sophisticated in its uses. Moreover, by providing ready access to digital information and services, staff members believe that the service agency's drop-in has been enriched while largely preserving its fundamental values.

**Figure 4.7**

The four prototypes. The Rolling Case (top left) holds information resources (brochures, fliers, etc.) organized into categories for easy and consistent access and
presentation. The value of respect is conveyed through attention to detail and
consistency of information organization and presentation. The Rolling Case fits on
the InfoBike (top right), which is equipped with portable chairs (not shown) and
an umbrella, along with a laptop computer (not shown). The value of trust is built
with staff members from service agencies engaging in outreach activities around an
information-rich resource. The information resources in the Rolling Case can be un-
packed and placed on a slat wall display (bottom left), which promotes the values of
autonomy and self-service. Finally, the Rolling Case also contains an in-fold (bottom
right), which organizes miniature versions of many of the fliers presented on the slat
wall. Thus, each of these four presentation devices makes the information resources
available in a different format, according to a consistent overall organizational and
presentation scheme.

A third project involving personal digital artifacts and homeless young people naturally followed from the NTYS courses: when young people successfully completed a NTYS class, we gave them an iPod. This incentive provided us with an opportunity to ask a critical question: how do young people make use of, hold on to, and part with iPods and other personal digital artifacts? To address this question, we interviewed a sample of NTYS graduates and asked them to recount what happened to their iPods (Woelfer & Hendry, 2011b). We also asked: how might the safety of homeless young people be improved with mobile phones? Here, using value sketches and value scenarios (see the discussion of these methods in chapter 3, and especially figures 3.3–3.5), we engaged with a different sample of young people about the safety of their neighborhood and asked them to envision how mobile phones might improve their safety (Woelfer et al., 2011; Yoo et al., 2013). One overarching finding of these projects was that young people's retention of digital artifacts is often contingent on the meeting of immediate needs, including food and money for expenses (e.g., rent), as well as the need to create and reciprocate goodwill among friends, family, and associates. A second finding was that the tethering of devices to infrastructure and institutions creates new forms of vulnerability when, for example, young people are required to find electricity or Internet access in public venues. One far-reaching consequence of these projects is that the design of mobile applications for safety must account for contingent forms of ownership; that is, mobile devices will come and go frequently while the challenge of keeping safe is always present.

### Homeless Young People: Contributions

Young people who are homeless use digital media and personal digital technology in ordinary ways, for many purposes, but they do so under extraordinary conditions. Homeless young people seek to construct places in public that are used for private things, such as watching a movie on a DVD player before going to sleep or charging a mobile phone at a secluded power outlet on private property. However, such public activities can prompt scrutiny that, in turn, can lead to stigma and even being arrested for trespassing. Similarly, homeless young people, like most young people in the United States, use social networking sites and desire digital media and technology in many forms (Woelfer & Hendry, 2010). At the same time, however, this ordinary use of social media can be a further source of stigma when the presentation of self includes photographs, videos, and writings of street life. These examples illustrate some tensions that must be engaged when designing for this community.

To conclude, we summarize our four contributions to value sensitive design. First, value scenarios have been extended from written narratives to video prototypes that represented the values of trust, respect, and caring for the purpose of eliciting stakeholder feedback (Woelfer & Hendry, 2009). The video form—its concreteness and affordances for shared viewing—was an excellent tool for catalyzing conversations with stakeholders and collecting data.

Second, in a project focused on the value of safety, value scenarios were also extended from designer-written to stakeholder-written narratives where homeless young people were prompted to write value scenarios to envision how mobile phones might be designed and used to keep safe. This empirical use of value scenarios identified and clarified several value tensions, for example, the possibility of being seen as a "snitch" when seeking help or that the police can be seen as both a potential benefit and threat (Woelfer et al., 2011). In contrast to the carefully designed and scripted video prototypes, stakeholders can be positioned to write value scenarios which, through additional analysis, lead to design insights.

In a third contribution, we developed a design stance with precaution as the main designer value (Woelfer & Hendry, 2011a). We did this in order to guide our interactions with stakeholders and community organizations. With this approach, we offer an example of how a design team can orient themselves to a complex sociotechnical setting, particularly involving special populations who may be perceived as vulnerable. This stance makes a commitment to proceed carefully, with circumspection and humility, when deciding how, and indeed if, to intervene, providing a form of legitimation for taking no action under some conditions.

In a fourth contribution, most broadly, we and our colleagues have used value sensitive design to investigate a complex social problem with multiple direct and indirect stakeholders, myriad value tensions, and many opportunities to intervene. As digital tools and technologies diffuse into this setting, value sensitive design is being used to understand this problem and create opportunities to act. The work continues with ongoing community-based projects, including Music is My Life (Woelfer & Lee, 2012; Woelfer, 2014), an art exhibit of drawings and stories by 129 homeless young people, and the deployment of a mobile payment system for Real Change, a street newspaper in Seattle (Guzmán, 2015).

## Privacy in Public

Author: Batya Friedman

Privacy in public spaces and online continues to be a contested issue. While some groups cry "privacy is dead" (e.g., Rauhofer, 1998), others assert its ongoing importance in human society (e.g., Schneier, 2006). The battleground often takes the form of technological developments and corresponding regulation, be they privacy-encroaching (e.g., drones and cameras in urban spaces, legal meta-analyses of big data and digital surveillance) or privacy-enhancing (e.g., Tor technologies and encryption, data-protection laws). The scale, pervasiveness, and interconnectedness of current challenges to privacy may be unprecedented. Yet the pattern of technological advances enabling new human capabilities and actions that, in turn, upset the balance among historical privacy protections is a familiar one; in these transitional periods, the public's perceptions may undergo change, new conventions and social expectations may emerge, and new rights and associated regulations may be clarified and enacted into law. As a case in point, consider the United States circa 1890: Samuel D. Warren and Louis Brandeis's seminal argument for a right to privacy was precipitated by a technological advance at the time—the development of cameras that could be used to take photographs in public without the subjects of the photographs being aware that their images had been captured. Warren and Brandeis (1890) described it as a form of "surreptitious" activity.

Beyond issues tied to technological advance, privacy as a construct in and of itself is nuanced and complex. What, when, and why someone considers some act to be a privacy violation depends in part on the underlying definition and rationale for privacy. Definitions often include one or more of the following diverse aspects: the ability to withdraw from society (e.g., to go somewhere in which you cannot be observed or others agree not to observe you), to be in society but left alone (e.g., to be in some semi-public or public space but to be allowed to go about one's activities anonymously or without being recorded), and to control information about oneself (e.g., to be informed about and able to consent to what information is collected about you and how that information is stored, maintained, and used). To this complexity of definition, the philosophical and legal rationale for privacy varies considerably (see Schoeman [1984] for a discussion of these differing viewpoints). One form of rationale draws on human rights, either arguing that privacy is a fundamental right in and of itself (Warren & Brandeis, 1890) or a right that is derived from other fundamental human rights, such as that of property (Thomson, 1975). Within this framing, a privacy violation constitutes a violation of human rights, and the machinery for dealing with rights violations gains purchase. Another form of rationale is psychologically grounded, either in the nature of the human psyche or of human society. From the perspective of the human psyche, privacy can be seen as a necessary mechanism for healthy human development and maturation (e.g., one way to psychologically distinguish self from other is to think a thought, keep it to yourself, and know that you know that thought but no one else does; Fried, 1968); from the perspective of human society, privacy can be seen as a necessary mechanism for smooth social functioning among people who might otherwise hold strong disagreements (e.g., people with right- and left-wing political beliefs can come together peaceably in the workplace in part because they are able to keep their political beliefs to themselves during the workday; Rachels, 1975). Within this framing, a privacy violation undermines human flourishing; here, discussions of healthy development, psychological well-being, and societal thriving come to the fore. Finally, and importantly, there are culturally relevant dimensions to privacy tied to what people in a given society at a given point in time expect to be private and what sorts of actions or signals they expect to indicate that something is intended to be private (Murphy, 1964). That is, different societies consider different types of actions and information to be private (e.g., in some societies and contexts financial information is considered largely private, in other societies and contexts less so), and different societies use different conventionally shared markers to indicate a desire for privacy (e.g., facing toward or away from the wall of an igloo in Inuit society, closing a bedroom door in a Western society).

When researchers and designers move forward with technological designs that implicate privacy, particularly privacy in public, in one way or another they engage this complexity of definition, rationale, context, and shifting societal expectations. Value sensitive design offers a number of useful tools for making meaningful inroads here. First among these are direct and indirect stakeholder analyses, since, often, in the process of optimizing information access for direct stakeholders, the implications for privacy of indirect stakeholders may be overlooked. Explicitly taking into account the granularity of information and locus of access can also be useful, since for these and other scalable dimensions some amounts and some contexts may be acceptable and other amounts and contexts less so, and understanding these pivot points can guide design insights. As information systems often cross regional and national boundaries in which there may be different expectations about and signals for privacy, value sensitive design methods (e.g., value scenarios, value sketches, value-oriented semi-structured interviews) can help to surface these cultural and contextual differences early in the research and design process. To briefly demonstrate how a value sensitive design approach might be used to engage implications for privacy in public, consider the following projects.

### Privacy in Public: Specific Projects

One of the first value sensitive design projects to investigate privacy in public was not initially framed as a project about privacy; rather, the project sought to investigate the effects of a real-time display of a local natural scene for people working in inside offices (Kahn et al., 2008a). The project's location was a major university in the Pacific Northwest of the United States. The goal was to see if such a real-time display would improve worker's mood, stress levels, and sense of community. Privacy was not on the research agenda. That said, the value sensitive design approach invoked a stakeholder analysis early on which, in turn, surfaced an important group of indirect stakeholders: those individuals who would walk through the scene and have their images captured and displayed in the inside offices. Thus, "the watcher and the watched" project (Friedman et al., 2006b) came into being, with an emphasis on understanding the implications of this technological intervention for privacy in public from the perspective of both direct (the people in the inside office "watching" the scene) and indirect (the people walking through the scene being "watched") stakeholders (see figure 4.8). Scalable assessments of proximity ("the camera displays live video from the fountain area on a screen … in an inside office with no windows in M[...] Hall; … in an apartment on University Ave.; … in an apartment in a residential neighborhood in Tokyo") and of pervasiveness ("the camera displays live video from the fountain area on a screen … in an apartment on University Ave.; … in the homes of thousands of people living

**Figure 4.8**
The "watcher" (top) and the "watched" (bottom).

in the local area; … in the homes of millions of people across the globe")
were included in surveys and semi-structured interviews with both direct
and indirect stakeholders. Findings showed consistent differences in the
perspectives of men and women about the large display. Specifically, more
women than men were uncomfortable with the large-display intervention
across all dimensions that were investigated (e.g., all variations of proximity and pervasiveness). Comparing the watchers (direct stakeholders) and
the watched (indirect stakeholders), among the men, indirect stakeholders were more often uncomfortable than direct stakeholders; interestingly,
among women, indirect and direct stakeholders were equally often uncomfortable. In terms of value sensitive design, the "watcher and watched"
project provides a concrete example of how to account for both direct and

indirect stakeholders as well as scalable dimensions such as proximity and pervasiveness, especially when privacy in public is at issue.

Cross-cultural aspects of privacy in public were investigated in a project that compared the "watched" results from the project above with a similar project conducted at a major university in Sweden by a team of Swedish and US researchers (Friedman et al., 2008c). While Sweden and the United States are both technologically advanced Western democratic societies, for purposes of this research they differ along important dimensions: the European Union, of which Sweden is a part, has well-articulated privacy and data-protection laws that do not have a parallel in the United States, and Sweden is known for its transparency of government. Care was taken to conduct the surveys and interviews in Swedish, and then to translate those results into English for analyses. One interview question tied to trust was added to tap issues of particular interest to Swedish team members. Cross-cultural differences were examined in two ways: (1) changes to the coding manual for the US interview data that needed to be made in order to adequately account for data from the Swedish interviews (e.g., new coding categories, new subcategories); and (2) differences in patterns of responses to the survey and interview questions. Findings were as follows. For the coding manual, no changes were required at the highest level of the coding scheme, suggesting that as a group the same set of concerns were expressed by the Swedish as by the US participants; though some changes were needed at lower levels of the coding scheme. In terms of patterns of responses, overall the Swedish participants were more concerned about privacy in public than their US counterparts; and qualitatively, in more nuanced analyses, Swedish participants emphasized the need to be "informed" about the camera and large display, while US participants emphasized the need to be able to "consent" to having their images captured. Though gender differences were not as pronounced as in the United States, more Swedish women than men were uncomfortable with the camera and display intervention.

The reach of privacy into public arenas pertains not only to physical aspects of a person but also to informational ones. In another project about public records in the United States, Munson and his colleagues (2011, 2012) investigated Pacific Northwest residents' perspectives on the publicness and privateness of public records when that information becomes available online and is downloadable and searchable. Historically in the United States, accessing information contained in public records has required some amount of sustained effort and intent in the form of a physical trip to a courthouse; online access to these same records increases ease of access and convenience at the risk of upsetting a well-established balance among the values of transparency, access, and privacy. Residents were surveyed about their views and values toward online public records in two contexts: political campaign contributions and real estate transactions. Paralleling the scalable assessment approach to identifying harms in the watcher and watched projects described above, the survey questions carefully explored the granularity of information that participants felt it is appropriate to be able to access online versus access only in person. Thus, questions probed participants' comfort with searching online for political campaign contributions and for real estate transaction information at, for example, the level of state, city, zip code, neighborhood name, home address, last name only, or first and last name. In addition, scalable assessment questions probed the residency status (e.g., US citizen, US permanent resident, not a US citizen or permanent resident) and proximity (e.g., in the same neighborhood, in the same state, in the United States, outside of the United States) of the individuals who would be accessing the information. Findings showed that respondents were more comfortable with information being searched at the broader geographic-area level than at the individual level for both real estate and campaign contributions. The only attributes on which respondents' comfort differed significantly between real estate purchases and campaign contributions were with searching by neighborhood and by home address. As one might expect, respondents were more comfortable with real estate transactions being searchable by neighborhood or home address than campaign contributions. Respondents also drew a distinction between access to information about themselves that was part of the public record by those who were fellow US citizens or legitimately living within the United States, and those who were not citizens or were illegally living in the United States. As Munson et al. note, though these technological advances have great benefits for values of transparency, accountability, and democracy, these same advances have also disrupted the existing balance among these values and personal privacy and are at odds with many of the survey respondents' expectations for how this data is and should be distributed. This research confirms that at least some people perceive privacy violations when public records are made available online.

**Privacy in Public: Contributions**

Though some might claim otherwise, the research reviewed here suggests that, at least in some Western countries and at least in some contexts, people's ideas about and expectations for privacy extend into their lives in public—be it physical or online spaces. Moreover, people continue to have nuanced conceptions of what information about themselves and their activities in public they want to be readily accessible to others, in which contexts, and at what level of detail. As evidenced by the research about online public records in which respondents sought actively to balance "enough" transparency while preserving "as much" privacy as possible, privacy in public does not exist in isolation but rather sits in a delicate relationship with other important human values. As evidenced by the research about watchers and the watched in the United States and in Sweden, men and women may experience technology that implicates privacy in public differently, and people experience technology that implicates privacy in public within the context of their societal, cultural, and institutional norms. Researchers and designers who engage such technologies would be advised to conduct careful stakeholder analyses with particular attention to indirect stakeholders (e.g., bystanders and others) who might be affected positively or negatively, as well as to incorporate into their user studies measures of scalable dimensions (e.g., granularity of information, ease of access to information), closely related values (e.g., transparency, trust, safety), and cultural practices and expectations. Importantly, such user studies should involve reasonable numbers of both men and women.

In terms of value sensitive design, the work reported here makes several contributions. First, the watcher and the watched projects conducted in the early 2000s were the first of their kind to take up questions of privacy in public in the physical-digital realm. Second, the research demonstrated not only the importance of conducting direct and indirect stakeholder analyses, but also how to use those analyses to bring indirect stakeholders (e.g., the watched) into the research and design process. Third, the research developed an initial understanding of scalable dimensions—those tied to granularity of information, proximity, and magnitude—and provided specific questions to tap those understandings that could be used in interviews and surveys. Fourth, for the human-computer interaction community, the research demonstrated the importance of collecting data from both men and women about privacy in public and analyzing that data for differences tied to gender. And fifth, the research provided one approach for conducting cross-cultural investigations into privacy in public, specifically using the coding manual as a means to identify cultural overlap and divergence. Numerous open questions remain for value sensitive investigations of privacy in public. Foremost among these is how to enumerate and account for diverse and potentially diffuse groups of indirect stakeholders; how to determine which scalable assessments are most relevant for a particular technology and in what ways; and to develop a better understanding of similarities and differences of men's and women's experiences of privacy in public.

### Land Use, Transportation, and the Environment

Authors: Alan Borning and Kari Watkins

Urban land use and transportation is a complex and value-laden arena. At the regional level, it involves decisions about land, infrastructure, and the built environment, including major long-term investments such as bridges, roads, and rail lines as well as zoning and other regulations that shape housing, retail space, industrial space, schools, parks and open space, and much else. At the individual level, it involves choices about whether and how to travel around the region for work, school, shopping, visiting friends, and many other purposes. The projects described in this section operate at these two levels: at the regional level, providing tools to support long-term land use and transportation planning in urban areas, and at the personal level, providing tools to make public transit more convenient, safe, and enjoyable.

Regarding support for regional planning, in many regions worldwide, there is great concern about such issues as traffic congestion, resource consumption, greenhouse gas emissions from transportation, walkability and public health, and sprawl. Elected officials, planners, and citizens grapple with these difficult issues as they develop and evaluate alternatives for major land use and transportation decisions and ultimately decide on a course of action (or inaction). The consequences of these decisions unfold over decades. To help make more informed decisions, we thus want to provide modeling and simulation tools that help stakeholders assess the long-term effects of different plans on land use, transportation, and the environment, and to do so in such a way that respects key values.

At a personal level, many people in urban areas use public transit to get to work, school, visit friends, go to medical appointments, and much else. In addition to the societal benefits of transit (such as reduced congestion and greenhouse gas emissions), for some people it is essential for basic mobility; for others it provides such benefits as a less stressful commute or time to read. However, public transit is not always as usable or sometimes even safe as one might like, and the process can be significantly improved by tools that provide real-time arrival information, trip planners, and alerts. Our second topic concerns providing such tools and the consequences of doing so.

Both of these projects have strong (although different) value components. Long-term land use and transportation decisions are often controversial, with the controversy reflecting underlying value conflicts among the different stakeholders. For example, for some stakeholders, a key criterion for evaluating alternatives is their impact on greenhouse gas emissions and other environmental effects; for others, a key criterion is impact on economic development. Another set of issues concerns how the decisions are part of an overall democratic process, thus implicating the values of legitimation, fairness, accountability, and transparency, among others. For the work on public transportation information systems, important values include fairness, access, health, community, and safety. In some cases, support for these values is unproblematic—few would argue against making the use of public transit safer for people waiting at night. In other cases, there are significant value tensions. For example, regarding fairness, given limited resources, how should these resources be used? How should we balance developing tools for high-end smartphones that might increase the number of people taking transit instead of driving alone with developing tools for riders who do not have such phones and who will be taking transit in any case, but for whom the safety and usability of transit could be greatly increased?

### Land Use, Transportation, and the Environment: Specific Projects
UrbanSim (Borning, Waddell, & Förster, 2008; Waddell, Wang, & Liu, 2008) is a state-of-the-art modeling system for simulating the development of urban areas over periods of 20 to 30 years under differing plans and assumptions. It includes component models for simulating such things as where households decide to live, where employers locate jobs, which areas

will have new or renovated buildings, and (in conjunction with an external travel model) how people travel in the region (i.e., by driving, public transit, walking, or bicycling). UrbanSim is typically run by a regional planning agency (or perhaps a research institution) using detailed input data, including demographic information, employment statistics, land ownership and building records, transportation network data, and environmental features. Given this data for a starting year and descriptions of differing plans, the system can then be run for 20 to 30 simulated years on each of the alternatives, allowing them to be compared. It is currently the most widely used land-use model in the United States, with applications in Europe, Asia, and developing regions as well.

As an example of UrbanSim's use, suppose that an urban region is considering several alternative proposals for dealing with heavy traffic congestion on a local freeway and other highways and arterials. One proposal focuses on building additional highway capacity; another involves building high-occupancy vehicle lanes and adding frequent bus service instead; and a third centers on adding a new rail system rather than road capacity, including zoning changes around the rail stations to encourage compact development and curb low-density sprawl. The planning agency would then encode these alternate proposals as scenarios for UrbanSim and simulate each of them. Indicators provide the means by which different stakeholders understand and compare the long-term impacts of the different alternatives. Typical indicators for this example include those that capture transportation usage (how many people are driving alone, how many are taking buses or trains, and how many are walking or bicycling); the availability and cost of housing and space for business, educational, and industrial uses; and the environmental impacts, including gasoline and diesel consumption for transportation, greenhouse gas emissions, water consumption, effects on open space, land cover, and biodiversity, and others.

The main focus of our value sensitive design work with UrbanSim has been laying the groundwork for public participation around the use of such systems in planning (Borning et al., 2005; Friedman et al., 2008a). Most planning agencies have long included substantial public participation in the overall planning process, but the modeling has been a back-room activity, the province of the expert modelers who use it. Our work has been concerned with opening up the "black box" of the modeling system in preparation for direct use by wider groups of stakeholders.

One activity has been documenting the available indicators. We originally sought a single, relatively neutral description of each indicator. However, advocacy plays a central role in the planning process, and when we sought to describe the different views on what an indicator represents and its desired direction, the result was unsatisfying: one group might want the indicator to increase, another have it decrease, and a third might maintain that it was not the right indicator in the first place. We thus took a different approach in which there was a relatively neutral *technical description* and, separately, a set of indicator perspectives written in a participatory process with different stakeholder groups (Borning et al., 2005). We then evaluated different combinations of the documentation (technical documentation alone, a perspective from just one group, from all groups, all documentation combined). The key finding was that stakeholders in all cases viewed the result as having greater legitimacy in the planning process as additional components were included.

A second contribution was a principled prioritization scheme for deciding which new indicators were the most important to implement next, where the prioritization was based on a triangulation among the topics of potential concern, stakeholder interest, and technical feasibility (Friedman et al., 2008a). Based on this, the group implemented and documented 13 new indicators. Davis (2006, 2008) reports additional work on personal indicators—those that provide information from the perspective of an individual stakeholder rather than the region. Personal indicators enable stakeholders to answer such questions as "how would my own commute be affected under different scenarios?" or "are my children likely to be able to afford a house in this neighborhood in 20 years?" The work on personal indicators thus lies between the two levels: it uses the regional-level data of UrbanSim and places it within a personal context.

In the realm of public transportation, value sensitive design has played a key role in research on the OneBusAway transit traveler information system[1] to help plan what transit rider information tools to build next using a modified version of the principled prioritization scheme from the UrbanSim work above. OneBusAway (Ferris, Watkins, & Borning, 2010; Watkins, Ferris, Borning, Rutherford, & Layton, 2011) is a set of transit

---

1. A related topic has been using value sensitive design as part of work with blind and deaf-blind transit riders; this is discussed in the Computers and Disabilities application section.

tools focused on providing real-time arrival information for transit riders via a website (https://onebusaway.org), smartphone applications, phone, and SMS (see figure 4.9). Originally deployed in the Puget Sound region of Washington State (Seattle and other nearby cities), as of 2015 it served over 100,000 riders per week in Puget Sound, with additional operational deployments in Atlanta (Georgia), New York City (New York), York (Ontario, Canada), Rogue Valley (Oregon), and Tampa (Florida), as well as experimental deployments elsewhere. The underlying goal of OneBusAway is to make it easier for riders to use public transportation and thereby increase rider satisfaction and increase transit ridership.

Through conceptual and empirical investigations, the OneBusAway team developed a list of potential transit information tools and began to prioritize projects based on the needs and values of transit riders of all types as well as impacts to indirect stakeholders, in particular bus drivers. Making use of value sensitive design in the design of OneBusAway has significantly

**Figure 4.9**
OneBusAway apps for Android, iPhone, and Windows phones. The Android app (left) is showing information for Tampa, while the iPhone and Windows phone apps (center and right, respectively) are showing information for Seattle. The iPhone version has also been extensively tested for accessibility for blind riders using the VoiceOver feature. Images courtesy of Sean Bareau, Aaron Brethorst, and Rob Smith.

changed the conceptualization of the overarching goals of the project and the decision-making process. Before using the value sensitive design approach, the focus was on a combination of new tools for high-end smartphones (i.e., the technology used in daily travel by the developers), but the decisions regarding which tools to work on was simply based on the intuitions of the designers. Now the prioritization of work is more systematic. One broadened focus is providing integrated tools, especially service alert notification along with real-time arrival information, on a full range of devices, from smartphones to the most basic phones. Another is a more systematic evaluation of deployed and potential technologies for indirect as well as direct stakeholders. Finally, the OneBusAway project team is investigating policies and programs (as well as technology) to help fill gaps, such as how best to serve people who have a prepaid phone service with limited minutes or have no mobile phone at all, or who have disabilities that make some of the interfaces less accessible to them.

The consideration of indirect stakeholders, as prompted by value sensitive design, has helped reveal the full spectrum of impact that OneBusAway may potentially have. Motivated by this stakeholder analysis, one of the most significant results has been the consideration of bus drivers in the design (Watkins et al., 2013a). Through bus driver interviews and value tension analyses, it became apparent that OneBusAway has a significant impact not only on the riders (the primary direct stakeholder), but also on the drivers as well (probably the most important indirect stakeholders) who are also the primary contacts riders have with the transit system. Further, basic questions of fairness dictate that we should consider the views and values of drivers in any case, as a group strongly affected by such technology. Therefore, the OneBusAway project team surveyed 500 bus drivers, with a response rate of over 50% (253 respondents) to investigate their views and values regarding existing real-time information systems, as well as potential future transit rider information applications. Almost all drivers were positive or neutral to the provision of real-time information. For example, a typical comment was "happier riders means happier drivers." In addition, drivers were receptive to building other new information applications for riders, with all applications in the survey being supported by at least 60% of the bus drivers. However, as revealed in their comments, drivers did not favor developing tools that would provide, for example, summaries to management of their on-time performance or ratings from riders, out of concern that this could be used in, for example, disciplinary actions. They also had concerns about tools such a "rate-my-route" tool that might stigmatize some areas or neighborhoods. This research provides a better understanding of the impact of rider information tools on bus drivers, including their values, harms, and benefits.

### Land Use, Transportation, and the Environment: Contributions

In terms of contributions to the domain, in the UrbanSim work we helped lay the groundwork for wider public participation around the use of such simulation systems in planning. In the OneBusAway work, we investigated the views and values of an important set of indirect stakeholders: bus drivers. In fact, a very common comment in the open-ended section of the survey was a note of appreciation for asking for their views. Regarding contributions to value sensitive design theory and methods, in the UrbanSim work we investigated providing information about a controversial domain via separate but linked technical descriptions and advocacy pieces. In addition, we introduced the key distinction among explicitly supported values, stakeholder values, and designer values. We also developed a principled prioritization scheme for further work, which was adapted for the OneBusAway work as well.

At the core of value sensitive design is the idea that we should systematically identify the values of stakeholders and take time to envision and investigate empirically the value tensions that may be created by any design, whether technological or otherwise. OneBusAway, as an application of information technology to solve transportation problems, was a natural use of value sensitive design. However, the principles of value sensitive design should be applicable throughout the transportation industry, especially when considering broader transportation planning goals. A first paper introducing value sensitive design in the transportation literature was presented in 2013 (Watkins et al., 2013b). Other stakeholder involvement techniques used in the transportation industry primarily focus on the context or surroundings of a corridor and specific projects within the corridor. By using the value sensitive design approach, transportation planners can better incorporate community values into transportation design and emphasize overall mobility and access solutions. As we strive for improved transport systems, it is imperative that we consider the human values of both the users of the system as well as other indirect stakeholders impacted by it.

## Engineering Design Practice

Authors: Jeroen van den Hoven and Ibo van de Poel

Engineering is a broad domain—ranging from the classical engineering disciplines, such as civil, mechanical, electrical, and chemical engineering, to disciplines like industrial design engineering, architecture, city planning, and the design of sociotechnical systems. In all of these, a wide variety of values play a part. General values important in almost all engineering include well-being, safety, health, and environmental care or sustainability. Within engineering and technology, approaches have been developed with aims similar to value sensitive design. One family of approaches, known as technology assessment (Grunwald, 2009), aims at predicting the social consequences of technological development. More recent approaches, such as constructive technology assessment, aim not only to anticipate potential consequences of technology but also to feed these back into the design and development process (Schot & Rip, 1997). A second family of approaches is based on ideas of concurrent engineering and "design for X" (DFX). In concurrent engineering, downstream considerations, such as production, use, and maintenance, are integrated into upstream decisions in engineering design and development. With DFX approaches, "X" can stand for a certain virtue or value or for a life phase. Typical virtues or values for which design for X haven been developed in engineering include the environment, quality, maintainability, reliability, cost, affective design, and inclusive design (Holt & Barnes, 2010).

Given the central place of human values in engineering design practice, moral philosophers have a number of important roles to play. First, they can help to identify and recognize moral issues and moral values that arise in design practice (e.g., Taebi & Kloosterman, 2008; Manders-Huits & van den Hoven, 2009; van Gorp, 2005). Second, they can study how designers come to judgments and decisions about such moral issues and how this judgment and decision-making process could be improved (e.g., van de Poel & van Gorp, 2006; van der Burg & van Gorp, 2005; Doorn, 2012). Third, they can contribute to approaches and methodologies that better help to identify and address moral issues in design practice, in particular the role of moral values in design (Doorn et al., 2013; Manders-Huits, 2011; van den Hoven, 2005, 2007). Fourth, they can address specific issues related to moral values in design, like design as a way of dealing with moral dilemmas (van den Hoven et al., 2012); conflicting values in design (van de Poel, 2009); the translation of values into design requirements (van de Poel, 2013); how to understand values such as privacy (van den Hoven, 1999, 2000), trust (Vermaas, Tan, van den Hoven, Burgemeestre, & Hulstijn, 2010), well-being (van de Poel, 2012), or human capabilities (Oosterlaken, 2009) in design; and the moral dilemmas raised by persuasive technology (Spahn, 2012). Fifth, they can develop more general theories about the value-ladenness of technology that are relevant to value sensitive design (for an overview, see Kroes & Verbeek, 2014).

## Engineering Design Practice: Specific Projects

Moral dilemmas pervade our daily life and our policy making. We are confronted regularly with situations in which different moral obligations or moral values identify different options as best, and in which there is no obvious easy choice. Such moral dilemmas have drawn considerable attention in moral philosophy, where philosophers tend to stress analysis, reasoning, and judgment to come to terms with these moral dilemmas. That said, a number of philosophers have observed that an undue emphasis on reasoning and analysis of individual choices has come at the cost of neglecting synthetic strategies for dealing with moral dilemmas. Thus, in the first project described here, we offer and explicate the general idea that the development of new technical options might solve or avoid previously identified value conflicts (van den Hoven et al., 2012; Whitbeck, 1998). For example, van den Hoven et al. (2012) have pointed out that innovation by means of value sensitive design may enlarge opportunity sets and thereby help to solve moral dilemmas. Such value sensitive innovation, they write, "can make the impossible possible, not in the sense of 'logically possible,' of course, but in the sense of 'feasible' or 'physically realizable'" (p. 150). According to van den Hoven et al., "technical innovation results in moral progress in those cases in which it means an improvement in all relevant value dimensions" (2012, p. 152). Of course, not all technical innovation implies improvement in all relevant value dimensions. Sometimes a gain in one value dimension comes at the cost of a loss in another value dimension. Sometimes the technical innovation creates new problems or side effects that, in turn, require new value dimensions to be taken into account. Sometimes the technical innovation only addresses the initial problem insofar as it is amenable to a technological solution. The values themselves might change as a result of technical development (e.g., changes with respect to sexual morality in some communities may be due to the development of contraceptives). Technical innovation may also create new choices and dilemmas that are challenging or undesirable for society at large, as in the case of prenatal diagnosis. For these reasons, innovation should be guided by the relevant moral values; accordingly, innovation by value sensitive design is at times an appropriate way to deal with moral dilemmas.

Turning now to a nationwide (and beyond) research program, in The Netherlands an important stimulus for value sensitive design research in engineering emerged in the form of The Netherlands Organisation for Scientific Research Program with a total budget of 13 million euros between 2009 and 2014. The program—themed "Responsible Innovation: Ethical and Societal Exploration of Science and Technology"—focuses on issues concerning technological developments that can reasonably be expected to have a dramatic impact, either positive or negative, on people or society. Developments studied in this program concern both new technologies (e.g., information and communication technology, nanotechnology, biotechnology, neural sciences) and technological systems in transition (e.g., agriculture, health care). The program aims at contributing to responsible innovation by increasing the scope and depth of research into societal and ethical aspects of science and technology in a proactive manner. The program has an international orientation and context: it not only involves Dutch innovation projects, but also innovation projects in other countries and other parts of the world, in particular those relevant to developing countries. Finally, it requires effective and close interaction among research in the humanities and technological and social sciences. Of import for the work reported here, the Responsible Innovation Program was written explicitly from a value sensitive design perspective and intentionally stimulates research that addresses value questions in innovation and engineering and systems design up front, in a multidisciplinary way (van den Hoven, 2013).

One predecessor project that helped to lay the foundation for the Responsible Innovation Program concerned waste water treatment. In this project, a value sensitive design approach was applied in parallel with the development of a new waste water treatment technology (van de Poel et al., 2005). The goal of the research was to experiment with conducting ethical research in parallel with an engineering R&D project. Specifically, the ethicists first used a network approach developed for the project purposes to map the relevant networks of actors (Zwart, van de Poel, van Mil, & Brumsen, 2006), then interviewed each of the main actors, and, finally, held a group session with the main actors in a computer facility that allowed for anonymous brainstorming and voting on key issues. In this way, the ethicists were able to identify the main risks of the project, the perceived severity of those risks, and whom the main actors considered responsible for addressing these risks (van de Poel et al., 2005). One key finding entailed the potential risks of so-called secondary emissions—emissions that are not regulated by law but potentially are harmful. In particular, typically the engineering researchers involved in the project thought these secondary emissions should be addressed during implementation of the technology, while the potential users thought these emissions should be addressed during R&D. This finding points to what may be called a problem of many hands: due to the number of people involved, it may be unclear who is responsible, and as a result the issue is not taken up (van de Poel & Zwart, 2010). When this insight was fed back to the main actors, it spurred the engineering researchers to include the issue of secondary emissions in subsequent research proposals (de Kreuk et al., 2010).

Another project investigated the meaning, roles, and uses of trust in the economic and public domain, particularly in relation to the task of designing systems for trust in information technology (Vermaas et al., 2010). The specific case concerned a real-world problem in economics: namely, the transfer of control for compliance with applicable regulations from customs agencies to companies. Previously, customs agencies exerted control at the level of individual items, however, this practice has become increasingly untenable and is being replaced by control at the level of companies. To do so, customs agencies must determine whether or not companies can be trusted to be in control of their business and in compliance with applicable regulations. In turn, companies have sought to use information systems as one means to establish this trust. Using a model proposed by Lewicki and Bunker (1995, 1996) and value sensitive design as a general framework, Vermaas and colleagues surveyed key stakeholders in an effort to understand what it means to them to have trust in the economic and public domain, and to identify the difficulties developers encounter when designing information systems for trust. Then, using their analysis of stakeholder perspectives in conjunction with existing engineering design methods, they provide a means to address these difficulties. Specifically, they argue that trust can be achieved by taking into account philosophical analyses of the value of trust and by including both parties in the trust relationship as clients for whom the information technology systems are to be designed.

### Engineering Design Practice: Contributions

The contributions of value sensitive design to work in engineering are manifold. In the specific engineering design work described above, value sensitive design has resulted in the better recognition of moral issues and moral values. Beyond these specific project outcomes, value sensitive design has led to changes in engineering research practice and to additional research or trials (e.g., the waste water treatment case above as well as in other cases; see Doorn [2011]). Value sensitive design and ethically parallel research have also been applied in a range of PhD projects funded by the 4TU Centre for Ethics and Technology (http://ethicsandtechnology.eu); these projects were carried out in close collaboration with the other centers of excellence at the three universities of technology in the Netherlands (Delft, Eindhoven, Twente) and engaged a range of engineering disciplines, including nanotechnology, sustainable energy, information and communication technology, high-tech systems, and fluid and solid mechanics. More broadly, the need for responsible innovation has been recognized in engineering. In addition to the Responsible Innovation grant program of The Netherlands Organisation for Scientific Research mentioned above, the European Commission has committed itself to promoting the responsible use of science and technology both within the European Union and worldwide (European Commission, 2012). It has coined the term "responsible research and innovation" (European Commission, 2012; von Schomberg, 2011, 2012), which consists of a combination of three themes: ethical acceptability, risk management, and human benefit yields (European Commission, 2012, p. 8).

Not only have moral values become incorporated more systematically in the last decades into engineering design, but design thinking has also become part of the study of moral values. The work of John Rawls

(1999) has probably played a role in this design turn. Rawls wanted to articulate defensible principles for the design of just basic institutions of society. Moral philosophers are gradually opening up to the idea that institutional and technological design shapes the space of action of individuals and have come to see that design is of moral importance. One of the rewards for thinking about values from a design perspective is that conflicts of values as they typically occur in moral dilemmas are often amenable to reconciliation in a new design in relevant parts of the world. Design is therefore a much-needed complement to moral projects about values, principles, and norms and their justification. Ultimately, design is about changing the world in such a way as to accommodate our values and moral preferences.

## Envisioning Criteria

Author: Lisa Nathan

Integral to value sensitive design is the position that the information systems we design can strongly influence our ways of being in the world. Yet we recognize that under the day-to-day pressures of design work, this positioning is easy to overlook. Information system designers have countless considerations to keep track of, including limited resources and short deadlines. Asking "real-world" designers to consider the longer-term, ethical implications of their designs for the human condition can easily come across as a frivolous, academic expectation. Although the projects referenced throughout this book have demonstrated the robust nature of value sensitive design methodology (i.e., the conceptual, empirical, and technical investigations), a small survey in 2010 corroborated our concern that the approach had not yet been widely influential outside of academia (Rotondo & Freier, 2010). This reflects an ongoing challenge for value sensitive design researchers. How can we offer insights from decades of value sensitive design research in a manner that is readily incorporated into everyday design practice?

### Envisioning Criteria: Specific Projects

As an initial step to address this challenge, the Value Sensitive Design Lab initiated a project in 2007 with the explicit goal of developing more accessible value sensitive design methods (or tools)—that is, methods that can be readily incorporated into everyday design practice. We sought to create design tools that would encourage designers to consistently reflect on the longer-term, societal-wide influence of their work. As part of the project we undertook an extensive review of the value sensitive design literature to discern the most critical components of the theory, methods, and other findings. We supplemented this review with an investigation of urban planning (Beveridge, 2002; Taylor, 1998) and Design Noir literature (Dunne, 2005; Dunne & Raby, 2001), two design perspectives that offer particularly strong insights concerning longer-term thinking and the potential negative influence of design. Combining these analyses, we identified four key criteria for evaluating the longer-term, society-wide implications of a design at any point during the design process. We labeled these envisioning criteria *time*, *pervasiveness*, *stakeholders*, and *values* (Nathan et al., 2008). The envisioning criteria serve as touchstones—tangible reminders of broader considerations. The criteria of time and pervasiveness remind designers to attend to the systemic qualities of their work, whereas the values and stakeholders criteria incorporate ethical dimensions. With the four envisioning criteria in hand we turned to crafting the first "off-the-shelf" value sensitive design toolkit, the Envisioning Cards.

The Envisioning Cards (Friedman et al., 2011), as described in the Envisioning Cards section in chapter 3, consist of a set of 32 three-by-five-inch cards, a small sand timer, and a brief instruction booklet. The timer is incorporated into some of the card activities; it also suggests that some progress can be made in just a short amount of time. All cards share the same structure, each having an image side and a text side. The cards are differentiated by themes, each card representing a unique theme. The themes are divided into four categories representing each of the four envisioning criteria (time, pervasiveness, stakeholders, and values). Each theme is described on the text side of its respective card. This elaboration consists of a title, a brief overview of the theme, and a design activity to engage the theme. The goal of the image side of the card is to provide possible scenarios related to the card's theme, yet without being prescriptive. To help designers who may choose to focus on a particular criterion, each has a distinct color scheme. As an example, all cards that fall within the values criterion are distinguished by the same color scheme: blue.

The first version of the Envisioning Cards was field-tested in human-computer interaction (HCI) design classes across the United States and in

Sweden. Additionally, the cards were featured in two professional devel-opment courses at HCI-related conferences. Feedback was gathered from phone interviews, an online survey, the HCI courses, email, and infor-mal discussions. Based on this feedback, changes were made to the cards throughout 2009–2010. Themes were added, activities were reworked, new images were produced, and a lightweight instruction booklet was crafted. In the beginning of 2011, the first professionally published version of the cards was released. Additional reporting by Friedman and Hendry (2012) suggests that the Envisioning Cards are useful for stimulating ideation and iteration in co-design and for conducting heuristic value analysis of exist-ing and proposed technologies. Further research is needed to investigate the adoption and use of the Envisioning Cards and how the cards might be systematically brought into design processes and educational settings.

### Envisioning Criteria: Contributions

To date, the key contributions to value sensitive design made by this line of inquiry are the four envisioning criteria and a physical format that can be incorporated into a range of design processes. The criteria show promise in terms of leveraging key insights from value sensitive design in a lightweight manner. Based on the criteria, the Envisioning Cards go some distance toward providing a design tool to help designers consider the longer-term, ethical implications of their work without taking on a rigorous tripartite investigation. Ongoing value sensitive design research in this area includes expanding the envisioning criteria to include, for example, multi-lifespan considerations, and incorporating the envisioning criteria into new meth-ods and toolkits. This includes card sets that are adapted to ethical consid-erations within specialized areas, such as computer security.

The envisioning criteria are directly tied to many open questions await-ing future research. In order of increasing complexity: (1) do design teams consider these sorts of values without any intervention (that is, is a toolkit like the Envisioning Cards even needed)?; (2) if so, what do these value processes look like?; (3) how might the effectiveness of the envisioning cri-teria be measured?; (4) what other criteria might be of import?; (5) do the Envisioning Cards evoke and fuel designers' ethical imaginations?; (6) what delivery mechanisms for the Envisioning Cards content are effective (e.g., paper cards, iPhone app, video tutorials)?

# 5 Conclusion

The next technologies are burgeoning forth. Some lead inwards, into our bodies, brains, and minds. Some lead outwards into our homes, neighborhoods, societies, and ecosystems. Together: designing technology and designing ways of being.

Will the next tools and technologies enhance or diminish human experience? Will they lead to more or less human well-being and dignity? Will they lead to more just societies or to more unequal ones?

The importance of engaging human values in the technical design process cannot be stated strongly enough. As we have seen, the theory and method of value sensitive design gives us tools for bringing our technical and moral imaginations together—and, in so doing, to expand the criteria by which we judge the quality of the technologies that we build.

In this final chapter, we step back and reflect on progress in value sensitive design. First, we consider the robustness of the framework, considering its comprehensiveness, durability, extensibility, and actionability. Then, we take up some common critiques and present future directions for extending value sensitive design. We conclude that through practice, we can make progress in accounting for human values in technical design.

## Assessing Robustness

Twenty years in, it is appropriate to inquire: "How robust a framework is value sensitive design?" To structure this inquiry, we invoke three established criteria for evaluating theory: comprehensiveness, durability, and extensibility. Then, because value sensitive design is a theory for practice, to those we add the fourth criterion of actionability.

*Comprehensiveness* refers to the coverage of a framework, where the greater the coverage, the more robust the framework. In the case of a framework to account for human values in the technical design process, coverage pertains to the breadth of values, technologies, level of analyses, populations, and contexts of use that can be accommodated adequately by the framework. In terms of values, rather than being specialized to a single value or short list—for example, solely privacy or security—value sensitive design can account for a wide range of values and webs of related values. In principle, the framework, while not adhering to any one normative ethical theory, can be used in the service of a diverse set of ethical theories (e.g., care ethics, just warfare, discursive ethics). In terms of technologies, as can be seen in the application sections, the framework can be employed insightfully to frame and to design for varied systems (from implantable medical devices to large-scale urban simulation), albeit, to date, the design of information technology has been the prominent concern. That said, newer work is beginning to engage a broader range of technologies, including those in energy and civil engineering (e.g., Mok & Hyysalo, 2018). Moreover, as can also be seen throughout this volume, rather than addressing a particular level of human experience, value sensitive design can account for levels of analysis spanning from the individual (e.g., implantable medical devices, human-robot interaction) to organizational (e.g., groupware knowledge-base systems) to global (e.g., information systems for transitional justice). In terms of populations, the framework creates space for bringing both direct and indirect stakeholders in a diversity of roles into the design process. In principle, there are no constraints on population. Work in the applications section includes homeless youth, medical patients, ordinary citizens, medical device providers, parents and their teenagers, blind and low-vision people, the public, and more. How to engage human populations with limited cognition (e.g., people with dementia, toddlers) as well as nonhumans are two directions for further exploration and could surface limitations in scope. Finally, and also in principle, there are no constraints on context of use. That said, the bulk of work in value sensitive design has been conducted within Western societies (in the United States and in Europe). Extending the framework to projects in diverse cultures and other geographies would help to surface Western worldviews in the value sensitive design framing, should such exist. For example, how would value sensitive design's even-handed, largely individualistic treatment of direct and indirect stakeholders be meaningfully appropriated in design contexts within primarily hierarchical or communal societies? On balance, we assess value sensitive design to be robust with respect to comprehensive coverage; there is, of course, more to be done.

*Durability* refers to standing the test of time. Value sensitive design offers a coherent foundation of theory and method, the core of which has remained quite stable over the past twenty years. Given that value sensitive design primarily has been developed in a technical field known for continuous, rapid change, this stability is particularly notable. The framework has been tested, and while some refinements have been made, its core commitments have remained largely intact. In addition, as discussed above, critiques have appeared in the literature that by and large have helped to refine, expand, and improve value sensitive design. However, flaws that undermine the core have not surfaced, at least at the time of writing. Moreover, because the framework at its core is not undergoing constant change, the mutual shaping of theory and method is possible. In the direction from theory to method, the theoretical distinction between direct and indirect stakeholders can guide the representation of values through, for example, Envisioning Cards (e.g., the "One Person, Multiple Roles" card helps designers identify ways in which a particular individual can experience a specific technology at times as a direct stakeholder and at other times as an indirect one). In the other direction, from method to theory, the invention and practical application of a method can clarify the meaning and usefulness of a theoretical construct. For example, the use of value dams and flows can clarify the conceptualization of a "value tension." Similarly, the use of stakeholder tokens can clarify the relationships among stakeholders (e.g., core versus peripheral). On balance, we assess the core commitments of value sensitive design to be robust with respect to durability.

*Extensibility* refers to the ability to adapt, extend, or develop a framework while retaining an intact core. That is, an extensible framework is one that can be extended without breaking its critical elements. At least two overarching aspects of the value sensitive design framework provide the bases for robust extensibility.

First, the level of abstraction of the theoretical constructs—interactional stance, stakeholders, values, value tensions, and so forth—is defined with a high degree of precision at a fairly high level of generality, allowing for flexibility of instantiation. Here we point to at least three ways in which the constructs can be extended. First, as specific new examples and cases are encountered, they can be fit into existing constructs. For instance, consider identifying direct and indirect stakeholders (an existing theoretical construct) for the emerging technology of brain-machine interfaces (a new technical case). In this way, the existing constructs account for a greater set of technologies, populations, settings of use, and so forth (sharing similarity with the criterion of coverage above). Second, within an existing theoretical construct, new subclasses can be identified that help to deepen and enrich our understanding of that construct. Here, to the extent useful, designers may also develop narrower subclasses of definitions to characterize particular instances that emerge from the design context. For example, by introducing the concept of indirect stakeholder and role, the framework can be extended, beyond "bystander" and "the human data point," to other specialized types of indirect stakeholders. In turn, this specialization of construct enables the framework to represent and accumulate design knowledge. Third, new constructs themselves can be added at the highest level of the framework. What these constructs entail and how they are conceptualized would require careful thought and likely arise through reflecting across design cases. To date, we have sought to keep the theoretical constructs to a smaller set of essential elements. While the framework can accommodate new constructs, such constructs should be added judiciously (and may not be needed at all).

The second overarching aspect of value sensitive design that affords extensibility stems from how the theoretical constructs and specific methods are related. In particular, new value sensitive design methods can be developed or adapted. Moreover, those methods are often closely aligned with the theoretical constructs. New methods can be developed in relation to existing constructs, as when new ways of investigating and addressing value tensions are invented. Likewise, when new subclasses are identified— so, for example, if a new subclass is identified, we would expect to eventually develop or adapt methods to engage that subclass (e.g., methods to engage indirect stakeholders who are bystanders in contrast to methods to engage indirect stakeholders who represent data points in a system). In this way, value sensitive design offers theoretical constructs that stimulate methodological innovation. Very practically, the framework can be extended, for example, by extending table 3.1 to add new methods under existing purposes, new purposes and methods, and so forth.

These two-overarching aspects, as illustrated by the above examples, provide reasonable evidence for robust extensibility of value sensitive design. In the future, additional dimensions may be identified that further contribute to extensibility.

*Actionability*, the fourth criterion, concerns a pragmatic usefulness and adoption. How readily can value sensitive design be taken up and appropriated by professional designers, engineers, and educators and their communities of practice? How do designers bring the framework's theoretical constructs into current design practice, if at all? Relatedly, how are value sensitive design methods adjusted to normative practices of an organization or community? How can the process of adoption and diffusion be supported?

In terms of design research, as evidenced by the publications cited in chapter 4 of this book, value sensitive design has been engaged, appropriated, and extended by a wide range of design researchers in academic and industry research labs. Moreover, this design approach is currently taught to graduate and undergraduate students in departments and programs including biomedical health informatics, civil engineering, communications, computer science, human-centered design, information, linguistics, media studies, and technology ethics at universities in Europe and North America.

Thought leaders have pointed to value sensitive design as a critical and worthy approach for advancing fields. For example, Liam Bannon (2011), writing in ACM *Interactions*, brings value sensitive design to bear in reimagining human-computer interaction. Gerhard Fischer (2018), also in ACM *Interactions*, positions value sensitive design alongside user-centered design and participatory design in the service of advancing quality of life in the digital age. Policy and legal scholars Kate Crawford and Ryan Calo (2016), in *Nature*, outline a four-pronged approach for tackling the social and ethical impacts of artificial intelligence systems, one prong of which builds on value sensitive design. In a collection on responsible innovation, Jeroen van den Hoven (2013) advocates value sensitive design as the practical way to deliver on the European Union charge for responsible innovation.

Turning to industry, given the constraints of proprietary practices, we do not know a great deal about the extent to which value sensitive design is being adopted and incorporated into professional practice. Descriptive models of design practices, such as that by Shilton (2012), will be invaluable for understanding current practices around adoption of value sensitive design and supporting further diffusion and appropriation. That said, leaders in computing engineering, drawing on Spiekermann (2015), have placed value sensitive design at the center of a new effort by the IEEE Software and Systems Engineering Standards Committee to develop Standard P7000, a model process for addressing ethical concerns during system design (IEEE Standards Association, 2016).

Taken together, these assessments—of comprehensiveness, durability, extensibility, and actionability—speak well to the overall robustness of value sensitive design.[1] No obvious fatal flaws or brittleness have surfaced. Moreover, the criteria are useful not only for evaluating the maturity and robustness of value sensitive design, but also for pointing to limitations and opportunities for improvement and next steps.

## Engaging Critique

In an indication of its maturity, value sensitive design has been the subject of a good deal of critique (e.g., Albrechtslund, 2007; Le Dantec et al., 2009; Alsheikh et al., 2011; Manders-Huits, 2011; Yetim, 2011; Borning & Muller, 2012). Davis and Nathan (2014) offer a comprehensive review of the critiques, organizing their analysis into four core areas summarized here:

1. *Ethical commitments.* What ethical commitments, if any, are made; that is, what ethical theory is used to adjudicate, for example, design options related to value tensions?
2. *Stakeholder participation and the emergence of values.* How do stakeholders participate, and how do their values emerge through participation?
3. *Voice.* How are designer and stakeholder views represented and distinguished?
4. *Universal values.* How should values, especially universal values, be conceptualized for design goals and processes?

These are critical questions for value sensitive design or any framework that seeks to comprehensively account for human values in the design process. That said, we do not believe that these questions, individually or as a group, present value sensitive design with insurmountable difficulty.

---

1. Beyond these four criteria, there may be additional dimensions that would be appropriate to consider.

To the contrary, these are stimulating questions that can be used to advance value sensitive design, as has been done by researchers outside of the framework's originators. For example, illustrating how ethical theory can be employed (question 1), Cummings (2006) employed just war theory to the user interface design for missile systems, and van Wynsberghe (2013) used care ethics to develop normative criteria for weighing options in the design of care robots for elderly persons. In regard to stakeholder involvement (question 2), Yetim (2011) addresses the challenge of legitimating stakeholders by recommending the use of discourse ethics. Deibel (2011) explores what qualify as good reasons for setting aside the views of certain stakeholder groups. Concerning the voice of designers and stakeholders (question 3), following the recommendation of Borning and Muller (2012), reporting on value sensitive design projects now often includes a section on "researcher stance," which goes some distance toward more clearly representing the designers' points of view.

Taking up question 4, a most challenging one, it is important to note that, as with any tool, while value sensitive design can be used for good or for harm, it is not neutral. On the question of universal values—whether they exist, how they are defined and obtain standing, how they might shape design processes, their potential for benefit and harm—value sensitive design does not articulate a definitive answer. That said, value sensitive design theory *does* nudge designers toward a focus on human well-being, dignity, and justice—values of a universal nature. To see how, consider these four commitments:

1.  to define human values by what is important to people in their lives, with a focus on ethics and morality;
2.  to consider and legitimate both direct and indirect stakeholders;
3.  to represent and address value tensions by appropriate means, and;
4.  to consider the co-evolution of technology and socio-structural aspects of the design situation.

During conceptual, empirical, and technical investigations, pursued iteratively and integratively, these and related commitments guide designers toward principled consideration of stakeholders' interests. In turn, as stakeholder interests are seen through potential harms and benefits and value tensions, focus is given to an overarching conceptualization of human well-being and dignity while positioning designers to act.

To concretize this somewhat abstract proposition—namely, that value sensitive design nudges designers toward a conceptualization of human dignity and justice—consider the following idealized account, in which one design subproblem leads to the next in an unfolding process. While not required, often designers begin with a conceptual investigation. Here, to identify key stakeholders and implicated values, they might conduct a direct and indirect stakeholder analysis with analytic and empirical components. Drawing on prior work, definitions for the values might be written, later to be revised based on an empirical investigation. This step is likely to result in a web of interrelated values. In turn, value tensions are likely to emerge, and the design team will be confronted with the circumstances that gave rise to them. Dimensions might include community and international norms, economics, individual and organizational preferences, individual rights, laws, limits of infrastructure, natural resources, technological effects, and so forth. In this work, the design team is prompted to consider the benefits and harms that both direct and indirect stakeholders might experience. In turn, designers are nudged toward making decisions about, for example, whose interests are more important or how opposing interests might somehow be reconciled. Similarly, this focus on value tensions leads designers to make their ethical commitments and reasoning explicit, perhaps, for example, through the method of value source analysis. Thus, in summary, as designers and engineers work back and forth between theory and method in the technical design situation, they take into account values, with a *focus on ethics and morality*.

## Looking to the Future

As we write, value sensitive design continues to develop as researchers, designers, engineers, and educators critique, apply, and extend it. Much remains to be done. In 2015 and 2016, two workshops[2] were held to

2. The first workshop, "Charting the Next Decade for Value Sensitive Design," at the Critical Alternatives 5th Decennial Aarhus Conference in Aarhus, Denmark, on August 17, 2015, was organized by Batya Friedman, David Hendry, Jeroen van den Hoven, Alina Huldtgren, Catholijn Jonker, and Aimee van Wynsberghe. Participant lists for each workshop can be found in the preface.

identify grand challenges for value sensitive design—relatively well-defined research questions that will take multi-year and multi-group efforts to address. Based on our own reflections and drawing on these workshops, we present open questions for moving forward, organized under theory, method, and practice.

Theory

• *Stakeholders.* In addition to direct and indirect stakeholders, are there other broad categories of stakeholders that would be helpful? Yoo (2018), for example, suggests the distinction between core and peripheral stakeholders may also be useful for framing the design space. Another dimension concerns very large and complex stakeholders, such as "emergent publics" (DiSalvo, Lukens, Lodato, Jenkins, & Kim, 2014; Yoo, 2018) and stakeholders that might span across multiple generations (Friedman & Nathan, 2010). How to account for these very large and complex stakeholder groups remains an open question.

• *Indirect stakeholders.* Several dimensions of the roles of indirect stakeholders remain unexplored. One dimension is the identification of common indirect stakeholder roles; for example, the "bystander" and "human data point" roles. What other recurring indirect stakeholder roles exist? What can we learn by surfacing these recurring roles, both in terms of identifying and engaging with indirect stakeholders as well as developing robust and potentially reusable design solutions?

• *Nonhuman stakeholders.* Direct and indirect stakeholders can be nonhuman. Such stakeholders might include pets or other service and domesticated animals, as well as wild animals, sacred mountain tops, historic buildings, oceans, ecosystems, the solar system, and beyond. How might such stakeholders be given standing in a design project? How are the interests of nonhuman stakeholders represented and engaged? What special considerations, if any, are needed to address value tensions among human and nonhuman stakeholders?

---

The second workshop, "Value Sensitive Design: Charting the Next Decade," held at the Lorentz Center in Leiden, The Netherlands, November 14–18, 2016, was organized by Batya Friedman, Maaike Harbers, David Hendry, Jeroen van den Hoven, and Catholijn Jonker. Participant lists for each workshop can be found in the preface.

• *Accounting for power.* Beyond the legitimation of direct and indirect stake-holders, which helps to some extent to legitimate those in less power-ful positions, value sensitive design has not explicitly addressed how to handle differences in power among respective stakeholders. Yet power dif-ferences pervade human experience—in family relations, in personalities and friendships, in villages and local communities, in institutional rela-tionships, within corporate structures, within government, and among nations. Moreover, technological solutions may instantiate, support, rebalance, or disrupt power relations. Thus, power relations cannot be ignored. How best to account for power relations within a value sensitive design framing remains an open question. What, if any, new theoretical constructs might be needed? How might existing value sensitive design methods better account for power? What could be adapted from other frameworks (e.g., participatory design)? Where might new methods be needed?

• *Conceptualizing policy.* In value sensitive design, policy is viewed as a tool or another form of technology. Accordingly, conceptual, empirical, and technical investigations will need to identify policy requirements. Still, how to develop policy within value sensitive design has not yet been fully theorized. What constructs and models will position designers to engage policy concerns? How can the design of policy be integrated with technical design? How might value sensitive design be used to develop policy? How might law, regulations, social norms, and other kinds of policy be engaged within value sensitive design?

• *Cultural responsiveness.* With some noteworthy exceptions (Alsheikh et al., 2011; Woelfer et al., 2011; Yoo et al., 2013b), value sensitive design has largely been employed with varied technologies and stakeholders in West-ern and urban contexts. Therefore, a major opportunity exists for develop-ing theory and practical approaches for applying value sensitive design to other sociocultural contexts. Some questions include: identifying, engag-ing, and respecting key cultural dimensions; and how to adapt methods aligned to communication practices and power differentials (e.g., reverence of elders). The challenges of entering and engaging any field site can be expected; it is unknown what, if anything, about value sensitive design cre-ates unique opportunities and difficulties.

Method

• *Eliciting human values.* Human beings have rich means for expressing what is important to them in their lives, including but not limited to modes that are verbal (e.g., telling stories), visual (e.g., drawing pictures), somatic (e.g., through gesture, touch, or facial expressions), and constructive (e.g., creating artifacts). A full range of value sensitive design methods would tap into this diversity of expression, with a variety of methods within each category of expression.

• *Navigating value tensions.* What is the full range of approaches for representing and engaging value tensions? Are different approaches appropriate for different kinds of value tensions? When in the design process is it productive to ask stakeholders directly about particular value tensions (e.g., using a slider or scale to indicate how the stakeholder balances among two competing values, say privacy and community)? Correspondingly, when in the design process is it productive to ask stakeholders about individual values and leave until later the synthesis of those responses (see Miller et al., 2007)? How can normative criteria and stakeholder views be considered when addressing value tensions?

• *Engaging with indirect stakeholders.* Because indirect stakeholders do not interact with a technology, per se, how to engage their views and values relative to the technology is typically not obvious. Accordingly, work is needed to develop a robust repertoire of methods to engage with indirect stakeholders that accounts for a diversity of technologies and a diversity of indirect stakeholder roles. A difficult special case is when an indirect stakeholder is a nonhuman—for example, an animal or an ecosystem.

• *Conducting policy analysis.* How might existing value sensitive design methods be used in the service of policy (see Miller et al., 2007)? Are there policy-specific methods that could and should be developed (see Magassa, Young, & Friedman, 2017; and Young, Magassa, & Friedman, in press)? If so, what do these look like? Moreover, policy affecting information and computing technologies can exist at various levels (Nathan & Friedman, 2010), from those that regulate the interface to those that govern the exchange of information that flows across national boundaries. Do different levels of policy require different types of value sensitive methods? If so, in what ways do they differ, and how can they be developed?

Practice

• *Reporting on value sensitive design projects.* Applying value sensitive design is part science, part art. When reporting on a research and design project, what should be conveyed and in how much detail? One recent step has been to include a "researcher stance" section in papers to make explicit designer worldview, personal values, and experience as appropriate (e.g., Borning & Muller, 2012; Woelfer et al., 2011); another step is to provide a reflective discussion of the rationale for employing a method (e.g., Yoo et al., 2013a). Developing common approaches and best practices for reflecting and writing about value sensitive design projects may help to advance practice.

• *Skillful practice.* How might the skills and sensibilities for applying value sensitive design be developed? In our experience, design studio techniques—pedagogically focused design activities, design critiques, reflective writing and discussion—are essential for teaching value sensitive design skills. How can pedagogical practices among designers, engineers, researchers, and students help diffuse common approaches and catalyze innovation in theory and method? Recognizing that only so much can be conveyed in writing, we envision interesting possibilities for using video and other media to advance skillful practice in value sensitive design.

• *Professional and industry appropriation.* Our tools and technologies ought to be designed responsibly, and value sensitive design has been recognized as offering a path for doing so (van den Hoven, 2013; Spiekermann, 2015). That said, while professional and industry uptake of value sensitive design has been increasing, widespread adoption and adaption has yet to be realized. How might value sensitive design be meaningfully appropriated within a professional or industry work environment, given the often shorter timeframes and balance to be struck with bottom-line economic justifications?

• *Community resources.* Related to the actionability criteria discussed above, community resources can play a key role in positioning researchers, designers, and engineers to build from each other's work. What resources are needed, and how might they be developed, disseminated, and maintained over time? Possible resources include working definitions of values, a method repository, bibliographies, and pedagogical resources.

• *Beyond information technology: Extending to other domains.* This future direction concerns the comprehensiveness criteria. While there are some exceptions (e.g., Watkins et al. [2013b] on public transportation technologies; de Kreuk et al. [2010], van de Poel et al. [2005], and Oosterlaken [2015] on civil engineering projects), the vast majority of work developing and applying value sensitive design has concerned information technologies. Accordingly, an open question is the extent to which value sensitive design can successfully be applied to other domains in, for example, energy, smart cities, transportation, government, and social services. Questions include: to what extent are the foundations of value sensitive design technology agnostic? Are new domain-specific methods needed? Can the engagement of new domains lead to theoretical extensions to value sensitive design?

### Through Practice, Progress

When value sensitive design was first conceived 20-plus years ago, a key question for the field of human-computer interaction concerned whether we could engage effectively with human values in the technical design process. Answering in the affirmative, this book shows that much progress has been made. From the onset, value sensitive design has sought to develop an approach—theory, methodology, specific methods, and practice—where human values are engaged systematically and brought into the process of technology development. Today, the questions are different. Before us are open frontiers in theory, method, and practice. Just as designers working on particular projects should aim for progress, not perfection, so, too, this commitment applies to the development of value sensitive design as a whole.

Recall, too, that value sensitive design moves us in important directions. It moves us toward the conceptualizations needed to identify shortcomings in current design processes and to seek remedies that promote human well-being. It moves us toward the language needed to discuss the often immense social consequences of our technical work with the public at large. And it moves us toward holding out human values as a design criterion—along with traditional criteria of reliability, efficiency, and correctness—by which systems may be judged poor and designers negligent.

Technology and human experience are together, with one shaping the other. In this mutual shaping, we observe that neither moves forward on its own, nor is technology value-neutral. Thus, design process matters. For researchers, designers, and engineers, at stake is nothing less than human dignity and just societies. As we strive to make progress in technical design and innovation, we need not require perfection, but commitment to practice—and through practice, progress.

# Envoi I: Visual Language for Value Sensitive Design Theory

Daisy Yoo, while a senior PhD candidate in the University of Washington Value Sensitive Design Lab working with Batya Friedman and David Hendry, developed the visual language for the theoretical constructs found in chapter 2. The idea for a visual language was inspired in part by Paul Klee's (1925) *Pedagogical Sketchbook*.

The language is comprised of three visual nouns.

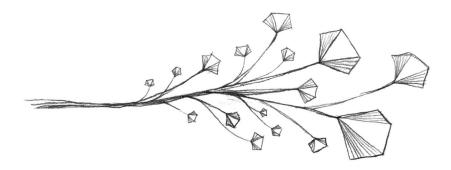

*Tools and technology.* The more linear edges and facets convey the artificial (human-made) aspects of tools and technology, as well as their assemblage and interleaving construction of infrastructure.

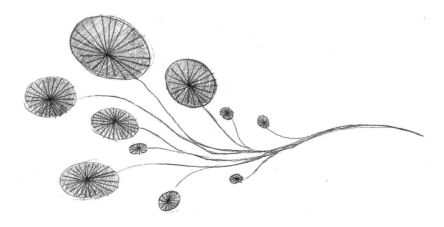

*Stakeholders.* The elliptical, more organic forms convey the living, organic dimensions of human and nonhuman stakeholders, as well as their assemblage and interleaving structure and relationships among families, communities, and societies.

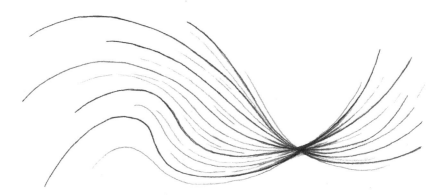

*Human values.* The threadlike forms convey the distinctness of each value of import; their nexus, how values are closely connected; and their twists and turns, how the values can change both individually and systematically.

From these three visual nouns, a generative set of compositions yields images for the six additional theoretical constructs: interactional stance; tripartite methodology; value tensions; multi-lifespan design; co-evolving technology and social structure; and progress, not perfection.

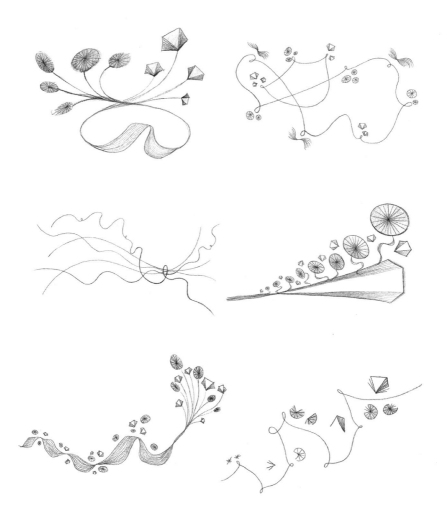

# Envoi II: Photo Poem

Cranes, stones, and pallets; hand, tool, and stone dust. As we have worked at this book, I have learned a little about carving stones from Batya's stories. There is a kinship between carving stone and value sensitive design: look for the details and the outline, look for the stopping point and the next way forward, look for the interaction between hand and tool and materials, look for process and outcome, look for the changing points of view.

—David G. Hendry

---

As with value sensitive design, stone carving is about transformation.

With stones, you cannot see or touch the stone in its entirety. From any standpoint, from every standpoint, something is occluded. Nonetheless, you need to act, to make a mark.

A light tap on the stone reverberates throughout. Doing small things can have huge impact.

The marks you make on the stone carry with them an impression of the tool and an impression of the stone carver. Tool user, tool, and artifact are inseparable.

Look carefully, patiently, before acting. Material removed from the stone cannot be put back. The response to an incomplete or misguided action is to act again, anew.

Though the outward form of the stone changes, the core elements endure.

It is possible to recognize when the carving is resolved but not to be able to speak about that resolution with words.

—Batya Friedman

---

All of the stones were carved by Batya Friedman, primarily with the hand tools shown in the first, seventh, and final photograph of the poem. The presentation of this photo poem was inspired by James Agee and Walker Evan's classic 1939 book *Let Us Now Praise Famous Men*, which opens with a series of uncaptioned black and white photographs of three tenant families in the deep South of the United States.

Photo on p. vi. Three tools: nine-point bushing hammer, brush, and
    mallet.

Photo on p. vii. *In Relation* (limestone from Texas).

Photo on p. viii. *Breath* (golden marble from British Columbia).

Photo on p. ix. Crane moving a stone (limestone fencepost from Kansas).

Photo on p. xxii. *Bicycle Seat* (travertine) and *Monolith* (limestone from
    Texas).

Photo on p. 18. *Monolith*—moon view (limestone from Texas).

Photo on p. 58. Fat point chisel.

Photo on p. 104. *Monolith*—in nature (limestone from Texas).

Photo on p. 166. *Mountain in Repose*—close up.

Photo on pp. 186–187. *Passages II*—four phases (limestone fencepost from
    Kansas).

Photo on p. 230. *Passages III* (limestone fencepost from Kansas), nine-point
    bushing hammer, and brush.

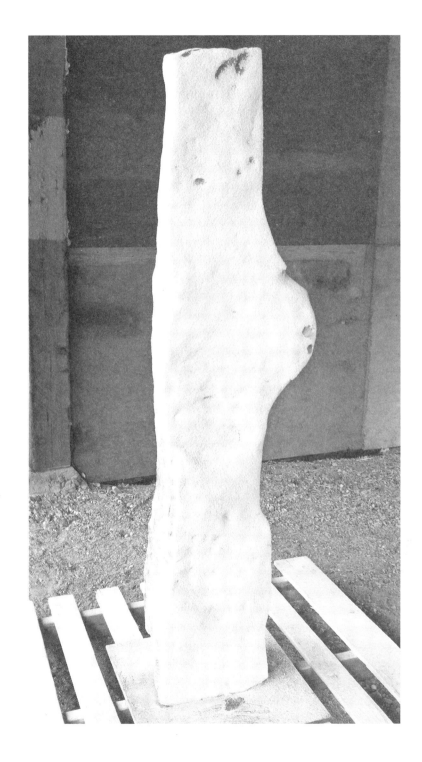

# References

Abokhodair, N., & Vieweg, S. (2016). Privacy and social media in the context of the Arab Gulf. In *Proceedings of the 2016 ACM Conference on Designing Interactive Systems* (pp. 672–683). New York, NY: ACM. doi:10.1145/2901790.2901873.

Albrechtslund, A. (2007). Ethics and technology design. *Ethics and Information Technology, 9*(1), 63–72. doi:10.1007/s10676-006-9129-8.

Alsheikh, T., Rode, J. A., & Lindley, S. E. (2011). (Whose) value-sensitive design: A study of long-distance relationships in an Arabic cultural context. In *Proceedings of the 2011 ACM Conference on Computer Supported Cooperative Work* (pp. 75–84). New York, NY: ACM. doi:10.1145/1958824.1958836.

Arendt, H. (1958/1998). *The Human Condition.* Chicago, IL: The University of Chicago Press.

Arkin, R. C. (2008). Governing lethal behavior: Embedding ethics in a hybrid deliberative/reactive robot architecture. Part I: Motivation and philosophy. In *Proceedings of the 2008 3rd ACM/IEEE International Conference on Human-Robot Interaction* (pp. 121–128). New York, NY: ACM.

Attewell, P. (1987). The deskilling controversy. *Work and Occupations: An International Sociological Journal, 14*(3), 323–346.

Azenkot, S., Prasain, S., Borning, A., Fortuna, E., Ladner, R. E., & Wobbrock, J. O. (2011). Enhancing independence and safety for blind and deaf-blind public transit riders. In *Proceedings of the SIGCHI Conference on Human Factors in Computing Systems* (pp. 3247–3256). New York, NY: ACM. doi:10.1145/1978942.1979424.

Baier, A. (1986). Trust and antitrust. *Ethics, 96*(2), 231–260.

Bannon, L. (2011). Reimagining HCI: Toward a more human-centered perspective. *Interactions, 18*(4), 50–57. doi:10.1145/1978822.1978833.

Bardzell, S. (2010). Feminist HCI: Taking stock and outlining an agenda for design. In *Proceedings of the SIGCHI Conference on Human Factors in Computing Systems* (pp. 1301–1310). New York, NY: ACM. doi:10.1145/1753326.1753521.

Bardzell, J., Bardzell, S., & Stolterman, E. (2014). Reading critical designs: Supporting reasoned interpretations of critical design. In *Proceedings of the SIGCHI Conference on Human Factors in Computing Systems* (pp. 1951–1960). New York, NY: ACM. doi:10.1145/2556288.2557137.

Barry, P. J., Ensign, J., & Lippek, S. H. (2002). Embracing street culture: Fitting health care into the lives of street youth. *Journal of Transcultural Nursing, 13*(2), 145–152. doi:10.1177/104365960201300208.

Bar-Tal, D. (1976). *Prosocial Behavior: Theory and Research*. Washington, DC: Hemisphere Publishing Corp.

Belman, J., Nissenbaum, H., Flanagan, M., & Diamond, J. (2011). Grow-A-Game: A tool for values conscious design and analysis of digital games. In *Proceedings of DiGRA 2011 Conference: Think Design Play* (pp. 14–17). Digital Games Research Association and Utrecht School of the Arts, Utrecht, The Netherlands.

Bender, E. M., & Friedman, B. (2018). Data statements for Natural Language Processing: Toward mitigating system bias and enabling better science. *Transactions of the Association for Computational Linguistics*.

Berdichevsky, D., & Neuenschwander, E. (1999). Toward an ethics of persuasive technology. *Communications of the ACM, 42*(5), 51–58. doi:10.1145/301353.301410.

Beveridge, C. E. (2002). Olmstead: His essential theory. *Nineteenth Century, 20*(2), 32–37.

Binder, T., De Michelis, G., Ehn, P., Jacucci, G., Linde, P., & Wagner, I. (2011). *Design Things*. Cambridge, MA: MIT Press.

Bjerknes, G., & Bratteteig, T. (1995). User participation and democracy: A discussion of Scandinavian research on system development. *Scandinavian Journal of Information Systems, 7*(1), 73–97.

Blevis, E. (2007). Sustainable interaction design: Invention & disposal, renewal & reuse. In *Proceedings of the SIGCHI Conference on Human Factors in Computing Systems* (pp. 503–512). New York, NY: ACM. doi:10.1145/1240624.1240705

Blythe, M., Wright, P., Bowers, J., Boucher, A., Jarvis, N., Reynolds, P., Gaver, B. (2010). Age and experience: Ludic engagement in a residential care setting. In *Proceedings of the 8th ACM Conference on Designing Interactive Systems* (pp. 161–170). New York, NY: ACM. doi:10.1145/1858171.1858200

Bødker, S. (1990). *Through the Interface: A Human Activity Approach to User Interface Design*. Hillsdale, NJ: Lawrence Erlbaum.

Bødker, S., Ehn, P., Sjögren, D., & Sundblad, Y. (2000). Co-operative design— Perspectives on 20 years with "the Scandinavian IT design model." In *Proceedings of NordiCHI* (pp. 1–9). Stockholm, Sweden: Royal Institute of Technology.

Bødker, K., Kensing, F., & Simonsen, J. (2004). *Participatory IT Design: Designing for Business and Workplace Realities*. Cambridge, MA: MIT Press.

Bonnar, C., Campbell, M., Drapeau, R., Bennett, C., & Borning, A. (2015). Contributing during the commute: Why transit riders submit information about bus stops with StopInfo (No. UW-CSE-15-09-04). Seattle, WA: Dept. of Computer Science & Engineering, University of Washington. https://www.cs.washington.edu/public _files/grad/tech_reports/main-tech-report.pdf.

Borning, A., Friedman, B., Davis, J., & Lin, P. (2005). Informing public deliberation: Value sensitive design of indicators for a large-scale urban simulation. In H. Gellersen, K. Schmidt, M. Beaudouin-Lafon, & W. Mackay (Eds.), *ECSCW 2005* (pp. 449–468). Dordrecht: Springer. http://doi.org/ 10.1007/1-4020-4023-7_23.

Borning, A., & Muller, M. (2012). Next steps for value sensitive design. In *Proceedings of the SIGCHI Conference on Human Factors in Computing Systems* (pp. 1125–1134). New York, NY: ACM. doi:10.1145/2207676.2208560.

Borning, A., Waddell, P., & Förster, R. (2008). UrbanSim: Using simulation to inform public deliberation and decision making. In H. Chen, L. Brandt, V. Gregg, R. Traunmüller, S. Dawes, E. Hovy, … C. A. Larson (Eds.), *Digital Government: E-Government Research, Case Studies, and Implementation* (pp. 439–464). Boston: Springer. doi:10.1007/ 978-0-387-71611-4_22.

Brand, S. (1999). *The Clock of the Long Now: Time and Responsibility*. New York, NY: Basic Books.

BrickHouse Security. (n.d.). GPS tracking device for kids. http://www.brickhousesecurity .com/gps-trackers/child-tracking.

Brodie, M., Lai, J., Lenchner, J., Luken, W., Ranganathan, K., Tang, J.-M., & Vukovic, M. (2007). Support services: Persuading employees and customers to do what is in the community's best interest. In Y. de Kort, W. IJsselsteijn, C. Midden, B. Eggen, & B. J. Fogg (Eds.), *Persuasive Technology: Proceedings of the Second International Conference* (pp. 121–124). Berlin: Springer. doi:10.1007/978-3-540-77006-0_16.

Brynjarsdottir, H. Håkansson, M., Pierce, J., Baumer, E., DiSalvo, C., & Sengers, P. (2012). Sustainably unpersuaded: How persuasion narrows our vision of sustainability. In *Proceedings of the SIGCHI Conference on Human Factors in Computing Systems* (pp. 947–956). New York, NY: ACM. doi:10.1145/2207676.2208539.

Burke, P. J. (2006). Identity change. *Social Psychology Quarterly*, *69*(1), 81–96. doi:10.1177/019027250606900106.

Burmeister, O. K. (2013). Achieving the goal of a global computing code of ethics through an international-localisation hybrid. *The International Journal of Communication Ethics*, *10*(4), 25–32.

Burmeister, O. K. (2016). The development of assistive dementia technology that accounts for the values of those affected by its use. *Ethics and Information Technology, 18*(3), 185–198.

Bynum, T. W. (1985). Editor's introduction. *Metaphilosophy, 16*(4), 263–265.

Calvo, R. A., & Peters, D. (2014). *Positive Computing: Technology for Wellbeing and Human Potential.* Cambridge, MA: MIT Press.

Camara, F., & Calvary, G. (2015). Worth-centered design in practice: Lessons from experience and research agenda. In J. Abascal, S. Barbosa, M. Fetter, T. Gross, P. Palanque, and M. Winckler (Eds.), *Human-Computer Interaction—INTERACT 2015. Lecture Notes in Computer Science, 9299* (pp. 123–139). Dordrecht: Springer.

Cantoni, L., Botturi, L., Faré, M., & Bolchini, D. (2009). Playful holistic support to HCI requirements using LEGO bricks. In *Proceedings of the First International Conference on Human Centered Design* (pp. 844–853). Dordrecht: Springer.

Carroll, J. M. (1999). Five reasons for scenario-based design. In *Proceedings of the 32nd Annual Hawaii International Conference on Systems Sciences.* doi:10.1109/HICSS.1999.772890.

Carroll, J. M. (2000). *Making Use: Scenario-Based Design of Human-Computer Interactions.* Cambridge, MA: MIT Press.

Cherukuri, S., Venkatasubramanian, K., & Gupta, S. K. S. (2003). BioSec: A biometric based approach for securing communication in wireless networks of biosensors implanted in the human body. In *Proceedings of the 2003 International Conference on Parallel Processing Workshops* (pp. 432–439). doi:10.1109/ICPPW.2003.1240399.

Cialdini, R. B. (2001). *Influence: Science and Practice* (4th ed.). Boston, MA: Allyn and Bacon.

Clough, P., & Corbett, J. (2000). *Theories of Inclusive Education: A Student's Guide.* London: Chapman.

Cockton, G. (2004). Value-centred HCI. In *Proceedings of the Third Nordic Conference on Human-computer Interaction* (pp. 149–160). New York, NY: ACM. doi:10.1145/1028014.1028038

Cockton, G. (2005). A development framework for value-centred design. In *CHI '05 Extended Abstracts on Human Factors in Computing Systems* (pp. 1292–1295). New York, NY: ACM. doi:10.1145/1056808.1056899.

Cockton, G. (2006). Designing worth is worth designing. In *Proceedings of the 4th Nordic Conference on Human-computer Interaction: Changing Roles* (pp. 165–174). New York, NY: ACM. doi:10.1145/1182475.1182493.

Consolvo, S., McDonald, D. W., & Landay, J. A. (2009). Theory-driven design strategies for technologies that support behavior change in everyday life. In *Proceedings of the SIGCHI Conference on Human Factors in Computing Systems* (pp. 405–414). New York, NY: ACM. doi:10.1145/1518701.1518766.

Cranor, L. F. (2000). Agents of choice: Tools that facilitate notice and choice about web site data practices. *Proceedings of the 21st International Conference on Privacy and Personal Data Protection* (pp. 19–25). Hong Kong, China. http://arxiv.org/abs/cs .CY/0001011.

Crawford, K., & Calo, R. (2016). There is a blind spot in AI research. *Nature, 538*(7625), 311–313.

Crilly, N., Blackwell, A. F., & Clarkson, P. J. (2006). Graphic elicitation: Using research diagrams as interview stimuli. *Qualitative Research, 6*(3), 341–366. doi:10.1177/ 1468794106065007.

Cummings, M. L. (2006). Integrating ethics in design through the value-sensitive design approach. *Science and Engineering Ethics, 12*(4), 701–715. doi:10.1007/ s11948-006-0065-0.

Czeskis, A., Dermendjieva, I., Yapit, H., Borning, A., Friedman, B., Gill, B., & Kohno, T. (2010). Parenting from the pocket: Value tensions and technical directions for secure and private parent-teen mobile safety. In *Proceedings of the Sixth Symposium on Usable Privacy and Security* (pp. 15:1–15:15). New York, NY: ACM. doi:10.1145/1837110 .1837130.

Davis, J. (2006). Value sensitive design of interactions with UrbanSim indicators (Doctoral dissertation). University of Washington, Seattle, WA.

Davis, J. (2008). Engaging and informing citizens with household indicators. In *Proceedings of the 41st Annual Hawaii International Conference on System Sciences.* doi:10.1109/HICSS.2008.145.

Davis, J. (2009). Design methods for ethical persuasive computing. In *Persuasive Technology: Proceedings of the Fourth International Conference* (p. 6:1–6:8). New York, NY: ACM. doi:10.1145/1541948.1541957.

Davis, J. (2011). From ethics to values in the design of mobile PINC. In *Proceedings of the Second International Workshop on Persuasion, Influence, Nudge and Coercion Through Mobile Devices 2011* (Vol. 722, pp. 27–30).

Davis, J., Lin, P., Borning, A., Friedman, B., Kahn, P. H., Jr., & Waddell, P. A. (2006). Simulations for urban planning: Designing for human values. *Computer, 39*(9), 66–72. doi:10.1109/MC.2006.324.

Davis, J., & Nathan, L. P. (2014). Value sensitive design: Applications, adaptations, and critiques. In J. van den Hoven, P. E. Vermaas, & I. van de Poel (Eds.), *Handbook of Ethics, Values, and Technological Design* (pp. 1–26). Dordrecht: Springer. doi:10.1007/978-94-007-6994-6_3-1.

De Kreuk, M., van de Poel, I., Zwart, S. D., & van Loosdrecht, M. C. M. (2010). Ethics in innovation: Cooperation and tension. In I. van de Poel & D. Goldberg (Eds.), *Philosophy and Engineering: An Emerging Agenda* (pp. 215–226). Dordrecht: Springer. doi:10.1007/978-90-481-2804-4_18.

Deibel, K. N. (2011). Understanding and supporting the adoption of assistive technologies by adults with reading disabilities (Doctoral dissertation). University of Washington, Seattle, WA. http://hdl.handle.net/1773/16349.

DeLoache, J. S., & Marzolf, D. P. (1995). The use of dolls to interview young children: Issues of symbolic representation. *Journal of Experimental Child Psychology*, *60*(1), 155–173.

Deng, X., Joshi, K. D., & Galliers, R. D. (2016). The duality of empowerment and marginalization in microtask crowdsourcing: Giving voice to the less powerful through value sensitive design. *MIS Quarterly*, *40*(2), 279–302.

Denning, T., Borning, A., Friedman, B., Gill, B. T., Kohno, T., & Maisel, W. H. (2010). Patients, pacemakers, and implantable defibrillators: Human values and security for wireless implantable medical devices. In *Proceedings of the SIGCHI Conference on Human Factors in Computing Systems* (pp. 917–926). New York, NY: ACM. doi:10.1145/1753326.1753462.

Denning, T., Friedman, B., Gill, B., Kramer, D. B., Reynolds, M. R., and Kohno, T. (2014). CPS: Beyond usability: Applying value sensitive design based methods to investigate domain characteristics for security for implantable cardiac devices. *Annual Computer Security Applications Conference (ACSAC)* (pp. 426–435). New York, NY: ACM.

Denning, T., Fu, K., & Kohno, T. (2008). Absence makes the heart grow fonder: New directions for implantable medical device security. In *Proceedings of the Third USENIX Workshop on Hot Topics in Security (HotSec)*. https://www.usenix.org/event/hotsec08/tech/full_papers/denning/denning_html.

DiSalvo, C. (2012). *Adversarial Design*. Cambridge, MA: MIT Press.

DiSalvo, C., Lukens, J., Lodato, T., Jenkins, T., & Kim, T. (2014). Making public things: How HCI design can express matters of concern. In *Proceedings of the SIGCHI Conference on Human Factors in Computing Systems* (pp. 2397–2406). New York, NY: ACM.

Doorn, N. (2011). Moral responsibility in R&D networks: A procedural approach to distributing responsibilities (Doctoral dissertation). Delft University of Technology, Delft, The Netherlands. http://repository.tudelft.nl/view/ir/uuid:6d7338a1-87ef-4cd1-94b3-47dcdd47ec16.

Doorn, N. (2012). Exploring responsibility rationales in research and development (R&D). *Science, Technology & Human Values*, *37*(3), 180–209. doi:10.1177/0162243911405344.

Doorn, N., Schuurbiers, D., van de Poel, I., & Gorman, M. E. (2013). *Early Engagement and New Technologies: Opening up the Laboratory*. Dordrecht: Springer.

Dörr, K. N., & Hollnbuchner, K. (2017). Ethical challenges of algorithmic journalism. *Digital Journalism, 5*(4), 404–419. https://dx.doi.org/ 10.1080/21670811.2016 .1167612.

Dreyfus, H. L. (1972). *What Computers Can't Do: The Limits of Artificial Intelligence*. New York, NY: Harper & Row.

Dunne, A. (2005). *Hertzian Tales: Electronic Products, Aesthetic Experience, and Critical Design*. Cambridge, MA: MIT Press.

Dunne, A., & Raby, F. (2001). *Design Noir: The Secret Life of Electronic Objects*. London: August.

Edwards, J. (1994). *The Scars of Dyslexia: Eight Case Studies in Emotional Reactions*. London: Cassell.

Ehn, P. (1988). *Work-Oriented Design of Computer Artifacts*. Stockholm: Almqvist & Wiksell International.

Ehn, P. (2008). Participation in design things. In *Proceedings of the Tenth Anniversary Conference on Participatory Design 2008* (pp. 92–101). Indianapolis, IN: Indiana University. http://dl.acm.org/citation.cfm?id=1795234.1795248.

Eisenberg, N., Fabes, R. A., & Spinrad, T. L. (2007). Prosocial development. In *Handbook of Child Psychology*. Hoboken, NJ: Wiley. http://dx.doi.org/ 10.1002/ 9780470147658.chpsy0311.

Elkind, J., Black, M. S., & Murray, C. (1996). Computer-based compensation of adult reading disabilities. *Annals of Dyslexia, 46*(1), 159–186. doi:10.1007/BF02648175.

European Commission. (2012). *Ethical and Regulatory Challenges to Science and Research Policy at the Global Level*. Luxembourg: Publications Office of the European Union. 10.2777/35203.

Felzmann, H., Beyan, T., Ryan, M., & Beyan, O. (2016). Implementing an ethical approach to big data analytics in assistive robotics for elderly with dementia. *ACM SIGCAS Computers and Society, 45*(3), 280–286. doi:10.1145/2874239.2874279.

Ferrario, M. A., Simm, W., Forshaw, S., Gradinar, A., Smith, M. T., & Smith, I. (2016). Values-first SE: Research principles in practice. In *Proceedings of the 38th International Conference on Software Engineering Companion* (pp. 553–562). New York, NY: ACM. doi:10.1145/2889160.2889219.

Ferris, B., Watkins, K., & Borning, A. (2010). OneBusAway: Results from providing real-time arrival information for public transit. In *Proceedings of the SIGCHI Conference on Human Factors in Computing Systems* (pp. 1807–1816). New York, NY: ACM. doi:10.1145/1753326.1753597.

Fischer, G. (2018). Exploring design trade-offs for quality of life in human-centered design. *Interactions*, *25*(1), 26–33. doi:10.1145/3170706.

Fitzpatrick, G., Huldtgren, A., Malmborg, L., Harley, D., & Ijsselsteijn, W. (2015). Design for agency, adaptivity and reciprocity: Reimagining AAL and telecare agendas. In V. Wulf, K. Schmidt, and D. Randall (Eds.), *Designing Socially Embedded Technologies in the Real-World* (pp. 305–338). London: Springer London. doi:10.1007/978-1-4471-6720-4_13.

Flanagan, M., Howe, D. C., & Nissenbaum, H. (2005). Values at play: Design tradeoffs in socially-oriented game design. In *Proceedings of the SIGCHI Conference on Human Factors in Computing Systems* (pp. 751–760). New York, NY: ACM. doi:10.1145/1054972.1055076.

Flanagan, M., Howe, D. C., & Nissenbaum, H. (2008). Embodying values in technology: Theory and practice. In J. van den Hoven & J. Weckert (Eds.), *Information Technology and Moral Philosophy* (pp. 322–353). Cambridge, UK: Cambridge University Press.

Floyd, C., Mehl, W.-M., Reisin, F.-M., Schmidt, G., & Wolf, G. (1989). Out of Scandinavia: Alternative approaches to software design and system development. *Human-Computer Interaction*, *4*(4), 253–350. doi:10.1207/s15327051hci0404_1.

Fogg, B. J. (2003). *Persuasive Technology: Using Computers to Change What We Think and Do*. Boston, MA: Morgan Kaufmann.

Fogg, B. J. (2006). Protecting consumers in the next tech-ade. Washington, DC: George Washington University. https://www.ftc.gov/sites/default/files/documents/public_events/protecting-consumers-next-tech-ade/transcript_061107.pdf.

Frankena, W. (1972). Value and valuation. In P. Edwards (Ed.), *The Encyclopedia of Philosophy* (Vol. 7–8, pp. 409–410). New York, NY: Macmillan.

Freeman, R. E. (1984). *Strategic Management: A Stakeholder Approach*. Boston, MA: Pitman.

Freeman-Benson, B., & Borning, A. (2003). YP and urban simulation: Applying an agile programming methodology in a politically tempestuous domain. In *Proceedings of the Agile Development Conference, 2003* (pp. 2–11). doi:10.1109/ADC.2003.1231447.

Freier, N. G. (2008). Children attribute moral standing to a personified agent. In *Proceedings of the SIGCHI Conference on Human Factors in Computing Systems* (pp. 343–352). New York, NY: ACM. doi:10.1145/1357054.1357113.

Freier, N., Billard, A., Ishiguro, H., & Nourbakhsh, I. (2010). Panel 2: Social responsibility in human-robot interaction. In *Proceedings of the 5th ACM/IEEE International Conference on Human-Robot Interaction* (p. 11). Piscataway, NJ: IEEE Press. http://dl.acm.org/citation.cfm?id=1734454.1734464.

Fried, C. (1968). Privacy. *Yale Law Journal, 77*(3), 475–493.

Friedman, B. (1996). Value-sensitive design. *Interactions, 3*(6), 16–23. doi:10.1145/242485.242493.

Friedman, B. (Ed.). (1997). *Human Values and the Design of Computer Technology.* Stanford, CA: CSLI Publications.

Friedman, B. (2004). Value sensitive design. In W. S. Bainbridge (Ed.), *Encyclopedia of Human-Computer Interaction* (pp. 769–774). Great Barrington, MA: Berkshire Publishing Group.

Friedman, B. (2013). *The Shape of Being: Technology Design, Human Values and the Future.* University Faculty Lecture, University of Washington, Seattle, WA, February 7, 2013.

Friedman, B., Borning, A., Davis, J. L., Gill, B. T., Kahn, P. H., Jr., Kriplean, T., & Lin, P. (2008a). Laying the foundations for public participation and value advocacy: Interaction design for a large scale urban simulation. In *Proceedings of the 2008 International Conference on Digital Government Research* (pp. 305–314). Montreal, Canada: Digital Government Society of North America.

Friedman, B., Felten, E., Grudin, J., Nissenbaum, H., & Winograd, T. (1999). Value-sensitive design: A research agenda for information technology. Unpublished report on the May 20–21, 1999, Value-Sensitive Design Workshop.

Friedman, B., Felten, E., & Millett, L. I. (2000a). Informed consent online: A conceptual model and design principles (CSE Technical Report No. 00-12-02). Seattle, WA: University of Washington, Department of Computer Science and Engineering.

Friedman, B., Freier, N. G., Kahn, P. H., Jr., Lin, P., and Sodeman, R. (2008b). Office window of the future?—Field-based analyses of a new use of a large display. *International Journal of Human-Computer Studies, 66*(6), 452–465.

Friedman, B., Harbers, M., Hendry, D. G., van den Hoven, J., & Jonker, C. M. (2016). Value sensitive design: Charting the next decade. Workshop organized for the Lorentz Center, November 14–18, 2016. Leiden, The Netherlands.

Friedman, B., & Hendry, D. (2012). The Envisioning Cards: A toolkit for catalyzing humanistic and technical imaginations. In *Proceedings of the SIGCHI Conference on Human Factors in Computing Systems* (pp. 1145–1148). New York, NY: ACM. doi:10.1145/2207676.2208562.

Friedman, B., Hendry, D. G., & Borning, A. (2017). A survey of value sensitive design methods. *Foundations and Trends in Human-Computer Interaction, 11* (23), 63–125. http://dx.doi.org/ 10.1561/1100000015.

Friedman, B., Hendry, D. G., van den Hoven, J., Huldtgren, A., Jonker, C., & van Wynsberghe, A. (2015). Charting the next decade for value sensitive design [Workshop]. Workshop organized for the Fifth Decennial Aarhus Conference on Critical Alternatives, August 17–21, Aarhus, Denmark.

Friedman, B., Hook, K., Gill, B., Eidmar, L., Prien, C. S., & Severson, R. (2008c). Personlig integritet: A comparative study of perceptions of privacy in public places in Sweden and the United States. In *Proceedings of the 5th Nordic Conference on Human-computer Interaction: Building Bridges* (pp. 142–151). New York, NY: ACM. doi:10.1145/1463160.1463176.

Friedman, B., Howe, D. C., & Felten, E. (2002a). Informed consent in the Mozilla browser: implementing value-sensitive design. In *Proceedings of the 35th Annual Hawaii International Conference on System Sciences, 2002*. doi:10.1109/HICSS.2002.994366.

Friedman, B., Hurley, D., Howe, D. C., Felten, E., & Nissenbaum, H. (2002b). Users' conceptions of web security: A comparative study. In *CHI '02 Extended Abstracts on Human Factors in Computing Systems* (pp. 746–747). New York, NY: ACM. 10.1145/506443.506577.

Friedman, B., & Kahn, P. H., Jr. (1992). Human agency and responsible computing: Implications for computer system design. *Journal of Systems and Software, 17*(1), 7–14. doi:10.1016/0164-1212(92)90075-U.

Friedman, B., & Kahn, P. H., Jr. (2003). Human values, ethics, and design. In J. A. Jacko & A. Sears (Eds.), *The Human-Computer Interaction Handbook: Fundamentals, Evolving Technologies, and Emerging Applications* (pp. 1177–1201). (Rev. ed. 2008). Mahwah, NJ: Lawrence Erlbaum.

Friedman, B., Kahn, P. H., Jr., & Hagman, J. (2003). Hardware companions?—What online AIBO discussion forums reveal about the human-robotic relationship. In *Proceedings of SIGCHI Conference on Human Factors in Computing Systems* (pp. 273–280). New York, NY: ACM. doi:10.1145/642611.642660.

Friedman, B., Kahn, P. H., Jr., & Borning, A. (2006a). Value sensitive design and information systems. In P. Zhang & D. Galletta (Eds.), *Human-Computer Interaction in Management Information Systems: Foundations* (pp. 348–372). Armonk, NY: M. E. Sharpe.

Friedman, B., Kahn, P. H., Jr., Hagman, J., & Severson, R. L. (2005a). Coding manual for "The watcher and the watched: Social judgments about privacy in a public place" (Technical Report No. IS-TR-2005-07-01). Seattle, WA: Information School, University of Washington. https://digital.lib.washington.edu/researchworks/handle/1773/2074.

Friedman, B., Kahn, P. H., Jr., Hagman, J., Severson, R. L., & Gill, B. (2006b). The watcher and the watched: Social judgments about privacy in a public place. *Human-Computer Interaction, 21*(2), 235–272. doi:10.1207/s15327051hci2102_3.

Friedman, B., Kahn, P. H., Jr., & Howe, D. C. (2000b). Trust online. *Communications of the ACM, 43*(12), 34–40. doi:10.1145/355112.355120.

Friedman, B., Lin, P., & Miller, J. K. (2005b). Informed consent by design. In L. F. Cranor & S. Garfinkel (Eds.), *Security and Usability: Designing Secure Systems That People Can Use* (pp. 495–521). Sebastopol, CA: O'Reilly.

Friedman, B., Nathan, L., Kane, S., & Lin, J. (2011). Envisioning Cards. Seattle, WA: University of Washington. http://www.envisioningcards.com.

Friedman, B., & Nathan, L. P. (2010). Multi-lifespan information system design: A research initiative for the HCI community. In *Proceedings of the SIGCHI Conference on Human Factors in Computing Systems* (pp. 2243–2246). New York, NY: ACM. doi:10.1145/1753326.1753665.

Friedman, B., Nathan, L. P., & Yoo, D. (2017). Multi-lifespan information system design in support of transitional justice: Evolving situated design principles for the long(er) term. *Interacting with Computers, 29*(1), 80. doi:10.1093/iwc/iwv045.

Friedman, B., & Nissenbaum, H. (1996). Bias in computer systems. *ACM Transactions on Information Systems, 14*(3), 330–347. doi:10.1145/230538.230561.

Friedman, B., & Nissenbaum, H. (1997). Software agents and user autonomy. In *Proceedings of the First International Conference on Autonomous Agents* (pp. 466–469). New York, NY: ACM. doi:10.1145/267658.267772.

Friedman, B., Smith, I., Kahn, P. H., Jr., Consolvo, S., & Selawski, J. (2006c). Development of a privacy addendum for open source licenses: Value sensitive design in industry. In P. Dourish & A. Friday (Eds.), *UbiComp 2006: Ubiquitous Computing* (pp. 194–211). Berlin: Springer. 10.1007/11853565_12.

Friedman, B., & Yoo, D. (2017). Pause: A multi-lifespan design mechanism. In *Proceedings of the SIGCHI Conference on Human Factors in Computing Systems* (pp. 460–464). New York, NY: ACM. doi:10.1145/3025453.3026031.

Froehlich, J., Dillahunt, T., Klasnja, P., Mankoff, J., Consolvo, S., Harrison, B., & Landay, J. A. (2009). UbiGreen: Investigating a mobile tool for tracking and supporting green transportation habits. In *Proceedings of the SIGCHI Conference on Human Factors in Computing Systems* (pp. 1043–1052). New York, NY: ACM. doi:10.1145/1518701.1518861.

Fuchs, L. (1999). AREA: A cross-application notification service for groupware. In S. Bødker, M. Kyng, & K. Schmidt (Eds.), *ECSCW '99* (pp. 61–80). Dordrecht: Springer. 10.1007/978-94-011-4441-4_4.

Gabrielli, S., & Maimone, R. (2013). Digital interventions for sustainable urban mobility: A pilot study. In *Proceedings of the 2013 ACM Conference on Pervasive and Ubiquitous Computing Adjunct Publication* (pp. 119–122). New York, NY: ACM. doi:10.1145/2494091.2494127.

Galegher, J. R., Kraut, R. E., & Egido, C. (Eds.). (1990). *Intellectual Teamwork: Social and Technological Foundations of Cooperative Work*. Hillsdale, NJ: Lawrence Erlbaum.

Gaw, S., Felten, E. W., & Fernandez-Kelly, P. (2006). Secrecy, flagging, and paranoia: Adoption criteria in encrypted email. In *Proceedings of the SIGCHI Conference on Human Factors in Computing Systems* (pp. 591–600). New York, NY: ACM. doi:10.1145/1124772.1124862.

Gollakota, S., Hassanieh, H., Ransford, B., Katabi, D., & Fu, K. (2011). They can hear your heartbeats: Non-invasive security for implantable medical devices. *Computer Communication Review*, 41(4), 2–13. doi:10.1145/2043164.2018438.

Goodrich, M. A., & Schultz, A. C. (2007). Human-robot interaction: A survey. *Foundations and Trends in Human-Computer Interaction*, 1(3), 203–275. doi:10.1561/1100000005.

Greenbaum, J. M., & Kyng, M. (Eds.). (1991). *Design at Work: Cooperative Design of Computer Systems*. Hillsdale, NJ: Lawrence Erlbaum.

Greif, I. (Ed.). (1988). *Computer-Supported Cooperative Work: A Book of Readings*. San Mateo, CA: Morgan Kaufmann.

Grudin, J. (1988). Why CSCW applications fail: Problems in the design and evaluation of organizational interfaces. In *Proceedings of the 1988 ACM Conference on Computer-supported Cooperative Work* (pp. 85–93). New York, NY: ACM. doi:10.1145/62266.62273.

Grünloh, C. (2018). Harmful or empowering? Stakeholders' expectations and experiences of patient accessible electronic health records (Doctoral thesis). KTH Royal Institute of Technology, Stockholm, Sweden.

Grunwald, A. (2009). Technology assessment: Concepts and methods. In A. Meijers (Ed.), *Philosophy of Technology and Engineering Sciences* (Vol. 9, pp. 1103–1146). Amsterdam: North Holland.

Gupta, S. K. S., Mukherjee, T., & Venkatasubramanian, K. (2006). Criticality aware access control model for pervasive applications. In *Proceedings of the Fourth Annual IEEE International Conference on Pervasive Computing and Communications (PERCOM), 2006*. doi:10.1109/PERCOM.2006.19.

Guzmán, M. (2015). Real Change 2.0: Seattle street paper goes digital with apps and mobile payments. *GeekWire*. https://www.geekwire.com/2015/real-change-2-0-seattle-street-paper-goes-digital-with-app-and-mobile-payments.

Halperin, D., Heydt-Benjamin, T. S., Ransford, B., Clark, S. S., Defend, B., Morgan, W., ... Maisel, W. H. (2008). Pacemakers and implantable cardiac defibrillators: Software radio attacks and zero-power defenses. In *Proceedings of the IEEE Symposium on Security and Privacy, 2008* (pp. 129–142). doi:10.1109/SP.2008.31.

Halperin, D., Kohno, T., Heydt-Benjamin, T. S., Fu, K., & Maisel, W. H. (2008). Security and privacy for implantable medical devices. *IEEE Pervasive Computing, 7*(1), 30–39. doi:10.1109/MPRV.2008.16.

Harbers, M., Detweiler, C., & Neerincx, M. A. (2015). Embedding stakeholder values in the requirements engineering process. In S. A. Fricker & K. Schneider (Eds.), *Requirements Engineering: Foundation for Software Quality: 21st International Working Conference, REFSQ 2015, Essen, Germany* (pp. 318–332). Cham: Springer International Publishing. doi:10.1007/978-3-319-16101-3_23.

Harbers, M., & Neerincx, M. A. (2017). Value sensitive design of a virtual assistant for workload harmonization in teams. *Cognition, Technology & Work, 19*(2–3), 329–343.

Harper, R., Rodden, T., Rogers, Y., & Sellen, A. (2008). Being human: Human-computer interaction in the year 2020. Cambridge, UK: Microsoft Research. http://research.microsoft.com/en-us/um/cambridge/projects/hci2020.

Hart, B. L., Hart, L. A., McCoy, M., & Sarath, C. R. (2001). Cognitive behaviour in Asian elephants: Use and modification of branches for fly switching. *Animal Behaviour, 62*(5), 839–884.

Hendry, D. G., Woelfer, J. P., Harper, R., Bauer, T., Fitzer, B., & Champagne, M. (2011). How to integrate digital media into a drop-in for homeless young people for deepening relationships between youth and adults. *Children and Youth Services Review, 33*(5), 774–782. doi:10.1016/j.childyouth.2010.11.024.

Himma, K. E., & Tavani, H. T. (2008). *The Handbook of Information and Computer Ethics.* Hoboken, NJ: Wiley.

Hirsch, E. A. (2008). Contestational design: Innovation for political activism (Doctoral dissertation). Massachusetts Institute of Technology, Cambridge, MA.

Hirsch, T. (2016). Surreptitious communication design. *Design Issues, 32*(2), 64–77. doi:10.1162/DESI_a_00383.

Holt, R., & Barnes, C. (2010). Towards an integrated approach to "Design for X": An agenda for decision-based DFX research. *Research in Engineering Design, 21*(2), 123–136. doi:10.1007/s00163-009-0081-6.

Huldtgren, A. (2015). Design for values in ICT: Information and communication technologies. In J. van den Hoven, P. E. Vermaas, & I. van de Poel (Eds.), *Handbook of Ethics, Values, and Technological Design* (pp. 739–767). Dordrecht: Springer. 10.1007/978-94-007-6970-0_35.

Huldtgren, A., Wiggers, P., & Jonker, C. M. (2014). Designing for self-reflection on values for improved life decision. *Interacting with Computers, 26*(1), 27–45. doi:10.1093/iwc/iwt025.

Iacono, S., & Kling, R. (1987). Changing office technologies and the transformation of clerical jobs. In R. E. Kraut (Ed.), *Technology and the Transformation of White-Collar Work* (pp. 53–75). Hillsdale, NJ: Lawrence Erlbaum.

IEEE Standards Association. (2016). P7000—Model process for addressing ethical concerns during system design. http://standards.ieee.org/develop/project/7000.html.

Irani, L., Vertesi, J., Dourish, P., Philip, K., & Grinter, R. E. (2010). Postcolonial computing: A lens on design and development. In *Proceedings of the SIGCHI Conference on Human Factors in Computing Systems* (pp. 1311–1320). New York, NY: ACM. doi:10.1145/1753326.1753522.

JafariNaimi, N., Nathan, L., & Hargraves, I. (2015). Values as hypotheses: Design, inquiry, and the service of values. *Design Issues, 31*(4), 91–104. doi:10.1162/DESI _a_00354.

Johnson, D. G. (1985). *Computer Ethics* (1st ed.). Englewood Cliffs, NJ: Prentice-Hall.

Johnson, D. G., & Mulvey, J. M. (1995). Accountability and computer decision systems. *Communications of the ACM, 38*(12), 58–64. doi:10.1145/219663.219682.

Kahn, P. H., Jr. (1999). *The Human Relationship with Nature: Development and Culture.* Cambridge, MA: MIT Press.

Kahn, P. H., Jr., Freier, N. G., Friedman, B., Severson, R. L., and Feldman, E. (2004). Social and moral relationships with robotic others? In *Proceedings of 13th International Workshop on Robot and Human Interactive Communication* (RO-MAN '04) (pp. 545–550). Piscataway, NJ: IEEE.

Kahn, P. H., Freier, N. G., Kanda, T., Ishiguro, H., Ruckert, J. H., Severson, R. L., & Kane, S. K. (2008b). Design patterns for sociality in human-robot interaction. In *Proceedings of the 3rd ACM/IEEE International Conference on Human Robot Interaction* (pp. 97–104). New York, NY: ACM. doi:10.1145/1349822.1349836.

Kahn, P. H., Jr., Friedman, B., and Alexander, I. S. (2005). *Coding Manual for "The Distant Gardener: What Conversations in the Telegarden Reveal about the User Experience of Human-Telerobotic Interaction"* (UW Information School Technical Report, IS-robotics_and_software_agents-2005-06-01). Seattle, WA: University of Washington, The Information School.

Kahn, P. H., Jr., Friedman, B., Alexander, I. A., Freier, N. G., and Collett, S. (2005). The distant gardener: What conversations in the Telegarden reveal about human-telerobotic interaction. In *Proceedings of 14th International Workshop on Robot and Human Interactive Communication* (RO-MAN '05) (pp. 13–18). Piscataway, NJ: IEEE.

Kahn, P. H., Jr., Friedman, B., Freier, N., and Severson, R. (2003). *Coding Manual for Children's Interactions with AIBO, the Robotic Dog—The Preschool Study* (UW CSE Technical Report No. 03-04-03). Seattle, WA: University of Washington, Department of Computer Science and Engineering.

Kahn, P. H., Jr., Friedman, B., Gill, B., Hagman, J., Severson, R. L., Freier, N. G., ... Stolyar, A. (2008a). A plasma display window?—The shifting baseline problem in a technologically mediated natural world. *Journal of Environmental Psychology, 28*(2), 192–199. doi:10.1016/j.jenvp.2007.10.008.

Kahn, P. H., Jr., Friedman, B., Pérez-Granados, D. R., & Freier, N. G. (2006). Robotic pets in the lives of preschool children. *Interaction Studies: Social Behaviour and Communication in Biological and Artificial Systems, 7*(3), 405–436.

Kahn, P. H., Kanda, T., Ishiguro, H., Freier, N. G., Severson, R. L., Gill, B. T., ... Shen, S. (2012). "Robovie, you'll have to go into the closet now": Children's social and moral relationships with a humanoid robot. *Developmental Psychology, 48*(2), 303–314. doi:10.1037/a0027033.

Kahn, P. H., Jr., Ishiguro, H., Friedman, B., Kanda, T., Freier, N. G., Severson, R. L., & Miller, J. (2007). What is a human?: Toward psychological benchmarks in the field of human-robot interaction. *Interaction Studies: Social Behaviour and Communication in Biological and Artificial Systems, 8*(3), 363–390. doi:10.1075/is.8.3.04kah.

Kaptein, M. (2015). *Persuasion Profiling: How the Internet Knows What Makes You Tick.* Amsterdam, The Netherlands: Business Contact.

Kaptein, M., & Eckles, D. (2010). Selecting effective means to any end: Futures and ethics of persuasion profiling. In T. Ploug, P. Hasle, & H. Oinas-Kukkonen (Eds.), *Persuasive Technology: Proceedings of the Fifth International Conference* (pp. 82–93). Berlin: Springer. doi:10.1007/978-3-642-13226-1_10.

Kaptein, M., Eckles, D., & Davis, J. (2011). Envisioning persuasion profiles: Challenges for public policy and ethical practice. *Interactions, 18*(5), 66–69. doi:10.1145/2008176.2008191.

Kaptein, M., Lacroix, J., & Saini, P. (2010). Individual differences in persuadability in the health promotion domain. In T. Ploug, P. Hasle, & H. Oinas-Kukkonen (Eds.), *Persuasive Technology: Proceedings of the Fifth International Conference* (pp. 94–105). Berlin: Springer. doi:10.1007/978-3-642-13226-1_11.

Kidd, S. A., & Davidson, L. (2007). "You have to adapt because you have no other choice": The stories of strength and resilience of 208 homeless youth in New York City and Toronto. *Journal of Community Psychology, 35*(2), 219–238. doi:10.1002/jcop.20144.

Kidd, S., & Shahar, G. (2008). Resilience in homeless youth: The key role of self-esteem. *American Journal of Orthopsychiatry, 78*(2), 163–172. doi:10.1037/0002-9432.78.2.163.

King, J. L. (1983). Centralized versus decentralized computing: Organizational considerations and management options. *ACM Computing Surveys, 15*(4), 319–349. doi:10.1145/289.290.

Kling, R. (1980). Social analyses of computing: Theoretical perspectives in recent empirical research. *ACM Computing Surveys, 12*(1), 61–110. doi:10.1145/356802.356806.

Kling, R. (Ed.). (1996). *Computerization and Controversy: Value Conflicts and Social Choices* (2nd ed.). San Diego, CA: Morgan Kaufmann.

Knight, J. (2008). Value-centred interaction design methods. *Journal of Information Communication and Ethics in Society, 6*(4), 334–348.

Knobel, C., & Bowker, G. C. (2011). Values in design. *Communications of the ACM, 54*(7), 26–28. doi:10.1145/1965724.1965735.

Koops, B.-J., & Leenes, R. (2014). Privacy regulation cannot be hardcoded. A critical comment on the "privacy by design" provision in data-protection law. *International Review of Law Computers & Technology, 28*(2), 159–171. doi:10.1080/13600869.2013.801589.

Kranzberg, M. (1986). Kranzberg's laws. *Technology and Culture, 27*, 544–560.

Kroes, P., & Verbeek, P.-P. (Eds.). (2014). *The Moral Status of Technical Artefacts*. Dordrecht: Springer.

Kyng, M., & Mathiassen, L. (1997). *Computers and Design in Context*. Cambridge, MA: MIT Press.

Le Dantec, C. A., Poole, E. S., & Wyche, S. P. (2009). Values as lived experience: Evolving value sensitive design in support of value discovery. In *Proceedings of the SIGCHI Conference on Human Factors in Computing Systems* (pp. 1141–1150). New York, NY: ACM. doi:10.1145/1518701.1518875.

Lewicki, R. J., & Bunker, B. B. (1995). Trust in relationships: A model of development and decline. In B. B. Bunker & J. Z. Zubin (Eds.), *Conflict, Cooperation, and Justice* (pp. 133–173). San Francisco, CA: Jossey-Bass Publishers.

Lewicki, R. J. and Bunker, B. B. (1996). Developing and maintaining trust in work relationships. In R. M. Kramer & T. R. Tyler (Eds.), *Trust in Organisations: Frontiers of Theory and Research* (pp. 114–139). Thousand Oaks, CA: Sage.

Lovett, B. J. (2010). Extended time testing accommodations for students with disabilities: Answers to five fundamental questions. *Review of Educational Research, 80*(4), 611–638.

Lynch, K. (1960). *The Image of the City*. Cambridge, MA: MIT Press.

Lytx. (n.d.). Teen driver safety system. https://www.lytx.com/our-markets/family/overview.

Magassa, L., Young, M., & Friedman, B. (2017). Diverse voices: A how-to guide for creating more inclusive tech policy documents. Tech Policy Lab. University of Washington, Seattle, WA. http://techpolicylab.org/diversevoicesguide/.

Maisel, W. H., & Kohno, T. (2010). Improving the security and privacy of implantable medical devices. *New England Journal of Medicine*, *362*(13), 1164–1166. doi:10.1056/NEJMp1000745.

Malpass, M. (2013). Between wit and reason: Defining associative, speculative, and critical design in practice. *Design and Culture*, *5*(3), 333–356.

Manders-Huits, N. (2011). What values in design? The challenge of incorporating moral values into design. *Science and Engineering Ethics*, *17*(2), 271–287. doi:10.1007/s11948-010-9198-2.

Manders-Huits, N., & van den Hoven, J. (2009). The need for a value-sensitive design of communication infrastructures. In P. Sollie & M. Düwell (Eds.), *Evaluating New Technologies* (pp. 51–60). Dordrecht: Springer.

Manders-Huits, N., & Zimmer, M. (2009). Values and pragmatic action: The challenges of introducing ethical intelligence in technical design communities. *International Journal of Information Ethics*, *10*(2), 37–45.

Marsden, G. (2008). Toward empowered design. *IEEE Computer*, *41*(6), 42–46.

Matthews, N. (2009). Teaching the "invisible" disabled students in the classroom: Disclosure, inclusion and the social model of disability. *Teaching in Higher Education*, *14*(3), 229–239. doi:10.1080/13562510902898809.

Melson, G. F., Kahn, P. H., Jr., Beck, A., & Friedman, B. (2009a). Robotic pets in human lives: Implications for the human-animal bond and for human relationships with personified technologies. *Journal of Social Issues*, *65*(3), 545–567. doi:10.1111/j.1540-4560.2009.01613.x.

Melson, G. F., Kahn, P. H., Jr., Beck, A., Friedman, B., Roberts, T., Garrett, E., & Gill, B. (2009b). Children's behavior toward and understanding of robotic and living dogs. *Journal of Applied Developmental Psychology*, *30*(2), 92–102. doi:10.1016/j.appdev.2008.10.011.

Millar, J. (2016). An ethics evaluation tool for automating ethical decision-making in robots and self-driving cars. *Applied Artificial Intelligence*, *30*(8), 787–809. doi:10.1080/08839514.2016.1229919.

Miller, J. K., Friedman, B., Jancke, G., & Gill, B. (2007). Value tensions in design: The value sensitive design, development, and appropriation of a corporation's groupware system. In *Proceedings of the 2007 International ACM Conference on Supporting Group Work* (pp. 281–290). New York, NY: ACM. doi:10.1145/1316624.1316668.

Millett, L. I., Friedman, B., & Felten, E. (2001). Cookies and web browser design: Toward realizing informed consent online. In *Proceedings of the SIGCHI Conference on Human Factors in Computing Systems* (pp. 46–52). New York, NY: ACM. doi:10.1145/365024.365034.

Mitchell, R. K., Agle, B. R., & Wood, D. J. (1997). Toward a theory of stakeholder identification and salience: Defining the principle of who and what really counts. *Academy of Management Review, 22*(4), 853–886. doi:10.2307/259247.

Mok, L., & Hyysalo, S. (2018). Designing for energy transition through value sensitive design. *Design Studies, 54*(January), 162–183.

Moor, J. H. (1979). Are there decisions computers should never make? *Nature and System, 1*, 217–229.

Moor, J. H. (1985). What is computer ethics? *Metaphilosophy, 16*(4), 266–275. doi:10.1111/j.1467-9973.1985.tb00173.x.

Moore, G. E. (1978). *Principia Ethica*. Cambridge: Cambridge University Press. Originally published 1903.

Muller, M. J. (1995). Diversity and depth in participatory design: Working with a mosaic of users and other stakeholders in the software development lifecycle. In *Conference Companion on Human Factors in Computing Systems* (pp. 385–386). New York, NY: ACM. 10.1145/223355.223734.

Muller, M. J. (2003). Participatory design: The third space in HCI. In J. A. Jacko & A. Sears (Eds.), *The Human-Computer Interaction Handbook: Fundamentals, Evolving Technologies, and Emerging Applications* (pp. 1051–1068). Mahwah, NJ: Lawrence Erlbaum.

Muller, M. J., & Kuhn, S. (1993). Participatory design. *Communications of the ACM, 36*(6), 24–28.

Mumford, L. (1934). *Technics and Civilization*. New York, NY: Harcourt, Brace and Co.

Munson, S. A., Avrahami, D., Consolvo, S., Fogarty, J., Friedman, B., & Smith, I. (2011). Attitudes toward online availability of US public records. In *Proceedings of the 12th Annual International Digital Government Research Conference: Digital Government Innovation in Challenging Times* (pp. 2–9). New York, NY: ACM. doi:10.1145/2037556.2037558.

Munson, S. A., Avrahami, D., Consolvo, S., Fogarty, J., Friedman, B., & Smith, I. (2012). Sunlight or sunburn: A survey of attitudes toward online availability of US public records. *Information Polity: The International Journal of Government & Democracy in the Information Age, 17*(2), 99–114.

Murphy, R. F. (1964). Social distance and the veil. *American Anthropologist, 66*(6), 1257–1274.

Nardi, B. A., & O'Day, V. (1999). *Information Ecologies: Using Technology with Heart*. Cambridge, MA: MIT Press.

Nathan, L. P. (2012). Sustainable information practice: An ethnographic investigation. *Journal of the American Society for Information Science and Technology*, *63*(11), 2254–2268. doi:10.1002/asi.22726.

Nathan, L. P., & Friedman, B. (2010). Interacting with policy in a political world: Reflections from the voices from the Rwanda tribunal project. *Interactions*, *17*(5), 56–59. doi:10.1145/1836216.1836231.

Nathan, L. P., Friedman, B., Klasnja, P., Kane, S. K., & Miller, J. K. (2008). Envisioning systemic effects on persons and society throughout interactive system design. In *Proceedings of the Seventh ACM Conference on Designing Interactive Systems* (pp. 1–10). New York, NY: ACM. doi:10.1145/1394445.1394446.

Nathan, L. P., Klasnja, P. V., & Friedman, B. (2007). Value scenarios: A technique for envisioning systemic effects of new technologies. *Extended Abstracts of CHI 2007 Conference on Human Factors in Computing Systems* (pp. 2585–2590). New York, NY: ACM.

Nathan, L. P., Lake, M., Grey, N. C., Nilsen, T., Utter, R. F., Utter, E. J., ... Friedman, B. (2011). Multi-lifespan information system design: Investigating a new design approach in Rwanda. In *Proceedings of the 2011 iConference* (pp. 591–597). New York, NY: ACM. doi:10.1145/1940761.1940841.

National Commission for the Protection of Human Subjects of Biomedical and Behavioral Research. (1978). The Belmont report: Ethical principles and guidelines for the protection of human subjects of research. Bethesda, MD: National Commission for the Protection of Human Subjects of Biomedical and Behavioral Research.

Nilsen, T. T., Grey, N. C., & Friedman, B. (2012). Public curation of a historic collection: A means for speaking safely in public. In *Proceedings of the ACM 2012 Conference on Computer Supported Cooperative Work Companion* (pp. 277–278). New York, NY: ACM. doi:10.1145/2141512.2141601.

Novitzky, P., Smeaton, A. F., Chen, C., Irving, K., Jacquemard, T., O'Brolcháin, F., ... Gordijn, B. (2015). A review of contemporary work on the ethics of ambient asssisted living technologies for people with dementia. *Science and Engineering Ethics*, *21*(3), 707–765. doi:10.1007/s11948-014-9552-x.

Oinas-Kukkonen, H. (2010). Behavior change support systems: A research model and agenda. In T. Ploug, P. Hasle, & H. Oinas-Kukkonen (Eds.), *Persuasive Technology: Proceedings of the Fifth International Conference* (pp. 4–14). Berlin: Springer. doi:10.1007/978-3-642-13226-1_3.

Oosterlaken, I. (2009). Design for development: A capability approach. *Design Issues*, *25*(4), 91–102.

Oosterlaken, I. (2015). Applying value sensitive design (VSD) to wind turbines and wind parks: An exploration. *Science and Engineering Ethics*, *21*(2), 359–379. doi:10.1007/s11948-014-9536-x.

Orlikowski, W. J. (2000). Using technology and constituting structures: A practice lens for studying technology in organizations. *Organization Science, 11*(4), 404–428.

Page, R. E., & Kray, C. (2010). Ethics and persuasive technology: An exploratory study in the context of healthy living. In *Proceedings of the First International Workshop on Nudge and Influence Through Mobile Devices 2010* (Vol. 690, pp. 19–22).

Pakrasi, S., Burmeister, O., Coppola, J. F., McCallum, T. J., & Loeb, G. (2015). Ethical telehealth design for users with dementia. *Gerontechnology, 13*(4), 383–387.

Papanek, V. (1971). *Design for the Real World: Human Ecology and Social Change.* New York, NY: Pantheon Books.

Papert, S., & Solomon, C. (1971). *Twenty Things to Do With a Computer.* Report from the Artificial Intelligence Lab, Massachusetts Institute of Technology (A.I. Memo No. 248; LOGO Memo No. 3). Cambridge, MA: MIT.

Pereira, R., & Baranauskas, M. C. C. (2015). A value-oriented and culturally informed approach to the design of interactive systems. *International Journal of Human-Computer Studies, 80*(Supplement C), 66–82. doi:10.1016/j.ijhcs.2015.04.001.

Philip, K., Irani, L., & Dourish, P. (2012). Postcolonial computing: A tactical survey. *Science, Technology & Human Values, 37*(1), 3–29.

Piaget, J. (1960). *The Child's Conception of the World.* Paterson, NJ: Littlefield, Adams. Originally published 1929.

Pommeranz, A., Detweiler, C., Wiggers, P., & Jonker, C. (2012). Elicitation of situated values: Need for tools to help stakeholders and designers to reflect and communicate. *Ethics and Information Technology, 14*(4), 285–303. doi:10.1007/s10676-011-9282-6.

Pritts, J. (2014). *ONC launches challenge to create easy-to-understand privacy notice.* http://www.healthit.gov/buzz-blog/privacy-and-security-of-ehrs/onc-launches-challenge-create-online-notice-privacy-practices.

Pruitt, J., & Grudin, J. (2003). Personas: Practice and theory. In *Proceedings of the 2003 Conference on Designing for User Experiences (DUX '03)* (pp. 1–15). New York, NY: ACM. doi:10.1145/997078.997089.

Purao, S., & Wu, A. (2013). Towards values-inspired design: The case of citizen-centric services. In *ICIS 2013 Proceedings.* http://aisel.aisnet.org/icis2013/proceedings/ResearchInProgress/78.

Rachels, J. (1975). Why privacy is important. *Philosophy & Public Affairs, 4*(4), 323–333.

Ramachandran, D., Canny, J., Das, P. D., & Cutrell, E. (2010). Mobile-izing health workers in rural India. In *Proceedings of the SIGCHI Conference on Human Factors in Computing Systems* (pp. 1889–1898). New York, NY: ACM. doi:10.1145/1753326 .1753610.

Rasmussen, K. B., Castelluccia, C., Heydt-Benjamin, T. S., & Capkun, S. (2009). Proximity-based access control for implantable medical devices. In *Proceedings of the 16th ACM Conference on Computer and Communications Security* (pp. 410–419). New York, NY: ACM. doi:10.1145/1653662.1653712.

Rauhofer, J. (2008). Privacy is dead, get over it! Information privacy and the dream of a risk-free society. *Information & Communications Technology Law, 17*(3), 185–197. doi:10.1080/13600830802472990.

Rawls, J. (1999). *A Theory of Justice* (Rev. ed.). Cambridge, MA: Harvard University Press.

Rector, K., Milne, L., Ladner, R. E., Friedman, B., & Kientz, J. A. (2015). Exploring the opportunities and challenges with exercise technologies for people who are blind or low-vision. In *Proceedings of the 17th International ACM SIGACCESS Conference on Computers and Accessibility* (pp. 203–214). New York, NY: ACM. doi:10.1145/ 2700648.2809846.

Reed, M. S. (2008). Stakeholder participation for environmental management: A literature review. *Biological Conservation, 141*(10), 2417–2431. doi:10.1016/j. biocon.2008.07.014.

Reed, M. S., Graves, A., Dandy, N., Posthumus, H., Hubacek, K., Morris, J., … Stringer, L. C. (2009). Who's in and why? A typology of stakeholder analysis methods for natural resource management. *Journal of Environmental Management, 90*(5), 1933–1949. doi:10.1016/j.jenvman.2009.01.001.

Rice, E., Milburn, N. G., & Monro, W. (2011). Social networking technology, social network composition, and reductions in substance use among homeless adolescents. *Prevention Science, 12*(1), 80–88. doi:10.1007/s11121-010-0191-4.

Robeyns, I. (2011). The capability approach. In E. N. Zalta (Ed.), *The Stanford Encyclopedia of Philosophy* (Summer 2011). https://plato.stanford.edu/archives/sum2011/ entries/capability-approach.

Rode, J. A. (2011). A theoretical agenda for feminist HCI. *Interacting with Computers, 23*(5), 393–400. doi:10.1016/j.intcom.2011.04.005.

Rotondo, A., & Freier, N. G. (2010). The problem of defining values for design: A lack of common ground between industry and academia? In *CHI '10 Extended Abstracts on Human Factors in Computing Systems* (pp. 4183–4188). New York, NY: ACM. 10.1145/1753846.1754123.

Rushanan, M., Rubin, A. D., Kune, D. F., & Swanson, C. M. (2014). SoK: Security and privacy in implantable medical devices and body area networks. In *Proceedings of the*

*2014 IEEE Symposium on Security and Privacy* (pp. 524–539). Washington, DC: IEEE Computer Society. doi:10.1109/SP.2014.40.

Sandel, M. J. (2009). *Justice: What's the Right Thing to Do?* New York, NY: Farrar, Straus and Giroux.

Sanders, E. B.-N. (2009). Exploring co-creation on a large scale. In *Proceedings Designing for, with, and from User Experience* (pp. 10–26). Delft, The Netherlands: StudioLab Press.

Sanders, E. B.-N., Brandt, E., & Binder, T. (2010). A framework for organizing the tools and techniques of participatory design. In *Proceedings of the 11th Biennial Participatory Design Conference* (pp. 195–198). New York, NY: ACM.

Sanders, E. B.-N., & Westerlund, B. (2011). Experiencing, exploring and experimenting in and with co-design spaces. In *Proceedings of the Nordic Design Research Conference* (pp. 298–302). Helsinki: NORDES.

Savage-Rumbaugh, E. S., Williams, S. L., Furuichi, T., & Kano, T. (1996). Language perceived: Paniscus branches out. In W. C. McGrew, L. F. Marchant, & T. Nishida (Eds.), *Great Ape Societies* (pp. 173–184). Cambridge: Cambridge University Press.

Schecter, S. (2010). Security that is meant to be skin deep: Using ultraviolet micropigmentation to store emergency-access keys for implantable medical devices. In *Proceedings of the First USENIX Workshop on Health Security and Privacy (HealthSec)*. https://www.usenix.org/conference/healthsec10/security-meant-be-skin-deep-using-ultraviolet-micropigmentation-store.

Schikhof, Y., Mulder, I., & Choenni, S. (2010). Who will watch (over) me? Humane monitoring in dementia care. *International Journal of Human-Computer Studies, 68*(6), 410–422. doi:10.1016/j.ijhcs.2010.02.002.

Schneider, F. B. (Ed.). (1999). *Trust in Cyberspace.* Washington, DC: National Academy Press.

Schneier, B. (2006). The eternal value of privacy. May 18, 2006. *Wired.com.* https://archive.wired.com/politics/security/commentary/securitymatters/2006/05/70886.

Schoeman, F. D. (Ed.). (1984). *Philosophical Dimensions of Privacy: An Anthology.* Cambridge, UK: Cambridge University Press.

Schot, J., & Rip, A. (1997). The past and future of constructive technology assessment. *Technological Forecasting and Social Change, 54*(2–3), 251–268. doi:10.1016/S0040-1625(96)00180-1.

Schön, D. A. (1987). *Educating the Reflective Practitioner: Toward a New Design for Teaching and Learning in the Professions.* San Francisco, CA: Jossey-Bass Publishers.

Schroeder, D. A., & Graziano, W. G. (Eds.). (2015). *The Oxford Handbook of Prosocial Behavior.* New York, NY: Oxford University Press.

Sengers, P., Boehner, K., David, S., & Kaye, J. (2005). Reflective design. In *Proceedings of the 4th Decennial Conference on Critical Computing: Between Sense and Sensibility* (pp. 49–58). New York, NY: ACM. doi:10.1145/1094562.1094569.

Sharkey, N. (2007). Automated killers and the computing profession. *Computer, 40*(11), 124–123. doi:10.1109/MC.2007.372.

Shilton, K. (2012). Value levers: Building ethics into design. *Science, Technology & Human Values, 38*(3), 374–397.

Shilton, K. (2018). Values and ethics in human-computer interaction. *Foundations and Trends in Human-Computer Interaction, 12* (2), 107–171.

Shneiderman, B., & Rose, A. (1996). Social impact statements: Engaging public participation in information technology design. In *Proceedings of the Symposium on Computers and the Quality of Life* (pp. 90–96). New York, NY: ACM. doi:10.1145/238339 .238378.

Singley, K., Lai, J., Kuang, L., & Tang, J.-M. (2008). BlueReach: Harnessing synchronous chat to support expertise sharing in a large organization. In *CHI '08 Extended Abstracts on Human Factors in Computing Systems* (pp. 2001–2008). New York, NY: ACM. 10.1145/1358628.1358630.

Slesnick, N., Dashora, P., Letcher, A., Erdem, G., & Serovich, J. (2009). A review of services and interventions for runaway and homeless youth: Moving forward. *Children and Youth Services Review, 31*(7), 732–742. doi:10.1016/j.childyouth.2009 .01.006.

Snyder, J., Shilton, K., & Anderson, S. (2016). Observing the materiality of values in information systems research. In *Proceedings of the 49th Hawaii International Conference on System Sciences* (pp. 2017–2026). Kauai, HI: IEEE.

Solomon, D. B. (2014). Employee and organization security value alignment through value sensitive security policy design (Doctoral dissertation). Nova Southeastern University. http://nsuworks.nova.edu/gscis_etd/4.

Spahn, A. (2012). And lead us (not) into persuasion…? Persuasive technology and the ethics of communication. *Science and Engineering Ethics, 18*(4), 633–650. doi:10.1007/s11948-011-9278-y.

Sparks, P., & Shepherd, R. (1992). Self-identity and the theory of planned behavior: Assessing the role of identification with "green consumerism." *Social Psychology Quarterly, 55*(4), 388–399. doi:10.2307/2786955.

Spiekermann, S. (2015). *Ethical IT Innovation: A Value-Based System Design Approach.* Boca Raton, FL: Auerbach Publications.

Spinuzzi, C. (2005). The methodology of participatory design. *Technical Communication, 52*(2), 163–174.

Stark, L., & Tierney, M. (2014). Lockbox: Mobility, privacy and values in cloud storage. *Ethics and Information Technology, 16*(1), 1–13. doi:10.1007/s10676-013 -9328-z.

Taebi, B., & Kloosterman, J. L. (2008). To recycle or not to recycle? An intergenerational approach to nuclear fuel cycles. *Science and Engineering Ethics, 14*(2), 177–200. doi:10.1007/s11948-007-9049-y.

Tagore, R. (1922). *Creative Unity.* London, England: MacMillan and Co., Limited.

Taylor, N. (1998). *Urban Planning Theory Since 1945.* Thousand Oaks, CA: SAGE Publications.

Teipel, S., Babiloni, C., Hoey, J., Kaye, J., Kirste, T., & Burmeister, O. K. (2016). Information and communication technology solutions for outdoor navigation in dementia. *Alzheimer's & Dementia, 12*(6), 695–707. doi:10.1016/j.jalz.2015.11.003.

Thomson, J. J. (1975). The right to privacy. *Philosophy & Public Affairs, 4*(4), 295–314.

Tomlinson, B., Blevis, E., Nardi, B., Patterson, D. J., Silberman, M. S., & Pan, Y. (2008). Collapse informatics and practice: Theory, method, and design. *ACM Transactions on Computer-Human Interaction, 20*(4), 24:1–24:26. doi:10.1145/2493431.

Turiel, E. (1983). *The Development of Social Knowledge: Morality and Convention.* Cambridge, UK: Cambridge University Press.

Turkle, S. (1984). *The Second Self: Computers and the Human Spirit.* New York, NY: Simon and Schuster, Inc.

Van de Poel, I. (2009). Values in engineering design. In A. Meijers (Ed.), *Philosophy of Technology and Engineering Sciences* (Vol. 9, pp. 973–1006). Amsterdam: North-Holland.

Van de Poel, I. (2012). Can we design for well-being? In P. Brey, A. Briggle, & E. Spence (Eds.), *The Good Life in a Technological Age* (pp. 295–306). New York, NY: Routledge.

Van de Poel, I. (2013). Translating values into design requirements. In D. P. Michelfelder, N. McCarthy, & D. E. Goldberg (Eds.), *Philosophy and Engineering: Reflections on Practice, Principles and Process* (pp. 253–266). Dordrecht: Springer. doi:10.1007/978-94-007-7762-0_20.

Van de Poel, I., & van Gorp, A. C. (2006). The need for ethical reflection in engineering design: The relevance of type of design and design hierarchy. *Science, Technology & Human Values, 31*(3), 333–360.

Van de Poel, I., & Zwart, S. D. (2010). Reflective equilibrium in R&D networks. *Science, Technology & Human Values, 35*(2), 174–199. doi:10.1177/0162243909340272.

Van de Poel, I., Zwart, S. D., Brumsen, M., & van Mil, H. G. J. (2005). Risks of aerobic granular sludge technology: Ethical and methodological aspects. In S. Bathe, M. de Kreuk, B. McSwain, & N. Schwarzenbeck (Eds.), *Aerobic Granular Sludge* (pp. 143–154). London: IWA Publishing.

Van de Waal, F. (2006). *Primates and Philosophers: How Morality Evolved*. Princeton, NJ: Princeton University Press.

Van den Hoven, J. (1999). Privacy and the varieties of informational wrongdoing. *Australian Journal of Professional and Applied Ethics*, *1*(1), 30–43.

Van den Hoven, J. (2000). Privacy and health information: The need for a fine-grained account. *International Journal for Quality in Health Care*, *12*(1), 5–6.

Van den Hoven, J. (2005). Design for values and values for design. *Information Age*, *4*, 4–7.

Van den Hoven, J. (2007). ICT and value sensitive design. In P. Goujon, S. Lavelle, P. Duquenoy, K. Kimppa, & V. Laurent (Eds.), *The Information Society: Innovation, legitimacy, Ethics and Democracy in Honor of Professor Jacques Berleur* (pp. 67–72). Hoboken, NJ: Springer. doi:10.1007/978-0-387-72381-5_8.

Van den Hoven, J. (2013). Value sensitive design and responsible innovation. In R. Owen, J. Bessant, & M. Heintz, *Responsible Innovation* (pp. 75–83). Hoboken, NJ: Wiley. 10.1002/9781118551424.ch4.

Van den Hoven, J., Lokhorst, G.-J., & van de Poel, I. (2012). Engineering and the problem of moral overload. *Science and Engineering Ethics*, *18*(1), 143–155. doi:10.1007/s11948-011-9277-z.

Van der Burg, S., & van Gorp, A. (2005). Understanding moral responsibility in the design of trailers. *Science and Engineering Ethics*, *11*(2), 235–256. doi:10.1007/s11948-005-0044-x.

Van Gorp, A. (2005). Ethical issues in engineering design: Safety and sustainability (Doctoral dissertation). Delft University of Technology, Delft, The Netherlands. https://repository.tudelft.nl/view/ir/uuid%3A39e544ba-15dc-4154-a6fc-e25106320e90.

Van Wynsberghe, A. (2013). Designing robots for care: Care-centered value-sensitive design. *Science and Engineering Ethics*, *19*(2), 407–433. doi:10.1007/s11948-011-9343-6.

Venable, J. R., Pries-Heje, J., Bunker, D., & Russo, N. (2011). Design and diffusion of systems for human benefit: Toward more humanistic realization of information systems in society. *Information Technology & People*, *24*(3), 208–216.

Vermaas, P., Tan, Y.-H., van den Hoven, J., Burgemeestre, B., & Hulstijn, J. (2010). Designing for trust: A case of value-sensitive design. *Knowledge, Technology & Policy*, *23*(3), 491–505. doi:10.1007/s12130-010-9130-8.

Vines, J., Clarke, R., Wright, P., McCarthy, J., & Olivier, P. (2013). Configuring participation: On how we involve people in design. In *Proceedings of the SIGCHI Conference on Human Factors in Computing Systems* (pp. 429–438). New York, NY: ACM. doi:10.1145/2470654.2470716.

Von Schomberg, R. (Ed.). (2011). Towards responsible research and innovation in the information and communication technologies and security technologies fields. Luxembourg: Publications Office of the European Union. doi:10.2777/58723.

Von Schomberg, R. (2012). Prospects for technology assessment in a framework of responsible research and innovation. In M. Dusseldorp & R. Beecroft (Eds.), *Technikfolgen abschätzen lehren* (pp. 39–61). Wiesbaden: Springer. 10.1007/978-3-531 -93468-6_2.

Waddell, P., Wang, L., & Liu, X. (2008). UrbanSim: An evolving planning support system for evolving communities. In R. K. Brail (Ed.), *Planning Support Systems for Cities and Regions* (pp. 103–138). Cambridge, MA: Lincoln Institute of Land Policy.

Walldius, C. Å., & Lantz, A. (2013). Exploring the use of design pattern maps for aligning new technical support to new clinical team meeting routines. *Behaviour & Information Technology, 32*(1), 68–79. doi:10.1080/0144929X.2011.553749.

Walldius, C. Å., Sundblad, Y., & Borning, A. (2005). A first analysis of the UsersAward programme from a value sensitive design perspective. In *Proceedings of the 4th Decennial Conference on Critical Computing: Between Sense and Sensibility* (pp. 199–202). New York, NY: ACM. doi:10.1145/1094562.1094598.

Warren, S. D., & Brandeis, L. D. (1890). The right to privacy. *Harvard Law Review, 4*(5), 193–220. doi:10.2307/1321160.

Watkins, K., Ferris, B., Borning, A., Rutherford, G. S., & Layton, D. (2011). Where is my bus? Impact of mobile realtime information on the perceived and actual wait time of transit riders. *Transportation Research Part A: Policy and Practice, 45*(8), 839–848.

Watkins, K. E., Borning, A., Rutherford, G. S., Ferris, B., & Gill, B. (2013a). Attitudes of bus operators towards real-time transit information tools. *Transportation, 40*(5), 961–980. doi:10.1007/s11116-013-9450-0.

Watkins, K. E., Ferris, B., Malinovskiy, Y., & Borning, A. (2013b). Beyond context-sensitive solutions: Using value-sensitive design to identify needed transit information tools. In S. L. Jones Jr. (Ed.), *Urban Public Transportation Systems 2013: Proceedings of the Third International Conference* (pp. 296–308). American Society of Civil Engineers. http://doi.org/ 10.1061/9780784413210.026.

Weibert, A., Randall, D., & Wulf, V. (2017). Extending value sensitive design to off-the-shelf technology: Lessons learned from a local intercultural computer club. *Interacting with Computers, 29*(5), 715–736. doi:10.1093/iwc/iwx008.

Weizenbaum, J. (1972). On the impact of the computer on society. *Science*, *176*(4035), 609–614.

Whitbeck, C. (1998). *Ethics in Engineering Practice and Research*. Cambridge, UK: Cambridge University Press.

Whitbeck, L. B. (2009). *Mental Health and Emerging Adulthood Among Homeless Young People*. New York, NY: Psychology Press.

White, C. (2007). *Bladerunner GPS tracker jacket locates kids, replicants*. https://gizmodo.com/314515/bladerunner-gps-tracker-jacket-locates-kids-replicants.

Whitten, A., & Tygar, J. D. (1999). Why Johnny can't encrypt: A usability evaluation of PGP 5.0. In *Proceedings of the Eighth USENIX Security Symposium* (pp. 169–184). https://www.usenix.org/conference/8th-usenix-security-symposium/why-johnny-cant-encrypt-usability-evaluation-pgp-50.

Wiener, N. (1985). *The Human Use of Human Beings: Cybernetics and Society* (Reprint of revised 2nd ed., originally published 1954). Garden City, NY: Doubleday.

Wiener, N. (1985). The machine as threat and promise. In P. Masani (Ed.), *Norbert Wiener: Collected Works and Commentaries* (Vol. IV, pp. 673–678). Cambridge, MA: The MIT Press.

Wilson, E. O. (2006). *The Creation: An Appeal to Save Life on Earth*. New York, NY: Norton.

Winograd, T., & Flores, F. (1986). *Understanding Computers and Cognition: A New Foundation for Design*. Boston, MA: Addison-Wesley.

Wobbrock, J. O., Gajos, K. Z., Kane, S. K., & Vanderheiden, G. C. (2018). Ability-based design. *Communications of the ACM*, *61*(6), 62–71. doi:10.1145/3148051.

Woelfer, J. P. (2014). Engaging homeless young people in HCI research. *Interactions*, *21*(1), 54–57. doi:10.1145/2543580.

Woelfer, J. P., & Hendry, D. G. (2009). Stabilizing homeless young people with information and place. *Journal of the American Society for Information Science and Technology*, *60*(11), 2300–2312. doi:10.1002/asi.21146.

Woelfer, J. P., & Hendry, D. G. (2010). Homeless young people's experiences with information systems: Life and work in a community technology center. In *Proceedings of the SIGCHI Conference on Human Factors in Computing Systems* (pp. 1291–1300). New York, NY: ACM. doi:10.1145/1753326.1753520.

Woelfer, J. P., & Hendry, D. G. (2011a). Designing ubiquitous information systems for a community of homeless young people: Precaution and a way forward. *Personal and Ubiquitous Computing*, *15*(6), 565–573. doi:10.1007/s00779-010-0341-5.

Woelfer, J. P., & Hendry, D. G. (2011b). Homeless young people and living with personal digital artifacts. In *Proceedings of the SIGCHI Conference on Human Factors in Computing Systems* (pp. 1697–1706). New York, NY: ACM. doi:10.1145/1978942 .1979190.

Woelfer, J. P., Iverson, A., Hendry, D. G., Friedman, B., & Gill, B. T. (2011). Improving the safety of homeless young people with mobile phones: Values, form and function. In *Proceedings of the SIGCHI Conference on Human Factors in Computing Systems* (pp. 1707–1716). New York, NY: ACM. doi:10.1145/1978942.1979191.

Woelfer, J. P., & Lee, J. H. (2012). The role of music in the lives of homeless young people: A preliminary report. In *Proceedings of the 13th International Society for Music Information Retrieval Conference (ISMIR '12)* (pp. 367–372).

Woelfer, J. P., Yeung, M. W.-M., Erdmann, C. G., & Hendry, D. G. (2008). Value considerations in an information ecology: Printed materials, service providers and homeless young people. In *Proceedings of the American Society for Information Science and Technology* (Vol. 45, pp. 1–9). doi:10.1002/meet.2008.1450450370.

Yetim, F. (2011). Bringing discourse ethics to value sensitive design: Pathways toward a deliberative future. *AIS Transactions on Human-Computer Interaction, 3*(2), 133–155.

Yoo, D. (2018). Stakeholder Tokens: A constructive method for value sensitive design stakeholder analysis. *Ethics and Information Technology* (pp. 1–5). doi.:10.1007/ s10676-018-9474-4.

Yoo, D., Derthick, K., Ghassemian, S., Hakizimana, J., Gill, B., & Friedman, B. (2016). Multi-lifespan design thinking: Two methods and a case study with the Rwandan diaspora. In *Proceedings of the 2016 CHI Conference on Human Factors in Computing Systems* (pp. 4423–4434). New York, NY: ACM. doi:10.1145/2858036.2858366.

Yoo, D., Huldtgren, A., Woelfer, J. P., Hendry, D. G., & Friedman, B. (2013a). A value sensitive action-reflection model: Evolving a co-design space with stakeholder and designer prompts. In *Proceedings of the SIGCHI Conference on Human Factors in Computing Systems* (pp. 419–428). New York, NY: ACM. doi:10.1145/2470654.2470715.

Yoo, D., Kantengwa, O., Logler, N., Interayamahanga, R., Nkurunziza, J. & Friedman, B. (2018). Collaborative reflection: A practice for enriching research partnerships spanning culture, discipline, and time. In *Proceedings of the 2018 CHI Conference on Human Factors in Computing Systems* (CHI '18). ACM, New York, NY, USA, Paper 279, 11 pages. doi:10.1145/3173574.3173853.

Yoo, D., Lake, M., Nilsen, T., Utter, M. E., Alsdorf, R., Bizimana, T., … Friedman, B. (2013b). Envisioning across generations: A multi-lifespan information system for international justice in Rwanda. In *Proceedings of the SIGCHI Conference on Human Factors in Computing Systems* (pp. 2527–2536). New York, NY: ACM. doi:10.1145/ 2470654.2481349.

Young, M., Magassa, L., & Friedman, B. (in press). Toward inclusive tech policy design: A method for underrepresented voices to strengthen tech policy documents. *Ethics and Information Technology*.

Zapico, J. L., Turpeinen, M., & Brandt, N. (2009). Climate persuasive services: Changing behavior towards low-carbon lifestyles. In *Persuasive Technology: Proceedings of the 4th International Conference* (pp. 14:1–14:8). New York, NY: ACM. doi:10.1145/1541948 .1541968.

Zuboff, S. (1988). *In the Age of the Smart Machine: The Future of Work and Power*. New York, NY: Basic Books.

Zwart, S. D., van de Poel, I., van Mil, H., & Brumsen, M. (2006). A network approach for distinguishing ethical issues in research and development. *Science and Engineering Ethics*, *12*(4), 663–684. doi:10.1007/s11948-006-0063-2.

# Index

Page numbers with f and t refer to figures and tables, respectively.